The proceeds from the sale of this book benefit THINK Together, a 501c3 nonprofit organization whose vision is to provide educational excellence and equity for all kids.

Let's THINK Together!

Praise for THINK Together

Randy Barth gets it right when he says most school reform strategies in the era of No Child Left Behind are overly focused on the wrong drivers such as accountability, human capital, and technology. Randy points out that more than ever our public school systems need to focus on building the skills and capacity of educators doing the hard work with children, and provide real time information and data to inform communities on the state of their public schools and to drive continuous improvement. It is only through information (data on student learning), support (capacity building and professional learning), and pressure (community transparency), that public schools can see the sustained improvement so needed to prepare children for college, career, and life.

—Jonathan Raymond
Former Superintendent,
Sacramento City Unified School District
President, Stuart Foundation

Little Lake City School District invests in professional development for teachers, staff, and administrators. We value and encourage teachers as instructional decision-makers by empowering them with research-based strategies, structures and tools to effectively reach each student. THINK Together has been an active and willing partner in this critical endeavor, spreading successful practices and understanding that real reform goes beyond "change du jour."

—Phillip Perez, EdD
Superintendent
Little Lake City School District

Successful low-income students thrive in a community that meets their varying needs through dedicated teachers and schools teamed with 21st century quality expanded learning opportunities. Santa Ana Unified School District and THINK Together created an impactful partnership that provides these sorts of opportunities for our students.

—Jane Russo
Retired Superintendent
Santa Ana Unified School District

Motivated by a drive to erase achievement gaps, Randy Barth demonstrates the powerful role extended learning plays to keep students on grade level. When students fail to master core cognitive concepts during the school day, they are at risk of falling behind and, ultimately, dropping out of school. These students need help to master these concepts in order to move on. THINK Together is not merely a random after-school tutoring program, but a highly customized service designed to extend the instructional day by reinforcing teachers' lesson plans. This approach has worked to solidify student learning by assuring that their core knowledge is strong and they are able to think critically and solve problems. It is with confidence that I highly recommend this book.

—Al Mijares, PhD
Orange County Superintendent of Schools

As an advocacy organization working to convince policymakers that expanded learning opportunities are a critical investment, we are extremely grateful to the THINK Together team for their focus on data and evaluation. In a field that is making a significant difference in children's lives, but often lacks the resources to evaluate impact thoroughly, THINK Together's well-documented results have been invaluable in communicating to a wide range of stakeholders the power of learning outside the classroom, after school, and in the summer.

—Jennifer Peck
Executive Director
Partnership for Children & Youth

THINK Together

How <u>YOU</u> can play a role in improving education in America

RANDY BARTH & JENNIFER DELSON

THINK Together: How YOU can play a role in improving education in America

Copyright © 2015 Randy Barth and Jennifer Delson. All rights reserved. No part of this book may be reproduced or retransmitted in any form or by any means without the written permission of the publisher.

Published by Wheatmark®
1760 East River Road, Suite 145, Tucson, Arizona 85718 USA.
www.wheatmark.com

ISBN: 978-1-62787-192-1 (paperback)
ISBN: 978-1-62787-193-8 (ebook)
LCCN: 2014948321

To all people who believe a high-performing public education system in America is everyone's responsibility.

Introduction

I wanted to write this book because I felt that we, as a nation, are having the wrong conversation about how to improve public education in America, especially for poor kids. The conversation, in my opinion, is too heavily influenced by the experiences in the large urban school districts and charter schools located in the major media markets.

Innovation in education is often happening elsewhere and so is poverty. According to a study released in 2013 by the Brookings Institution, the nation's poor are now more likely to be found in the suburbs than in cities or rural areas. Poverty in suburbs is rising faster than in any other setting in the country. By 2011, there were 3 million more people living in poverty in suburbs than in inner cities, an increase of 64 percent between 2000 and 2011.

There are also innovative strategies that are being implemented in low-income suburban schools that are achieving great results. These strategies are often more scalable than the charter school models that garner so much media attention. Not that we shouldn't examine innovations that are working wherever we find them. It's just that there are interesting things that are happening in the public school system in low-income suburbs and urban areas outside of the major media markets that deserve to be part of the conversation. This book brings several of these strategies to light.

I also felt that all too often an important voice is missing in the education reform discussions: that of the system's leaders. Over the years, many people, including many policy makers and education philanthropists, became frustrated working with "the system." I certainly understand that because the system is hard to work with and in. In our chapter on the education gauntlet we talk about why that is and what might be done about it. However, even with the growth in charter schools and the 10 percent of the population that attends private schools, 87 percent of America's K–12 student population attends traditional public schools. So, it seemed to me that more of the education reform conversation about low-income students needed to include what is working in these settings. And, it turns out there are things that *are* working.

THINK Together has a unique perspective. We currently work in more than 450 low-income schools across forty-two California school districts. Approximately two-thirds of these districts provide us with a nightly upload of all their student data so that we can measure the impact of our work and foster continuous improvements. This qualitative and quantitative look, over a number of years, provides us with a unique view into what is working and not working on the ground in our schools.

What we see working is very similar to what noted school change leader, Michael Fullan, advocates. Current school reform efforts have not gotten the increases in student achievement we as Americans hoped for, according to Fullan, because we are concentrating on four wrong drivers of change: negative accountability, individualistic strategies, technology, and ad hoc policies. The places that we see getting results are focusing on strategies that are based on capacity building, social capital, deep pedagogy, and systemic development. Technology can serve to augment these strategies, but it cannot effectively replace them. Fullan's view resonates with THINK Together because in our two decades of working with schools, the schools that have made sustained progress are the ones that have focused on this latter course.

As we have gone on this educational journey, our data repeatedly pointed to an organization called The Principal's Exchange, as one of the most effective organizations in helping schools and school districts build the capacity of their staff to do great work, foster trust and collaboration among the staff and the board (social capital), help teachers to strengthen their pedagogy, and build effective systems to efficiently operate the district and sustain excellence over time. So, their work became part of the story that we wanted to tell.

As Fullan says, "The key to effective whole-system reform is to center the effort on capacity building—the development of skills, competencies, and motivation of individuals and groups, at all levels of the system. This means taking a development stance compared to an accountability stance. *When you combine non-judgmental capacity building with transparency of results and practices, you get the best of both support and pressure.* There is a sense of urgency about the student achievement agenda but it plays itself out through action and implementation and the spread of good practice. Internal accountability grows (where the group holds itself accountable) and external accountability gets ramped up to focus on the smaller percentage of schools that are not moving forward. *Quality capacity building replaces a preoccupation with compliance.*" THINK Together's experience on the front lines of education has found this to be true. And, while we at THINK Together are big advocates of accountability, we have observed that you have to equip folks first to deliver the outcomes that you are seeking. Practically speaking, with 3.2 million teachers in America, you simply can't fire your way to success.

I also wanted to write a book that was interesting and accessible enough to engage the average reader while rigorous enough to provide important information to policy makers and practitioners. Paul Tough's books, *Whatever It Takes* and *How Children Succeed* were models that I had in my head as I started down the path to write this book.

Writing a book like Paul's is harder than it looks because you are writing for two different audiences. After working on the book for about a year, I felt that I was lost in the weeds. I set it aside for a few weeks and when I picked it up and re-read it, even I was bored by it. It read like a federal grant application.

At that point I reached out to Jennifer Delson, a former *Los Angeles Times* reporter who had done a story on THINK Together some years earlier. Jennifer had left the *Times* and was working on various projects in and around Santa Ana. She read what I had written and proposed the basic framework for what became this book. The first draft that I had written became research for what came later.

Jennifer enriched the book in multiple ways and solved a gnarly problem for me, how to write about myself.

Jennifer also had the time (and the experience) to interview a variety of stakeholders that were involved in our journey over the years. Prior to covering Orange County, Jennifer had been a reporter in Mexico and Central America, so her background helped to enrich the immigrant perspective that is very much a part of the THINK Together journey.

Because both Jennifer and I wrote portions of the book, we have adopted the third person voice in an effort to be consistent. Jennifer's content and my content were fused together by our story editor, Steve Reich.

Engaging the broader community is an important part of the story. We can and do talk about systems change work and what approaches we see working and not working in schools. But schools reside in communities. Good communities often have good schools and tough communities often have poorer performing schools. People have different views as to which is the cause and which is the effect, but it seems reasonable to say that there is a symbiotic relationship there.

In most cities and towns in America, the school district is the largest business in town. Most people don't think about it that way. It often is the largest employer, it usually owns the most real estate, it produces arguably the most important product, and it's owned by the taxpayers. The quality of the schools has a big impact on property values and economic development, yet few people know what is going on with their local school district. In most cities in America, fewer than 20 percent of people vote in their local school board elections in a presidential election year and often half of that in a non-presidential election. So part of the problem with our schools is you!

The more hopeful news is that you can be part of the solution too. As a voter and taxpayer you can get informed and vote. As a community member, you can volunteer to be a tutor or a mentor. If your experience is anything like the people on these pages, your efforts will be rewarded beyond your wildest dreams. If you are a state or federal policymaker, what you read in this book about what is working on the ground will help you to make informed policy decisions. If you are a local school board member, or thinking about running for one of those seats, this book may help you become a more effective board member. If you are a systems leader, hopefully this book gives you a peek into what is working elsewhere that may inform your work. Or, it may encourage you to get involved in an ongoing dialogue with other superintendents that you can share ideas and challenges with. If you're a teacher or a school employee, this book may help you understand better what goes on downtown. If you are a parent or grandparent, hopefully the book provides you with some things that might illuminate your way as you prepare a path for your child's journey through school. Finally, if you are a person of faith, hopefully you will feel a call to action as I have, in a way that you can be the salt and the light for others and be a reflection of God's love in your local community.

I have been very blessed to have the opportunity to do work with low-income schools. It is extremely challenging work, but we've had enough success and observed enough success in others working with this large group of students, that in the end, it is very hopeful work. We've seen some incredible successes and seen lives change. Along the way, my life has changed for the better too. So, in the end, it is this sense of hope that I wanted to share with you: that brighter days lay ahead for even our most challenging kids and their communities. If we come together as communities and as a nation, America will remain both great and good.

Randy Barth
Santa Ana, California
August, 2014

Contents

1

Randy

Shots rang out in the Shalimar neighborhood of Costa Mesa, California. Another teen had fallen victim to the gang wars epidemic in cities across America in 1994.

The Vario Little Town Gang was at war with the Shalimar Street Gang. But this time the gunfire awakened unexpected rivals—three mothers who were tired of the drug dealing, the threats, and the escalating violence. They decided to organize and take action.

A few weeks later, a successful stockbroker named Randy Barth was reading the *Daily Pilot* over lunch in a small deli in nearby Corona del Mar. He was captivated by an article headlined "Westside Story" that chronicled the problems in Shalimar, an area only a few miles from him but a world away. The article told of efforts by a group of local mothers to take their neighborhood back from the gangs, though Randy couldn't imagine how exactly these brave women planned to do that.

Randy had recently become an elder at St. Andrew's Presbyterian Church in Newport Beach, where he was head of the church's Mission Committee. At the time he was focused on helping the local homeless population, but something about this story opened Randy's eyes to the bigger picture. Why wait until people are homeless before trying to help them? Why wait until gangs are formed before trying to stop them? Why not try to solve the problem before it happens?

Randy would later realize that the solution was an education system that not only left no child behind, but one that lifted every child up.

Randy couldn't know it then, but this simple shift in perspective would eventually lead to the creation of THINK Together, one of the nation's largest nonprofit providers of academic support programs for low-income students, serving more than 140,000 youth at over 450 locations across California. Working with a wide variety of public and private agencies, including more than forty-two public school districts, THINK Together is based on the belief that education is the single most important factor in helping young people achieve their full potential. THINK stands for Teaching, Helping, Inspiring, Nurturing Kids. Today, THINK Together not only offers a safe place for children to do their homework after school, but a full range of in-school and expanded learning opportunities from ages zero to eighteen.

But all of that would come years later. Today, Randy's mission was closer to home. The mothers of Shalimar were facing a huge challenge.

Randy turned to a friend, Father Jerome Karcher, a priest at St. Joachim Catholic Church, whose parish encompassed Shalimar. Father Jerome knew the mothers who were taking back their neighborhood, and within a few days, he arranged for Randy to meet them.

Randy usually worked long hours, arriving at his penthouse office by 6:30 a.m. and staying until late afternoon or early evening. But on this day, when the bell rang at 1 p.m., he jumped in his car and headed inland to Costa Mesa.

Costa Mesa is home to many of the service workers employed in the restaurants, hotels, country clubs, and yacht clubs of nearby Newport Beach. Though neighborhoods like Shalimar were just a short bus ride from the prosperous areas they served, they were light years away in terms of resources and living anything close to the American Dream.

Shalimar was two blocks long and filled with some sixty-five apartment buildings housing over 1,500 people. But that was just a guess. There likely were two to three times as many people crammed into individual units to save money.

THINK Together

3

Randy and Father Jerome found themselves in the tidy apartment of Eva Marin, the manager of a midsized complex adjacent to Shalimar Drive. Eva had four children, three of whom were still school age. With her were Maria Alvarez and Paty Madueño.

The three mothers described the challenges the neighborhood faced. The residents were primarily recent immigrants from Mexico, Guatemala, and El Salvador who had come to America in search of a better life. They spoke mostly Spanish and lived two or three families per apartment. Many of the buildings were owned by absentee landlords and showed signs of neglect. Police struggled to keep up with the crime. Drug dealing ran rampant and fueled the turf war between the gangs.

All of the resources for kids—schools, parks, and libraries—were outside Shalimar and in a different gang territory where it wasn't safe to venture. The children were bused to school and dropped back into the neighborhood after classes with nowhere to go and nothing to do.

"What we need is a place for the children to go after school," Paty Maduenño told Randy. "It has to be very close by, because we're afraid of the kids walking around here. We need something, though— something positive. Something that will help them latch on to the American Dream."

Randy looked into the three sets of hopeful eyes and decided to do whatever it took to turn things around. He spent every free moment in Shalimar putting together a plan. He met with parents, youth, the police, city officials, and church leaders. The local churches were supportive, but only Randy's church, St. Andrew's, had enough money to get the job done.

St. Andrew's was on board, but the church treasurer worried about the liability: "What if somebody gets shot over there? The church is the deep pocket that will be sued." So Randy proposed locating the afterschool center in an industrial space safely away from the Shalimar apartments. This plan may have worked for the treasurer, but not for the mothers.

"We'd be sending them on a walk right in front of the drug dealers," said Maria Alvarez. She had another idea. "Come to the building I manage. I'll put you in a three-bedroom apartment downstairs from where I live. That way I can keep an eye on things," she added.

Randy wasn't sure that this was an alluring place for a learning center, but he figured that the mothers knew best. When they toured the three bedroom apartment Maria suggested, they found more than fifteen people living there. The primary tenant paid $750 a month but was subleasing each bedroom for three hundred dollars and made a profit by sleeping on a cot in the living room. Cockroaches scurried over worn carpeting. Frayed electrical cords snaked through piles of dust to give each bedroom a single light bulb. It was hardly ideal, but it was Randy's if he wanted it.

The wheels were now set in motion.

Randy rounded up a group of friends from St. Andrew's with whom he had served with on previous building projects in Mississippi and Mexico to help turn the apartment into a learning center. They took out the closets and created a ledge around the walls to serve as desk space. They fixed the electrical problems and tented the patio so students could study outside in any kind of weather. Finally, they filled the apartment with classroom furniture.

The preparation for the center's launch was a wonderful exercise in team building. The mothers continued to meet and plan with other parents in the neighborhood. Local church members, several of them teachers, met to set up the curriculum. The only group missing was the fathers, so the mothers organized a painting party. But in the end, no one came except Randy and Roger Cetina, Eva Marin's husband. With the opening just four days away, the two worked as fast as they could. Meanwhile, the pressure was building.

Now, each day after the stock market closed, Randy would dash off to Shalimar to tend to final details. And every day, he had the treasurer from St. Andrew's breathing down his neck. Even though the church elders had approved the project, the treasurer wouldn't back off.

On opening day, the treasurer made one last run at killing the project. "St. Andrew's cannot take on this kind of liability. There are just too many things that could go wrong here, Randy," he said.

"We just can't have it." He forbade Randy from opening the learning center and told him that under no circumstances would St. Andrew's be involved.

"I understand your position," replied Randy, calmly. "But remember, the elders have approved this project. I see risk differently than you do. I think the greatest risk in this situation lies in not providing these kids the support they need. I think that is what is biblical. We are moving this project forward."

If the church would not sign the lease, he would. With that, the treasurer relented.

At 1 p.m., the stock market bell rang, and Randy raced to Shalimar from his Newport Beach office. The big moment had arrived: The Shalimar Learning Center was opening! A school bus dropped students off at the corner, but only a modest number trickled in. Randy was disappointed, but he remained hopeful. He prayed that once the word got out, more kids would come. It was only a matter of time.

That evening, a ceremony was held for the families of Shalimar. Over sixty people squeezed into the small apartment in celebration. Rev. Bill Flanagan from St. Andrew's, one of the project's great champions, and Father Jerome offered prayers for the facility and the families. Randy spoke eloquently about the partnership between the parents, the students, the community, the churches, and the city of Costa Mesa. A wonderful spirit and new sense of hope filled the room.

When the evening was over, Randy climbed into his car and began to weep. He wept for the children of Shalimar who had so little. He wept for their parents who had come to America to make a better life for their children, only to face an uphill battle. He wept in relief that all the hard work, the perseverance to push past the many obstacles, looked like it was going to lead to something righteous and good. And finally, maybe even subconsciously, Randy wept because he had found his purpose in life.

It was a moment that just a year earlier, Randy could have only hoped to imagine.

The year before the Shalimar Learning Center's opening, Randy went through an emotional wringer that turned his world upside down.

Randy Barth was living the good life. He enjoyed regular meals in the finest restaurants. He traveled the world: the Amalfi coast of Italy, the hill towns north of Rome, Florence, Lake Como, Dublin, London and the English countryside, Portugal's Algarve coast. And then there were the tropics: Bora Bora, Kapalua, Poi Pu Beach, the Kona Coast, and Cancun. Closer to home, Randy hit the US Open in New York, where he often had box seats for his clients. There were tickets to Lakers games, and skiing in Aspen and Park City.

None of this raised an eyebrow in Corona del Mar, California. It was here that Randy fit in, or so it appeared. He was a successful stockbroker, good-looking, affable, and adept at servicing people who were among the richest in America. His clients were friends, and his friends were clients. At 33, he was earning a healthy six-figure income, enough to place him in the top 10 percent of wage earners at a pretty young age. He exuded confidence from a spate of good luck bolstered by hard work that he never minded. After all, it was the hard work that helped Randy to afford the good life.

It hadn't always been this way. He grew up the middle of three boys in a modest two-bedroom house in the middle-class Los Angeles suburb of Downey. Randy had always worked. As a kid, he mowed lawns and pumped gas. Later, as a student at UCLA, he waited tables to help pay his tuition. Ultimately, he ended up working in a five-star Beverly Hills eatery, where he took in over one hundred dollars in tips each night. There, he learned about fine wines and the way wealthy people interacted and what they liked. Five nights a week, Randy was elbow-to-elbow with celebrities of the day, like football star Joe Namath, actress Linda Evans, California Lt. Gov. Mike Curb, and trumpeter Herb Alpert.

After graduating in 1981 with a degree in economics, Randy

launched his professional career as a stockbroker with E.F. Hutton & Co. He worked in Whittier, a suburb not far from his hometown of Downey. A girlfriend, who was already a successful executive at a large clothing retailer, ushered Randy into the world of his former customers, the diners who used to tip him big. She fed him large doses of fascinating people, terrific food from fantastic restaurants, and always great wine. At the same time, Randy began developing his own prominent clients with deep pockets, many of whom lived in coastal Orange County.

When E.F. Hutton refused his transfer request to the Newport Beach office, Randy jumped to Drexel Burnham, scoring a six-figure signing bonus in the process. He bought a townhouse in Corona del Mar, the toniest part of Newport Beach. He lived across the bay frequented by sailboats as they headed out to sea from the nearby marinas. The streets, named for plants and in alphabetical order, like Avocado, Begonia, Carnation, Dahlia and Goldenrod, were lined with multi-million-dollar homes that offered spectacular views. Average incomes were among the highest in the country. With the beach, golf, tennis, and all sorts of other outdoor activities combined with its growing status as a first-rate financial hub, Newport Beach offered an amazing lifestyle for someone like him.

While it was a lifestyle Randy enjoyed, the superficial fun ultimately wasn't fulfilling. Looking back, Randy reflected, the lifestyle "felt like eating dessert without the sustenance of the main course." Randy would later realize that he was seeking a greater purpose.

Now in his late twenties, a new girlfriend would put Randy's world to the test. Instead of the lifestyle debate being a private one, it became one between Randy and his new love, Marilyn. She looked at him with her deep blue eyes in a way that melted Randy's heart. Her long brown hair and supermodel smile were enchanting. Randy had known Marilyn since long before high school, where he'd always had a secret crush on her. She was radiating. He was in love.

Yet, Marilyn's family was far more religious than Randy's. Randy had been raised in the Lutheran Church, but in his twenties he had drifted away from his faith.

"I think it's going to be hard for us, Randy, because I can't move my life forward with a man who does not believe in Christ," Marilyn told him one evening over a romantic candlelit dinner. "To have a solid long-term relationship, it has to be grounded in shared values and beliefs."

"I agree," replied Randy, surprising himself as the words came out. "Faith is an issue a couple needs to be aligned on—or at least have an understanding around—in order to have a successful marriage." He felt proud that he was mature enough to envision a future together and realize what elements were important.

Randy began accompanying Marilyn to church each Sunday, though secretly, he remained on his own comfortable agnostic perch. But one day he heard the charismatic Tim Timmons give a sermon at the South Coast Community Church.

Timmons talked about *Mere Christianity*, a book by C.S. Lewis that championed the Christian faith on the basis of morality. Timmons boomed deep enough to reach Randy's soul as he described Lewis' transformation from longtime atheist to Christian. Randy would later read Lewis himself: "I cannot learn to love my neighbor as myself till I learn to love God." Randy took these words to heart and opened himself to renewal.

Over the next year and a half, Randy became not only a believer but a married man to the woman he loved. The newlyweds worshipped at St. Andrew's Presbyterian Church near their home in Corona del Mar. With a magnificent organ facing its 1,200 seats and a glass ceiling open to the heavens, St. Andrew's inspired leadership attracted worshippers from near and far. In the late 1980s, St. Andrew's congregation was the largest undesignated giving church to the national Presbyterian denomination. It supported a $4.5 million budget and gave $1.5 million to missions that fought poverty and spread the gospel around the globe.

Some of that money would eventually prove to be useful at Shalimar, but Randy was initially more interested in expressing his newfound Christian faith by helping the homeless. He went on to lead the church's Homeless Issues Task Force and became chairman of the board of a small nonprofit called SPIN—Serving People In Need.

One evening at a SPIN fundraiser, he overheard a man challenging a nun. "If there really is a God, why does He allow homelessness?" The nun turned the inquiry around. "I think that God asks us the same question: With all that he has given us, why do we allow homelessness?"

For Randy, the pivot in this question would be transforming. "With all the resources that we have been given, why do we allow these social problems to occur?" As much as he was enjoying the privileged life, he found more meaning and purpose in helping the less fortunate. By the early 1990s, Randy was named an elder at St. Andrew's, where he worked closely with its senior pastor, the Rev. Dr. John A. Huffman Jr., a distinguished leader in the Christian church. John also chaired the board of World Vision International, a global Christian relief, development, and advocacy organization dedicated to working with children, families, and communities to overcome poverty and injustice. John became something of a mentor to Randy, helping him deepen his faith and teaching him how to how to run a nonprofit organization. Juggling his duties as an elder and chairing the board of SPIN, while at the same time working long hours as a stockbroker, Randy was finally becoming the man Marilyn always wanted him to be. Or, so he thought.

Four and a half years into the marriage, it began to quickly crumble. After a couple of feeble attempts at counseling, the marriage was over. Randy didn't know what hit him.

To describe Randy as devastated would be an understatement. He'd had a crush on Marilyn since the fourth grade though they didn't date until after their ten-year high school reunion. When she agreed to his marriage proposal at the Hotel Bel-Air, Randy was in heaven. Now, after only a few years of bliss, life felt like an empty hell. He sat listlessly in his Newport Beach office for weeks, wondering what was next.

One morning on his way to work, he heard an ad on the radio. When he got to his office he quietly closed the door and dialed 1-800-

CLUB-MED. Randy figured some time out of town would provide the escape he needed. He had hit a wall in the examination of his life with both his pastor and his therapist. Club Med felt right because it was someplace he could visit alone, yet still interact with others if he chose to. There were lots of Club Meds near places he'd been. But Randy wanted to go to someplace new, where he wasn't likely to run into anyone from Newport Beach. His wounds were too fresh and raw, and he didn't want to explain to anyone he knew what he was doing there alone.

Randy landed on the idea of Martinique in the French West Indies. The Club Med there is called Buccaneer's Creek and is at the southern tip of a tropical paradise. Its small bungalows are positioned between a lush coconut grove and one of the most beautiful beaches in the Caribbean. Randy went swimming and snorkeling in the clear waters. He sailed and he windsurfed. Yet, nothing could fully wash away the memories of Marilyn. Compounding his despair was the knowledge that he was nearly broke. Although he had been making a six-figure income for more than ten years, most of his investments were now upside down thanks to the recession of the early 1990s. Randy could escape his geography but not his reality.

On his way out of town, Randy had picked up Stephen Covey's *7 Habits of Highly Effective People*. One passage really spoke to him: "Picture yourself at your funeral. What was your life about? What are people saying about you? What is your legacy?"

Randy Barth was not a person to simply think about doing things. As he sat on that beach in Martinique, he made a list of his values and what he wanted from his next chapter in life. "I can continue to be a good-time Charlie, or I can do something more meaningful with my life," he thought. Randy began, for the first time, to think about what he wanted his legacy to be, and what changes he would need to make to turn his thoughts into a reality.

A year on, hundreds of children were coming to the Shalimar

Learning Center each day. Randy's role in the center did not involve helping them directly—after all, he still had a day job as a stockbroker. He gave himself the role of organizing the resources and navigating the politics so the people on the front lines could support the students. He would be the guy who would introduce members of the business community to Shalimar. He would be the one to show city officials that the center wasn't going to increase problems in Shalimar but rather reduce them. Paty Madueño says the center became "the golden ticket" for the neighborhood. While obtaining permits and seeking support, Randy and the St. Andrew's congregation brought influential people to Shalimar, people who in turn drew more people and even greater support.

If you're a kid growing up in Shalimar, it's difficult to envision much of a future for yourself. But, over time, teenagers from the neighborhood trickled into the newly opened Teen Center, where Director Kristina Wright told the girls: "You can waitress, or you can take school more seriously, have a career, and make a really good salary."

One thirteen-year-old girl from Guatemala, Nadia Flores, heeded these words. She promised herself that she would never become a teen mom like many of the other girls she knew. Yet, there were so many temptations on those streets and so many dead ends. Such were the hurdles the volunteers faced as they sought to change the lives of the Shalimar youth.

In 1994 on Shalimar Drive, young men lingered in abandoned cars to peddle drugs, leering at the girls who passed by. One night, a group went out, stabbed a teen with a screwdriver, and dumped him in the dry Santa Ana River bed. Left for dead, he was found by a jogger the next morning, still alive.

Despite the daunting challenges, the Shalimar Learning Center not only survived, it thrived. Volunteers flooded in, and more than one hundred youth came every day to learn and to grow. The humanitarian organization World Vision has a saying that it seeks to place the hand of the at-risk poor into the hand of the at-risk rich, so that they can both be transformed. That was what was beginning to occur at Shalimar.

There were days, however, when the students and volunteers had to take a few steps back. At a Christmas gathering, the celebration was cut short by a dreaded pop-pop-pop and the squealing of tires. Everyone dropped to the newly carpeted floor, afraid to get up because they knew it was another drive-by shooting.

Still, there were so many kids who wanted to come to the center that they took turns inside waiting for available tables and chairs. The center had become an oasis from the neighborhood chaos and their cramped apartments, where rats scratching along floorboards can destroy a night's sleep if there isn't already a fight among family members or roommates to wake them up first.

In response to the Christmas violence, the police closed off two nearby intersections to reduce the possibility of more drive-bys. Neighbors protested the closures, fearful of being caged in with criminals, but later breathed easier as the shootings declined.

Ever since the learning center had opened, police officers had stepped up patrols. Yet, the vandalism remained. The neighborhood thugs expertly used spark plugs to cut car windows without a sound. They made spider-web designs with the plugs, then pushed the glass out and reached in to the cars. They sold whatever they grabbed to buy drugs.

Mothers would make sure they had everything they needed by early evening so they didn't have to go out after dark. Yet, they wouldn't move out of the neighborhood because they didn't know where else to go. They imagined there could be places worse.

Volunteer tutor Bobbi Dauderman showed her eight-year-old student a picture of a bed. The word in Spanish was underneath: *cama*. The boy couldn't understand what the object was. A classmate turned to Bobbi and piped up: "That's because he has never slept in a bed."

Still, there was hope. Apartment manager Maria Alvarez would say many times that the center was a ray of light in darkness: *una rayita de luz en la oscuridad.*

Paty Madueño never forgot Randy's bold step into the Shalimar neighborhood. She and the others continued to help him in every way they could. During an early community mobilization effort, there weren't enough telephone lines for the phone bank. Randy took the women to his office in the shadows of John Wayne Airport. They nervously entered the sparkling elevators and stepped lightly down the plush carpeting in an uncomfortable silence. Paty looked out at the empty airfield and saw far beyond.

"I always remember that moment," Paty said recently. "Looking out through his window was a view I had never seen before. I could not recall seeing through a bigger window. I realized that the world was a very big place, and there were people in it whose lives were so very different than ours in Shalimar, and that Randy Barth didn't have to do what he was doing. He was doing all of this to really help, to make a difference."

The mothers of Shalimar knew Randy had taken a risk. And not just a financial one. He had reached across a seemingly colossal chasm—between the rich and poor of Orange County, California—to help generations to come.

Randy bridged their neighborhood with the pillars of the local community like the Tarbell family, owners of one of the largest residential real estate brokerage firms in Southern California and strong leaders in both Christian circles and local philanthropy. Betsy Tarbell once told Randy about an organization she was helping launch called Women of Vision, an arm of World Vision that was founded to help mothers and children around the world. Randy remembered Betsy saying that if he ever knew of a local project that would be a good fit for volunteers from the organization, to let her know.

After one call to Betsy, members of Women of Vision streamed in to Shalimar. Several volunteers including Karen French and Jean Wenke had once been public school teachers. Shalimar became their new school. It wasn't long before the center grew to three apartments in two buildings. Residents took note, and soon the place was affectionately called "la escuelita," the little school.

The Women of Vision worked side by side with other volunteers from St. Andrew's and neighboring communities. Together, they were a potent group. They included leaders in education, business, and government. Yet, the volunteers were getting as much from the Shalimar students as the students were getting from them. Providing these kids academic support and exposure to broader opportunities—support that middle- and upper-middle-class kids often take for granted—gave each volunteer a great sense of purpose. The volunteers brought resources and life experiences to the children that they might not have found otherwise.

"We had a network. I think it attracted people, and people saw the value in doing it. It was a way for people to make a difference, said Bobbi Dauderman, who has been a volunteer for close to twenty years. "For me, working with these kids and getting them to find the answers and helping them down that path is really rewarding."

During Bobbi's time with the group, she promoted a literacy project inside the Shalimar Learning Center and brought financial support. "The tutoring has definitely come a long way over time," she said. "At the beginning, it was very chaotic, with few protocols in place. The children were so happy for the help, though."

Bobbi made a mental note each time she heard a heartbreaking story. Too often, at least in those early days, the student's father was in prison and the mother worked a second job at night. "I gave those kids a lot of credit because they were trying to get ahead," she said. "They would go home, and there wasn't a table to put their homework down on. Many of the parents couldn't help them with their homework. We got so much from helping them."

Their success, coupled with media coverage of the center's opening, led to calls from all over Southern California from folks who wanted to replicate Shalimar. Some came from close by, including other neighborhoods of Costa Mesa and nearby Santa Ana. Randy, always one to think big, began to wonder, "Was this a one-time accident where a lot of things came together? Or could this work be replicated?"

The answer to the second question turned out to be yes.

2

Javier, Joe, Ernest, Nadia, and Paolo

Javier Diaz had two choices growing up in Shalimar gang territory: join the gang or be a lookout "in the know." He was already fourteen and still hadn't made a decision, even though his uncle had run with the gang, enjoying nice clothes, nice cars, and not-so-nice girls. Everyone expected Javier would soon join up too.

When Javier got to Estancia High School, the gangbangers began to give him a rough time. As a resident of Shalimar territory, gang member or not, he qualified as a crosstown rival. There were a few fights. Most of the time, Javier watched, but sometimes he threw some punches. He could hold his own if he had to, but he didn't want to. He didn't want trouble.

In order to stay safe, Javier requested a transfer across town to Newport Harbor High School. But he wondered if he would ever really be safe. Javier's struggle, and those of his classmates and neighbors, became the struggle of the Shalimar Learning Center as it sought to help its first generation of students, scarred by the economics of their families and the violence outside their doors.

By the time he was fourteen, Javier had seen five drive-by shootings from his bedroom window. The fiery burst of automatic weapons would be followed by screeching tires and ghastly screams. Then came the drive-by that caught his friend. Let's call him, Joe, because he doesn't really want to be on these pages. Joe wants to forget all of this ever happened.

Javier, Joe, and another friend, whom we'll call Ernest, knew that rival gangs had it in for the neighborhood. Things were actually better since the Shalimar Learning Center had opened. The police had erected blockades to curb drive-bys, and city officials now required derelict property owners to bring their buildings up to code. Javier, Joe, and Ernest even went to the center after school. There, they met Sam Anderson, a volunteer tutor who in the summer of 1994 paid the three of them to clean his boat.

Sam, an early retiree, was a man of considerable means, and could be both unapologetic and modest. He drove a top-of-the-line Mercedes, but he would not mind picking up Shalimar teens and their mothers and bringing them home. He raised a few eyebrows when he drove through Shalimar in the shiny black car; drug dealers would come running, thinking he was a potential customer. Behind his thick glasses, the teens recognized the eyes of a man who truly wanted to help. Sam spoke in a soft Southern accent with a clear message on the importance of finishing high school and setting both personal and professional goals. In a neighborhood with so many rough edges, Sam's fatherly concern felt like love.

On the day the boys were set to clean his boat, Sam picked them up at Shalimar and headed for his home in Beacon Bay. In Shalimar, the boys' apartments faced a crowded street. Sam's home faced Newport Harbor, and his boat was docked in front. When the boys finished the work, Sam took them out for a cruise and showed them the upscale islands that dot the harbor: Balboa, Collins, Harbor, Lido, Linda, and Bay. From the deck of the boat, the teens gazed at the waterfront homes, many as large as the apartment buildings where they lived. With lawn furniture outside nicer than anything they'd ever seen indoors, they couldn't help but realize they lived a world away.

Life in Shalimar may have been improving, but a few things remained the same. Early one evening in February 1995, Javier, Joe, and Ernest watched as a white Blazer with tinted windows circled the block repeatedly. Nothing happened, but the three remained alert just in case. Then just a few minutes after 10 p.m., Javier was working outside on a car radio when the silence was shattered. *Bamamama-mam. Bamamamamam. Bamamamamam. Bamamamamam!*

The Blazer was still a block away, but the gunfire had already arrived. Joe looked up, surprised, as 15 more shots blasted out of an automatic weapon. No one could really see it, but they knew it had a long barrel. Ernest threw his only weapon, a beer bottle, at the car but missed. Javier choked, stunned that he was part of a melee that seemed more like a movie than real life. The sound of the Blazer's tires screeched through the dark neighborhood. It felt like time had stood still, until…

Joe looked down at his shirt and saw blood.

"I've been shot!" he cried.

Javier quickly removed Joe's shirt, then his own, and instinctively applied pressure to the two bullet wounds in Joe's stomach. He later wondered how he knew to do this. Blood soaked through both of their shirts, but Javier would not let up.

"It's going to be all right," he assured Joe. "Those guys are freaking idiots. I can't believe this."

Police took Javier and Ernest in for questioning, holding them in the station until just before dawn. While Joe opted to forget the entire night, the shooting remained etched in Javier's and Ernest's memories, changing both of their lives forever.

For Ernest, the hope and promise of the Shalimar Learning Center was overshadowed by the gang wars. He had grown up watching people fighting in the alleys and then at Estancia High, where he learned to hold his own against rival gang members. Ernest was a strong fighter and perfected his skills so he could send a guy to the ground with a single punch.

Ernest now believed he needed to defend Shalimar, his home since he was a baby. He joined the gang. He stopped going to school. He ran away from home. By the time he was sixteen, Ernest and his girlfriend were staying a week at a time in different motels. He was using and selling crack cocaine and earning over two hundred dollars for less than two hours of work.

Randy, Sam, and the other volunteers at the Learning Center who had known Ernest were saddened. The loss made them look more closely at what they and others could do to help save young men like him.

Then Randy read about Geoffrey Canada, who worked with the Rheedlen Centers for Children and Families in New York City. Canada later developed the Harlem Children's Zone, a nonprofit organization whose mission is "doing nothing less than breaking the cycle of generational poverty for the thousands of children and families it serves."

Their efforts to reach young people and change their futures resonated with Randy. He was learning how a support system could help offset some of the deficiencies found in low-income families: parents with limited education, parents struggling with addictions, and parents too busy working to put food on the table to effectively engage with their children. Randy's research led him to understand that doing well in school was not simply a question of intellectual ability or the quality of the school, but rather the product of all the influences in a child's life. Kids who were read to regularly and engaged in open-ended dialogue from an early age, in any language, entered school much more prepared to learn to read. This early preparation often led to more early success which, in turn, built confidence and a love for learning. Kids in low-income neighborhoods, from Shalimar to Harlem, often didn't start with that advantage.

Geoffrey Canada was well into his work in Harlem when Randy began his in Shalimar, and both would find that they would need to forge ahead and learn from trial and error. Geoffrey's work would involve a paid staff helping a mostly African American population. Randy's organization was still a group of unpaid volunteers who gave their all to build a support system for mostly Latino students, reflecting the changing demographics in Southern California. Along the way, they learned to accept the unfortunate fact that there would be teens like Ernest whom they would not be able to reach. Though they were saddened by what happened to Ernest's life, they remained hopeful for the lives of others. "We saw so much progress with so many kids, and that is what kept us all going," Sam recalled.

Over time, Randy and his team were discovering that the problems they encountered at Shalimar were similar to what was happening in low-income neighborhoods across America. They came to realize that the consequences of inaction for our communities and our country could prove to be tragic.

One evening Randy presented a set of surprising statistics to a group of donors. The academic performance of eighteen-year-old Latino and African American students in California was the same as that of thirteen-year-old Asian Americans and Caucasians. With the California student population now composed of 63 percent Latino and African American students (57 percent Latino and 6 percent African American), a crisis was brewing that would have a huge negative effect on the quality of California's workforce. It would later turn out that by 2012, according to state Superintendent Tom Torlakson's Blueprint for Education, the California workforce under the age of thirty-five was one of the least-educated in the developed world. This stood in sharp contrast to the state's current workforce over fifty, which is one of the world's best-educated. By 2020, it is expected that there would be a shortage of 1 million college graduates in California's labor market. Statistics like this were not good for anyone, rich or poor.

The issue for Randy was no longer about helping kids with their homework. It was evolving into a larger mission that could help build a "school support ecosystem" that would include comprehensive after-school programs, summer learning programs, small group tutoring programs, early learning programs, parent programs, and community engagement and health programs. But that would take more than a decade of trial and error, failure and success. In the early years, just taking SAT preparation classes was a radical idea in Shalimar. But love and dedication kept everyone moving forward.

Sadly, Ernest did not appreciate nor understand the outstretched arms at Shalimar as did his friend, Javier, who was drawn to the promise underlying the center's mission. The more Javier worked to improve his life, the less Ernest had anything to do with him. They used to be best friends, but now Ernest wouldn't even shoot hoops with Javier. Maybe that was just as well, Javier thought.

"Once you get into that life, you are in your own world," Javier recalled years later. "We had hit a fork in the road. He was headed on his path, and I was on a different path. Our relationship changed dramatically. It got to the point where I did not want to hang out with him anymore. No one was angry. We just knew who we were, and we were not the same."

Ernest looked back recently, too, and explained that he felt at the time that he needed to defend himself. He needed the gang to stand behind him. "I did get more involved in the gang because by then, rivals already knew who I was, and it was either get in or I would not be safe by myself," he said. "It wasn't just the shooting. By then I was already hanging out there and doing the things gangs do. I didn't really think I could keep going to the teen center, but let me tell you that every time I went, they welcomed me with open arms. I was one of the first ones that went there. It was my decision to make, and I chose the gang."

Even though he missed his friendship with Ernest, Javier made a clear decision the night Joe was shot.

"For me, that night was like, 'Holy crap. I do not want to get involved with gangs,'" Javier recalled.

Then he remembered Sam Anderson, the man with a big heart, the man who trusted him enough to bring him to his home. As Javier spent more time at the Shalimar Teen Center, Sam was there along with the other tutors who helped Javier make his way through school. Although born in the United States, Javier spoke Spanish at home. His mother, a native of Sonora, Mexico, immigrated to America at age seventeen. English was Javier's second language, and for a long time, it was also his nemesis.

"The hardest was writing essays," Javier recalled. "I would do the bare minimum, and the teachers didn't push me because they didn't expect much from me."

The only subject that really interested Javier was history. He told Sam about an assignment that would involve learning about the battles of the Civil War. Sam "got more excited than me," Javier recalled.

Sam's enthusiasm, "at first seemed a bit odd, but I was getting better grades thanks to him. All at once, I was doing better in every subject," Javier remembered. "With his support, I began to really believe in myself and in what I was doing," he added with a smile.

While Ernest remained on the streets dealing drugs, Javier ran for president of the Shalimar Teen Center and won.

When Javier graduated from Newport Harbor High School, the occasion was almost as grand as a presidential inauguration. Javier would be the first person in his family with a high school diploma. Sam, Javier's mother, his friends, and even his uncle joined the throng to watch him walk proudly across the stage in his cap and gown to receive his diploma. Javier had finally reached his goal.

But Javier had not thought much about what would come next. What would he do now? Even as he attended Orange Coast College, the local community college, the Shalimar gang still loomed large back in the neighborhood. Javier needed to get away.

He managed to get away all right, all the way to London. Javier enlisted in the US Marine Corps and served his country for four years, including two years in England. But once his time was up, he returned to Costa Mesa, where once again he was faced with gang members who could still draw him in.

So even though he was now a 22-year-old who didn't have a place in an afterschool center, he called his mentor Sam for guidance. Sam was always happy to help former students whenever he could.

"Sam told me I really needed to get back to school. So I did," Javier said.

Javier finished his associate degree at Orange Coast College and then earned a bachelor's in sociology at California State University, Fullerton. He volunteered at the Shalimar Learning Center and later received a teaching credential and a master's degree from Loyola Marymount University. Javier was hired by the Laguna Beach Unified School District to serve as the school community liaison. Today, he helps limited- and non-English-speaking children become successful in school. He's still hoping to become a teacher. In budget-strapped California, teaching jobs have been hard to come by, even for bilingual applicants like Javier.

Not long ago, the now-34-year-old Javier heard from Ernest, who has spent only five years outside a jail cell since they parted ways at age sixteen. Javier knows that Ernest's story could have been his own had he not clung to the path forged with the help of tutors at Shalimar.

Ernest's life has not been easy. He spent a lot of time in juvenile hall. Then, he found himself in county jail and later, state prisons. His first felony assault charge stemmed from a fight in 1998. The second and third stemmed from another fight in 2005 when he punched a sheriff's deputy and knocked him to the ground.

It was Ernest's third strike, and he was out. Just before Ernest's twenty-seventh birthday, a judge laid down his gavel and declared, "thirty years to life."

Ernest was sent to Pelican Bay State Prison, explicitly designed to house California's "worst of the worst" in solitary confinement. For five years, he spent twenty-three hours in a windowless 8-by-10-foot cell. His only view was through a crack in a perforated steel door that faced a solid concrete wall. He was later sent back into the general prison population in another facility, where he now spends his days reading anything he can get his hands on.

Ernest hopes to reduce his sentence because of a state initiative passed in late 2012 that changes the "Three Strikes Law." If there were a third conviction involving a nonviolent crime, the prisoner could petition the court for a reduced sentence. Ernest reached out to Javier for a written recommendation. His old friend was only too happy to comply.

Ernest also reached out for a recommendation from Nadia Flores, another old friend from Shalimar. Although she was a few years younger, he always remembered the pretty girl with coffee-bean eyes and shiny black hair. She was the Shalimar girl who used to spend her weekends going to wild house parties and cruising Bristol Street in Santa Ana.

Nadia never forgot Ernest, Javier, nor Joe. The hardship they all endured, as the children of recent immigrants with little education, is engraved in her memory and continues to shape her life today.

Growing up in Shalimar, Nadia couldn't imagine much of a future, besides work, and working, and working some more. Maybe, she thought, she could become a restaurant manager. But sometimes she wondered if she might not even live long enough for anything to matter. She recalled Joe getting shot and how she learned about it on the bus after school.

"Is he OK? Is he? He is alive, isn't he?" she asked her friends as they rode from Newport Harbor High back to Shalimar.

"Oh, he's fine now," said one. "Gangbangers, you know."

"Yeah," she said, remembering the frequent gunfire. "I know."

Nadia knew that kids all around her were being consumed by life on the street. Her parents provided few clues of what she ought to be doing. Her mother was rarely at home. She was a maid and babysitter for a family that lived nearly two hours away. Her father worked as a karate teacher, but would often drink so much that he was useless. Her sister spent her days playing with the neighbors, leaving Nadia frequently alone in the apartment. When she turned thirteen, her family sent her out to find a job to help with the bills. As soon as a school counselor helped her obtain a work permit, Nadia got a job in telemarketing. Her focus then became how to get from school to her apartment, and from her apartment to school and to work.

While crime and misfortune surrounded her family's tiny apartment, Newport Harbor High was filled with rich kids from neighboring Newport Beach who got BMWs for their sixteenth birthdays whose parents all belonged to the same yacht club. Her parents, immigrants from Guatemala who spoke mostly Spanish, didn't belong to anything.

While her classmates played water polo or football or swished pom-poms as cheerleaders, Nadia worked as a telemarketer. From there she found a job at Golden Spoon, then Togo's sandwiches, the Omelet Parlor, and even Costa Mesa City Hall. She wasn't picky. The Youth Employment Service referred her to the jobs, and she would take anything she could get.

When Nadia's classmates gathered for yogurt and smoothies after football games, they'd see her in a black apron emblazoned with the words "Golden Spoon" covering her white collared shirt. Nadia's hair was swept back under a black hat as she served her classmates. Sometimes the next day, Nadia's mother would clean their houses.

Money was always tight. Nadia was self-conscious of her clothes and those tell-tale blue tickets she used to pay for her lunches—the ones given to kids whose meals were federally subsidized.

"I just wanted to fit in, but I was showing up at Newport Harbor High School in my clothes from Target and K-Mart," she recalled. "My parents couldn't drive me to school, so they bought me this pink-and-purple bicycle, a K-Mart special. It was embarrassing. I'd roll in to school on this cheap bike, and my classmates were coming in their new cars."

Then one day Nadia and her friends were told about the idea for the Shalimar Learning Center, just blocks from her apartment.

"Neighborhood organizers asked us if we would go to such a place," she recalled. "I told them I would, but I wasn't thinking about doing homework. I thought the center would be a great place to hang out with friends and not get shot. I had no real interest in doing better in school. I really didn't see any reason to bother."

As time went on, though, Nadia began to see plenty of reason to bother. She was repulsed by the idea that she might end up like her parents or, even worse, out on the streets. She remembered Joe's shooting and reminded herself that she would need to keep busy to lessen the odds of being there the next time a shooting occurred.

When the Shalimar Learning Center opened, Nadia and her friends peered in through the door. The desks were shiny and clean. The walls were freshly painted, an unusual sight for Nadia and the Shalimar kids who lived in run-down apartments. Equally surprising was the team of volunteers. They were all white. And Nadia knew they were all rich because she could see their Mercedes and BMWs parked outside. The only other people she knew who had cars like that were drug dealers.

"I had to think, why had these people come to help us?" Nadia said.

They reminded her of the woman her grandmother worked for. Her grandmother was a maid in the upscale city of La Habra Heights. When Nadia was little, her grandmother had often brought her along because she knew the girl would be neglected at home.

Nadia and her grandmother kept quiet and to themselves in the woman's home and never ate at the dining room table if the family was present. Still, the woman was nice. When Nadia's grandmother couldn't help her with homework, the woman stepped in and provided a few tips or took Nadia to buy supplies for school projects. Nadia imagined these white people coming to Shalimar would be much like her. She wasn't intimidated—in fact she became increasingly intrigued.

Nadia immediately found support in Sam, who became like a second father. His Southern accent charmed her, and he made her think with his challenging questions. He asked her what she wanted to be when she was thirty-two. What did she want her life to be like? No one had ever asked her things like that before, and she quickly realized that she'd have to set some goals in order to pull herself out of Shalimar. Sam and the other tutors would frequently warn her about the consequences of not going to college. No matter what questions she had, they were there to help. If she couldn't make it to the center because she was working, the tutors would help her after hours. Ultimately it would take a village of gentlemen and kind ladies from Newport Beach to help Nadia.

Edna Rowe, a St. Andrew's volunteer, helped Nadia with geometry. Jill McWhertor, another St. Andrew's volunteer and a teacher in the Newport-Mesa Unified School District, provided Algebra II and Calculus support. Nicole Denholm tutored Nadia in French. Barbara Roberts proofed her essays. Judy Coyne filled Nadia with her knowledge of Biology and Physics. Judy had heard about Shalimar at church and felt she might be able to help students in science. After all, she had a degree in bacteriology and had worked in medicine for decades.

Judy was assigned to the teen center, and that's where she met Nadia, "I saw this young woman who wanted so badly to succeed. I had the time to help, so I did."

Nadia's work schedules meant she frequently could not come to the center during regular hours, so Judy and Nadia would meet at 10 p.m. and study until midnight. Both tutor and student made a conscious decision to plug through until graduation. "She really helped me fill every single gap," Nadia said.

One weekend, Judy and Nadia went to the nearby Back Bay, a scenic nature preserve home to migratory birds and endangered species that surrounds a boot-shaped slice of Newport Harbor. They were there to gather insects for Nadia's biology project. Nadia's parents would have never had the time. She remembers wondering, would they have even known where the Back Bay was or which bugs to collect? Together, Nadia and Judy carefully caught all the species they needed, then placed the insects in jars to dry, and later pinned them to a board, one by one.

"Without Shalimar, without people like Judy, I wouldn't have made it into college," Nadia said. "I wouldn't be where I am today."

Nadia was one of the first Shalimar students to participate in a SAT preparation class at the Shalimar Learning Center. Just studying for the test separated her emotionally from the neighborhood where most residents earned not much more than minimum wage. Believing that she had a shot at attending college lifted Nadia's heart. It made college seem closer than it ever had.

With the SAT under her belt, an army of tutors helped her with applications. Soon, the acceptance letters rolled in. They came from the University of Southern California, Chapman University, and the University of California, Santa Barbara. She chose Santa Barbara and graduated four years later. The volunteers and staff from Shalimar were all there, proudly watching as she walked in a sea of long black gowns and mortarboards. No one in Nadia's family had graduated from high school, and here she was, graduating from college. The challenges she overcame and her triumphs would serve as examples as Randy Barth and his volunteers worked to garner more support and to change more and more lives.

"Vilmaaaa! Veel-ma!"

Through an open window from inside her house, the neighbor was calling out for thirteen-year-old Vilma. "I'm coming, Auntie," Vilma yelled from her own little house in Santa Ana, the second-largest city in El Salvador. But you wouldn't know it from the looks of Vilma's neighborhood, a maze of cinderblock houses set on dusty, unpaved roads. Vilma lived in one of the colonias, a poor neighborhood that lacked public services and decent schools.

But Vilma wasn't moving very fast. The heat was oppressive. There was no food, little water, no air conditioning, or even a fan. Vilma loved Auntie, who was almost like a real relative. Often, she would have Vilma pick through her hair looking for gray strands. Vilma's job was to pull them out, and she loved to do it.

If Vilma pulled out enough strands, Auntie would reward her with a banana or a peach. One of nine children who often squabbled to get meals, Vilma would then slowly sink her teeth into the delicious fruit with glee. This was as close to paradise as she had ever known. Her father was a tile layer who, by the early 1980s, was having trouble making a living. Civil war tore through El Salvador, hurting the pocketbooks of big companies and the working poor alike. Her mother was stuck at home, taking care of her large brood. Vilma couldn't stand the constant focus on food, or the lack of it. They would eat tortillas and beans three times a day. But sometimes, not even that was available.

"I can buy you shoes, or we can eat," her mother would often say.

Struggles like these, coupled with civil wars, drought, hardship, and corruption, drove millions of Latino immigrants to the United States in the 1980s and 1990s. Most of the immigrants in Orange County came from Mexico, but there were pockets of Central Americans like the one in Shalimar that would later attract Vilma and her future husband.

Vilma's story is typical of many Shalimar residents and demonstrates the inherent disadvantages that their children faced as they tried to make their way through school. While the parents were mostly hardworking, often they did not have the resources to bring up children in America. It wasn't just that they didn't speak English. Many parents hadn't even finished elementary school in their own countries, and now they were faced with the bureaucracies inherent in public education in a foreign country. In their new neighborhoods in America, there were gangs they had never seen in their small villages back home. Before, they could manage on a meager income while still living in the family house. Now, they needed to pay rent, which in Orange County was so high that they would end up in overcrowded, run-down apartments just to get by.

Despite these hurdles, the stories that filtered back to Mexico, Guatemala, or El Salvador always focused on the positive aspects of life in America. Vilma heard that she could make enough money to feed all of her siblings. So with only a sixth-grade education and a small bag of clothes, she risked everything and headed north. Her plan was to make a new life and earn money to send back to her mother in El Salvador. She began her journey on land, riding buses and trains when she could. By the time she crossed the border into Guatemala, she had run into trouble. Fortunately, she met a man who came to her rescue in Guatemala City, the country's gritty capital. He offered her food and a place to stay.

Vilma's contagious smile and ink-black hair put a spell on Carlos Leon, the son of Chinese immigrants who owned several restaurants. Carlos had never known the poverty she was trying to escape from, but he was far from content in Guatemala. Civil war also plagued his country, and opportunities were limited. He studied to receive a vocational certificate to become an elementary school teacher, but he was working as a driver for a national soccer player.

After Vilma and Carlos married, they decided they would move to America. Carlos had already lived in Los Angeles back in 1967 and in Chicago in 1976. But each time, he returned to be with his family. This time, however, he wondered if he would ever come back. His sister had already moved to California and was living with her husband in Costa Mesa. Vilma and Carlos settled nearby. First, they would rent a bedroom in a Shalimar apartment for three hundred dollars. Then, they earned enough to rent the whole two-bedroom unit for five hundred dollars. They stayed in that same apartment for twenty years.

"It's not that we didn't know the neighborhood was a problem. We did," said Carlos. "But no one bothered us, and we didn't bother anyone."

Carlos always paid the rent on time. He always had steady work, and he always worked hard. Just days after arriving on a plane from Guatemala, he was offered a job to help a wealthy family who had renovated their home. Carlos would be the one to reorganize the house and place all the furniture back. That led to a second job as a groundskeeper for an even wealthier Newport Beach family. He would tend to their lawns and whatever they asked. At the end of each day, he would head back to Shalimar.

A downstairs neighbor worked as a sobador and healer who helped Shalimar neighbors with their aches and pains. When Vilma could not conceive a child, the couple went to him. He rubbed her belly and massaged her back. Before long, Vilma had one child and became pregnant a second time. At first Carlos was displeased. He already had two children in Guatemala from a previous marriage. Vilma wouldn't be able to work her factory job for months, and Carlos feared that two children would make their finances too tight.

Before too long, Carlos' attitude changed completely. Paolo, the second boy, born in 1986, was incredibly bright. He played soccer and the neighborhood's favorite pastime, Kick the Can. Carlos was amazed that his young boy already spoke like an adult and took his education so seriously.

Paolo got help with his homework at the Shalimar Learning Center, but he was often annoyed with the other kids. "Papa, they all talk too much. They are joking around. That won't help anyone in the long run," Paolo would report back to his parents.

Yet, Paolo knew the Shalimar Learning Center could help him. There were kids like Nadia Flores who had been in these same seats just a few years before who had not only graduated high school, but also graduated college. Paolo was never allured by the life of gang members; he knew they were up to no good. But could he do more than just menial jobs after graduating high school? His parents still hadn't learned English, nor did they have the time to read to him or take him to museums or cultural events. They loved him with all their hearts, but his parents simply didn't understand nor could they really help him get ahead. They didn't know about the importance of extracurricular activities or SAT preparation or college applications.

Paolo never got the opportunity to play with expensive Lego sets or with construction toys. But he dreamed that one day he would construct big buildings and maybe even design them. When he learned that a professional who designs buildings is a called an architect, he closely guarded the nearly impossible dream of becoming one. He wasn't much of an artist, but still he thought he might be able to create plans for buildings. Unfortunately, he hadn't a clue how he would reach his goal.

Like many children of immigrants, he would have to find the support he needed outside his home. But where would he find this help?

Despite Paolo's criticism of other students, he saw that the Learning Center could provide the personal attention he couldn't get at school. With help from employees, volunteers, and even Randy himself, he began to craft a plan for his future.

"At the center, they were telling me what I needed to do to get ready for high school, and I liked that. My parents were very, very supportive, but they couldn't help me with some things because of the language barrier," Paolo said.

Shalimar tutors had high expectations for Paolo. They wondered if he might be able to go to a new elite prep school, Sage Hill in Newport Beach. Sage Hill hosts small classes and a rigorous curriculum for students whose families can afford the $33,000-per-year tuition. To create some diversity, the school offers scholarships, and the competition is fierce. With the support of his tutors at Shalimar,

Paolo won one of the scholarships and was soon to be launched on a life-changing trajectory.

"I knew it meant leaving everything behind, but I was willing to do anything to get an edge. I thought Sage Hill would be critical to my success," Paolo said.

Paolo's father, Carlos, still worked as a groundskeeper in Newport Beach. Each morning, he would drop Paolo off at school seventy-five minutes early so he could still get to work on time. Meanwhile, with time on his hands, Paolo befriended a cafeteria worker who often would make him breakfast.

Initially, the experience was grueling. Paolo quickly realized that his Sage Hill classmates were far ahead of him in just about everything. His public school experience had not prepared him for anything like this. It was most obvious in English. Paolo did not grasp the underlying meanings in fiction. He read the words on the page and accepted them at face value.

When the class read *The Adventures of Huckleberry Finn*, Paolo said he might have missed the book's criticism of slavery if his teacher had not pointed it out. No character in the book is left undamaged by slavery, yet, Paolo said, "I would have missed those literary meanings if they weren't explained to me."

"Critical-thinking skills were not yet on my radar," he recalled. "My peers already understood that fiction may carry layers of meaning. I did not know that. In fact, I realized that my English language skills were likely limited compared to theirs. I was speaking Spanish at home."

Living in these two worlds had become second nature to Paolo. Crossing from one to another was almost seamless. From the Shalimar neighborhood, the route to Paolo's future took him down 17th Street a few miles to Dover Drive, then straight to the coast. Or, one could follow the Santa Ana River, which had created an estuary that became Upper Newport Bay, which flowed into Newport Bay. Before the turn of the twentieth century, new settlers with plans for tourism and shipping dredged this bay, turning it into a navigable harbor, and developed the sandbars, building luxury homes on them. For years, Newport Harbor was not much of a year-round residential area, but rather a place where wealthy people from Los Angeles and Pasadena might spend their summers.

In the 1950s, developers took a mudflat that the locals called Shark Island, leveled it, and subdivided it into 107 lots set in a horse-shoe so that each had its own dock and water views. They changed the name to Linda Isle. The island allows public access, yet it's pretty hard to find. An electronic gate controls access to the island in Newport Harbor. The houses here are big and bigger. Spanish, English Tudor, and sleek modern mansions sit side-by-side. The two-bedroom apartment where Paolo Leon and his parents lived was likely smaller than most of the guest quarters on the island.

Yet, on a sunny day in the spring of 2000, Paolo Leon and his father headed to Linda Isle. When they reached the gate in Carlos' Honda, they received clearance to head down the island's only street, Linda Isle Drive. The two parked, got out, and headed, tools in hand, toward one of the ubiquitous docks. Carlos, who worked during the week as a groundskeeper, would often work weekends, too. For this job, Carlos was to build a ramp that would lead down to the family's floating dock. He was to receive $1,500, a fraction of what a con-struction company might charge for the same job, but a lot more than he would have seen otherwise. Carlos was happy, not only for the opportunity to earn some extra money, but because Paolo was there, too.

And it was here on Linda Isle that Paolo got his first taste of being an architect. Carlos offered to pay his son for his help in both the design and construction of the ramp. But Paolo refused the money; he was there for the experience. Working with his dad on the weekends was the only way he could spend time with him.

The rest of the week Paolo was busy trying to fit in at Sage Hill. To smooth the way, he often spoke at the school's weekly "town meetings." On the day the upcoming school elections were announced, Paolo decided to run for student body president. He knew that he might not stand a chance, but if he won, it would look great on a college application. The election was an interesting test to see if a scholarship kid could really be accepted in a school like this. His classmates were driven to school in Ferraris, or they drove themselves in their own BMWs. They lived in sprawling homes that overlooked the ocean. Paolo, on the other hand, was still getting rides in his dad's older Honda. Paolo was up against five other candidates, but when the votes were counted, he was the winner. Even today, he still can't imagine how it happened.

"It might have been because they knew my story and they liked it," Paolo said.

But it wasn't only fellow students who admired him. A school administrator hired Paolo to tutor her children in math and later offered him the chance to buy her used car. Paolo would be given the car immediately and would work off the payments through tutoring. Paolo could not believe his good fortune. The black Honda Accord looked like new. Without this opportunity, he might not have owned a car for years.

Paolo continued to create his own good luck. At the end of high school, he won a full-ride academic scholarship to the University of Southern California. USC has one of the premiere architecture schools on the West Coast, and Paolo wanted to pursue his dream.

All of these accomplishments did not go unnoticed. Randy saw Paolo as a student who, even at a young age, could speak to potential donors of the organization that had grown into THINK Together. His former tutor Bobbi Dauderman also admired Paolo and his dream to become an architect. One year when she bought a table at a THINK Together fundraiser at the Balboa Bay Club, she invited Paolo to sit with her. She also invited a friend, Carl McLarand, chairman and chief executive officer of one of the most prominent architectural firms in Orange County, now known as MVE & Partners. Carl and Paolo hit it off instantly. Carl was impressed with Paolo's determination, while Paolo was just hoping to say the right things.

Obviously he did: Carl offered Paolo an internship contingent on the successful completion of Paolo's first year at USC. This offer would set the stage for the coming years. Carl co-chaired the board of councilors for the Architecture School at USC, which was also his alma mater. The summers after Paolo's freshman and sophomore years, he worked as an intern at MVE. By his junior year, Paolo was interning there year-round, happily driving his black Honda Accord back and forth between MVE and his classes at USC. Because Paolo was working nearly full-time at MVE and with his college paid for by scholarship, Paolo was able to help his parents buy a condominium in Tustin, the first home that the family had owned.

"This was a bright kid who would have made it somehow, some way," Randy remembers, "but I think it was through THINK Together that he was able to take advantage of opportunities and connections. We were able to help make his dreams come true."

When the day came for Paolo to receive his degree from USC, Randy and his THINK colleague Mia Castillo joined the Leon family and stood proudly in the audience to watch Paolo promenade in his graduation cap and gown. Later, they would join the family's festivities. A number of Leon relatives traveled from Guatemala for the celebration, joining family and friends from Shalimar, Sage Hill, USC, MVE, and elsewhere along the family's journey. The Leon family had come to America to make a better life, and their American Dream was coming true.

Soon after the graduation, Carlos built a special alcove with recessed lighting in the living room of the new family home. In this alcove hangs Paolo's diploma, along with the tassel from his graduation cap, in a beautiful frame. The recessed lighting, which Carlos learned to install during his thirty-five years working for that same Newport Beach family, illuminates the embossed black lettering. Paolo beams as he thinks back to the days he and his father spent working together on Linda Isle, a place they might never have belonged, but a place that joined them solidly together. It was this project that Paolo included in his application to USC. It remains the architectural project that brings him the greatest pride.

3

THINK Together

Don Moe was the sort of contact any nonprofit leader would relish. He was a senior consultant to the Irvine Company, which owns one-sixth of Orange County and is one of the largest owners of office buildings, apartments, and shopping centers in America. Randy had a natural cheerleader in Don, who was both his former brother-in-law and his client. They saw each other at least once a year for Don's annual investment portfolio review.

Wearing his stockbroker hat, Randy met the silver-haired Don one day for lunch in December of 1996 at the Pacific Club in Newport Beach. Here, the two could find an oasis in their otherwise over-scheduled lives. The club, founded by real estate tycoons George Argyros and William Lyon, along with industrialist J. Robert Fluor among others, was modeled on dinner clubs such as the University Club in New York. Members shelled out thousands of dollars to join and paid a few hundred more a month to dine and enjoy the facilities. The Pacific Club was a regular haunt for Randy, who had been a member there for years. Sitting in the richly paneled Grill Room, where many of Orange County's dealmakers work their magic, Randy and Don nibbled on the club's signature cheese sticks while waiting for their meals. Randy couldn't help from bringing up an obviously incongruous subject: his work at the Shalimar Learning and Teen Center.

"It's been really interesting because we keep getting calls about what we did and how we did it," Randy said. "Now we've learned from our experience and brought some staff in to give some structure to the program."

Randy's new wife, the former Mary Kessler, who had been a mining executive in Arizona before they married the previous year, was working (full-time and without pay) as the center's first director. Randy told Don about Mary's organizational skills and her fluency in Spanish, which she had picked up while working at an orphanage in Mexico during college. Her work at Shalimar enabled Randy to point his attention to a new center he was helping to launch.

Randy brought Don up to speed on other details of his personal life. He and Mary had adopted a girl, Emily Grace, and another girl, whom they'd name Kathryn Rose, was on the way. He told Don about the six-bedroom home in Santa Ana that they had bought recently that was now under renovation. There was a lot to catch up on. Much of this was the stuff of a normal, upper-middle-class life. But what was unique was Randy's newfound passion to combat poverty and gangs in a couple of the toughest neighborhoods in Orange County.

"We've started a new program in Santa Ana with Mariner's Church," another evangelical megachurch, Randy told Don. "We're in another dicey neighborhood filled with the same elements: drug dealers, prostitutes, domestic violence, and all sorts of crime. The whole street backs up to railroad tracks. All the apartments are one-bedrooms that were once military housing for the Tustin Marine Corps Air Base.

"It's a tumultuous area, much more so than Shalimar," Randy continued, his words coming out in a rush. "There's tension between the Cambodian immigrants and the Latino immigrants, and the population is so transient. There's nearly a 100 percent annual turnover in student population in the neighborhood schools. We've made a commitment to this neighborhood called Minnie Street, and I refuse to let them down. And we're looking at other sites, too."

Don was intrigued by Randy's newfound passion. He was visibly impressed with his friend's efforts and swayed by his message. Randy repeated the statistics he'd learned by heart: By the mid-1990s, nearly

25 percent of Orange County's students lived in impoverished conditions. Escalating poverty in this otherwise prosperous county meant that the future workforce could potentially be under-educated and under-prepared.

Randy may have sounded like a community activist, citing this sort of stuff to his former brother-in-law, but perhaps because of his deep understanding of economics and data and his ability to translate both to investors, he was able to drive the message home. Besides, Randy wasn't just repeating something he'd read or citing random statistics, he was speaking from personal experience.

More than that, Randy spoke from the heart. He spoke about the struggles to aid children who could not get the support they needed at home. He spoke about how too many people assumed that all students had a parent who could help. He spoke about how too many kids were falling through the cracks of an ailing public education system every single day.

Randy's timing was serendipitous. The Irvine Company was becoming increasingly concerned about the threat of gangs in Orange County and wondering how it could be curtailed. While similar debates were playing out nationally, Randy and his team were already creating solutions. He was able to provide concrete examples of how they were helping teens become good, and, in some cases, excellent students. Don knew instantly that Randy was on the right track at the right time.

Less than a month after his conversation with Randy, Don was on a plane with Sat Tamaribuchi, Irvine Company vice president in charge of environmental affairs. The two were flying back to California from Washington, DC, after a federal meeting on water quality, an issue important to the firm. Don decided to divert the conversation away from company business, which had taken center stage for days. He remembered that Sat had recently attended a presentation by the UC Irvine School of Social Ecology regarding gang activity. Don had hours on the plane to talk with Sat and shared with him the contagious enthusiasm Randy offered about the Shalimar Learning and Teen Center.

Within weeks, Sat met with Randy at Shalimar, getting to know the operation firsthand. It wasn't long before the two men began to discuss how the Irvine Company could help.

"If I can get the Irvine Company interested enough in your work, could you replicate your work in other areas?" Sat asked. "If you think you can do it, we think we can help you."

Randy smiled. He'd been preparing for an opportunity like this.

With the Irvine Company setting momentum, Randy began to solicit interest from leaders in the Orange County corporate and philanthropic worlds. He was trying to build a start-up board of directors that could help stake the organization with some funding and connections out of the gate. Judy Swayne, founder and CEO of the fledgling Orange County Community Foundation, was especially helpful with introductions. Randy was able to garner interest from some of the county's major players, including the *Orange County Register*, the *Los Angeles Times*, the Walt Disney Company, Pacific Life, the Fieldstone Foundation, the Sisters of St. Joseph, and Southern California Edison, along with the Community Foundation.

THINK Together was formed as a nonprofit organization in June of 1997. On July 20, 1997, the Orange County Register's Sunday paper featured a front-page article headlined "THINKing of Others" that detailed the story of Shalimar and Minnie Street and the launch of THINK Together to replicate those models. The front page lead-in read like this: "Thousands of Orange County's poorest kids have a new friend—a 39-year-old stockbroker whose vision of uniting people, churches and corporations is bearing fruit in some of the county's toughest neighborhoods. The new organization, THINK Together, has opened two new afterschool learning centers—with more to follow. Join reporter David Parrish on a journey into the frontiers of hope."

That same year, THINK Together won both the Disney Community Service Award as Orange County's top charity and the R.C. Hoiles Charity of the Year Award for its work at Shalimar and Minnie Street. The two recognitions brought THINK Together $90,000, and the organization was off to the races.

"What is with that girl?"
"Which girl?"
"La negrita. The dark one. She won't talk to anyone."
"How would I know? She doesn't talk to me, either."
"Shh! We are not supposed to be talking."
"But this isn't school. It's after-school."
"We are still doing school stuff, though. Homework."
"Aren't you smart enough to stop at 3 p.m.?"

The new THINK Together established two additional learning centers in another tough gang neighborhood near downtown Santa Ana. An elementary program, dubbed the "Noah Project," was opened at St. Joseph's school, and its companion teen center was opened down the street, in the basement of the Episcopal Church of the Messiah. Since the opening of Shalimar, Randy regularly fielded calls from people wanting the program in their neighborhood or church. Luan Mendel, a volunteer from Church of the Messiah, was a leader who got it, and Randy rightly surmised that THINK Together could build around Luan's volunteer leadership in that neighborhood. The wife of an auto executive who had moved around the country, Luan had been a teacher before coming to California. She later became part of THINK Together's paid staff, and her teaching experience and commitment to excellence in program quality became influential as the organization's culture was beginning to be established.

Mary Barth became the first executive director of THINK, and she and Luan established the organization's first office in a borrowed Sunday school classroom at Church of the Messiah. The church was built in 1889 and was the oldest continuous-use building in the county. The summer of 1997 was a hot one, and Mary and Luan toiled away without air conditioning in what amounted to a brick oven. But they were excited about the launch of the new programs and continued to field calls from others with interest.

One of those calls came from Lillian French, the principal at Davis Elementary, the neighborhood public school. "The kids need your support," Lillian told them, "but I'm not sure they'll find you if you set up in the church."

THINK kept its programs at the churches and set up an additional program inside Lillian's school in the fall of 1998. At this point, each program site had a paid full-time site coordinator, but the rest of the site staff was all volunteer. The neighborhood surrounding Davis was one of Santa Ana's most troubled. Gangs operated freely in the nearby streets. There were few places for students to play outside, and because families doubled up in apartments, there was little space for students to study. Nearly every student qualified for a federally subsidized lunch, and nearly every kid spoke Spanish at home.

"I heard the adults talking about that girl. Her name is Maria."

"What do they say?"

"Her mom was arrested, taken away by the police. Her dad is gone. She never knew him. It's hard for her abuela to raise her and her two brothers."

"Dios mio. No wonder why she doesn't talk. She is filled with too much sadness."

Lillian wanted her school to be a community hub to tackle the problems that children like Maria faced. She spent hours applying for grants and shopping for programs to help not only her students but also their families.

"Having the program on campus was a real learn-as-we-go experience," she later recalled. "Part of the challenge was having after-school programs use classrooms, which were used in a year-round schedule." Still, she was ecstatic at the results. "THINK Together fit in really well. What was so cool for me was that it was a free program to the school. I was impressed that people came to volunteer and help."

Jose Candelas was named Davis' site coordinator. He rounded up volunteers who could see that the students needed help with their English, but providing that help wasn't always easy. "There was some pushback from the students. They would say, 'Hey, don't tell me what to do.' At first, the 40 kids in the afterschool program didn't want to take help from strangers, yet they needed help with nearly every subject."

"Why does Maria stay in the corner during the afterschool program?"
"Why is she always standing in the corner?"
"She isn't standing. She is going up and down the stairs."
"She must be counting. One stair. Two stairs. Three stairs."
"Shh! We are supposed to be working on our homework."

Jose and his volunteers contended with all sorts of student idiosyncrasies, but one problem seemed omnipresent: The students and their parents were clearly intimidated by the idea of any direct communication with the school.

"What we saw was a major gap between the students and the school," Jose remembered. "We helped bridge that gap, because as an afterschool program, we could speak more informally to parents and to students. We could also tell them that the schoolteachers were there to help them."

Lillian knew that the parents, many of whom were immigrants from small villages with little more than grade-school learning, had no experience communicating with a governmental agency. Teachers, like other professionals in Mexico, were called *licenciados* to recognize their college education. They were people to be respected. It's a class issue; dialogue is not broached. So at Davis, if a child had a learning disability, it would need to be detected by the school. Parents might not think to say anything to anyone.

"I think that Maria must be very dumb. She never says anything."

"No te creas. I saw them giving her a test in Spanish. The teachers were saying she knew everything."

"If she knows everything, how come she doesn't brush her hair?"

"I don't know. She must like it like that."

"I never saw hair so bushy. Maybe it is hard to brush."

The more that Jose and the volunteers helped the students with their homework, the stronger their relationships grew. And the more kids began to go into the classrooms prepared for the lessons, the more confident they became. There were fewer arguments with parents at home because the children had already done their homework and even had time to do chores.

Jose then made a deal with an old high school friend who was running a city recreational program near Davis Elementary. He would help those kids with their homework if the rec program would provide physical activity for his kids. At the same time, classes were set up to help teach parenting skills to mothers who needed them as well as exercise programs for those who wanted them.

Early decisions like these became the seeds of the programs that THINK would later establish throughout California. Future strategies would seek to involve families, include physical education, and, most importantly, communicate with school staff so that after school lessons complemented classroom learning.

"Oye, I think you were wrong about Maria."
"What do you mean?"
"She's talking."
"Really? To whom?"
"She's talking to the señora, the tutor. Do you see?"
"I wonder what she is saying."

Emmanuel Rodriguez remembers when THINK Together began its program at Davis Elementary School. As a second-grader, he yearned for help with math and longed for recreational activities. His teacher gave him a registration form, and he ran all the way home and excitedly explained to his mom that she would have to sign it. Emmanuel would spend four years in THINK Together. He not only conquered math, his scores on standardized tests rose successively each time he took them. But THINK provided even more, expanding Emmanuel's world beyond his immediate neighborhood. He enjoyed trips to places like the Bowers Museum in Santa Ana, which he might never have visited otherwise.

The city recreation program soon partnered with THINK Together for events such as Thanksgiving and Christmas parties that included both students and their parents. There were even birthday celebrations and festivities including dunk tanks with teachers. The partners did whatever it took to make learning more fun than hanging out on the streets.

"THINK Together kept me off the streets, and that was a big thing because it was a very tough neighborhood," recalled Emmanuel, who today is a student at Santa Ana College and works as a THINK Together program leader. "The kids who hung out on the streets were rebellious, and they were doing bad stuff by the time they got into middle school."

In these early days of THINK Together, the organizers and the families had the proud sense of being pioneers. Lillian French was one of them. She had a vision for extending the school day long before it became part of the routine conversation about education in urban neighborhoods. She saw firsthand that many of her students came to school with disadvantages, and she sought to help them not only catch up, but to achieve their full potential.

At first, Lillian was not terribly successful in obtaining grants to realize her vision. She was determined to build a comprehensive program in which students could divide their time among help with homework, physical fitness, and a computer lab. In the end, with THINK's help, Lillian would achieve her goals, including a state-of-the-art computer lab built with the generous support of Bill Podlich, co-founder of Newport Beach-based Pacific Investment Management Company (PIMCO), one of the largest active global fixed-income managers in the world.

Lillian's vision and tenacity became the prototype for hundreds of THINK Together's public school sites that would eventually follow. "We came to be a big family, and, together, we were helping children who needed to learn more," Jose Candelas remembered.

Nearby, in the city of Tustin, the THINK Together team was having a similar experience. With support from the Irvine Company, Randy found a neighborhood with great need and a public school eager to have them. Nancy Lev, principal at Thorman Elementary School, had already tried every strategy she could to provide her low-income students the extra help they needed.

"Maria is spending a lot of time with the tutor. They go over stupid stuff that we learned last year."
"Well, if she doesn't go over it now, she won't learn it at all."
"At least she is talking."
"I talked to her, too. She is very nice."
"The tutor gave her a prize for all her work. They gave her stuff to fix her hair and make it very pretty."
"We need to stop talking and work so we get a prize, too."

Nancy paid teachers extra to work late and help students who were struggling. She asked them to regularly phone parents to discuss problems and instructed her staff to teach interested parents ways to better help their children at home.

When Randy asked if Nancy wanted to host an afterschool program at Thorman, she gladly accepted and opened her doors wide. Nancy used federal grant money to buy books and educational games. She conducted volunteer selection and training and provided school staff to monitor the operation.

Like Lillian French at Davis Elementary, Nancy Lev also invited THINK Together to staff meetings at her school. At these meetings, school staff and THINK site coordinators would discuss student needs and solutions together. Nancy's goal was a seamless integration of the nonprofit afterschool program and the school day. She fostered an environment where teachers and THINK staff could review the problems of individual students together, determining how the afterschool program could best supplement school-day learning for each of them. This collaboration and alignment became a foundational element of the culture of the organization as THINK continued to grow.

Kara Johnson, the site coordinator at Thorman, like Jose at Davis, was also trying to break down what she perceived as a wall between the school and the community. When she was a student at Vanguard University, Kara had volunteered at the Shalimar Learning Center, where she'd felt a close relationship with the students. But in this new community, THINK Together was an unknown. To convince students and parents that THINK was really there to help, she knocked on doors in the neighborhood and even accepted dinner invitations. Kara went the extra mile, providing students not only with tutoring and help they couldn't find at home, but with trips like "college day" to Vanguard, which she hoped would "give them a vision and remove the stigma that college couldn't be for them, too."

Years later, Omar, one of Kara's students, invited her to his high school graduation. She was the only one of his guests who was not a family member —or perhaps, as Kara believed, Omar now considered

THINK part of his family. Kara was thrilled to later learn that he would graduate from California State University, Fullerton.

"No one can say Maria is dumb now."

"Oh, yeah? I can: Maria is dumb now."

"Well, I guess you can say it, but it's not true."

"How do you know?"

"She worked on her English with the señora, the tutor. Maria is going to GATE."

"What's GATE?"

"Well, if you were as smart as Maria, you would know."

"GATE is a program of advanced classes, and I think Maria is going to be famous one day. Maybe we will tell people that we knew her."

Over the next five years, THINK Together would grow to fourteen locations, still all privately funded. In 2002, THINK commissioned the first formal study of the effects of its programs, and the results were promising.

At the end of 1997, Randy left the investment business to become the CEO of National Management (NMC), a regional transportation company that one of his clients owned. Her husband, the company's founder, had passed away, and they needed somebody to run it. NMC was a strong operating company, but it needed a leader with strategic and financial savvy and one who could address some of the problems within the culture of the organization.

In 1999, Randy gave a speech to the management team, laying out a vision for this culture shift. NMC was a very efficient company, but it was run like a sweatshop. In many ways, the more than one thousand drivers who worked for the company were similar to the parents of the THINK Together students—immigrants who came to America to build a better life for themselves. When Randy took over NMC, employees received no health benefits and not even paid vacation.

Because of the success of its business strategy and the remarkable efficiency of the operations, the company could well afford to pay these benefits and remain extremely competitive in its markets.

After the speech, one of NMC's managers, Todd Gurewitz, sent Randy a book, *The Soul of the Firm*, by C. William Pollard, chairman and CEO of the Service Master Company. "I think this is what your vision is," Todd said. Service Master, which provides everything from pest control to janitorial services, had by the 1990s grown to more than three billion in annual revenue. It had a terrific track record of not only earnings growth, but of customer satisfaction and the development of its people. Its employees often started as low-skilled or semi-skilled service workers, but were developed and grown by the organization.

Randy became committed to building a culture at NMC based on the same servant leadership principles deployed at Service Master. To help accomplish this, Randy hired Dr. Joe Maciariello, a professor from the Peter F. Drucker School of Management at Claremont Graduate University, as a consultant. Joe had consulted with Service Master to help export its culture, as it made acquisitions and expanded to China.

As they got to know each other, Randy told Joe about his work with THINK Together. Joe suggested that Randy take some graduate classes at CGU, where he could build his skill set to accomplish what he wanted with both NMC and THINK Together. Joe also offered to set up a meeting with Peter Drucker himself, and Randy jumped at the chance. Drucker, then ninety, but still teaching, writing and consulting, was incredibly sharp and inquisitive.

Over lunch in Claremont, at which the Austrian-born management icon still enjoyed a glass of wine, Randy was surprised that Peter's interest was directed more to THINK Together than in building a Service Master-like culture at NMC. Randy had laid out a vision for expanding NMC's delivery business as shoppers began to move online in the early dot-com era. It was a big opportunity and, after all, THINK Together was still tiny at the time. But a portion of Drucker's own work for years had been focused on America's transition to a knowledge-based economy. California was in the midst of a historic wave of immigration, with a preponderance of new immigrants being low-skilled and semi-skilled workers from Mexico and Central America. Drucker, in his gruff and direct manner, told Randy, "Never before in human history have peasants become knowledge workers in a single generation. But that is the challenge before us. It's a fascinating problem to work on."

Soon, Randy was taking classes at CGU, including several from Drucker himself. Randy learned much from Drucker about keeping an organization focused on its customers and key stakeholders and the importance of measuring results. In contrast, many top MBA programs were focused on maximizing shareholder return and financial engineering. Randy also learned about corporate strategy and implementation—and especially the impact of culture on implementation—from another professor, Vijay Sathe. This combination of mid-career learning and the skill set gained while running NMC would later serve Randy well as opportunities presented themselves to THINK Together.

Another Austrian-born icon would soon have an impact on Randy's world. Arnold Schwarzenegger was looking for his next act, post-Hollywood. He was contemplating a political career and looking to build a statewide platform from which to launch an eventual run for governor. While serving as chairman of the President's Council on Physical Fitness and Sports under President George H. W. Bush from 1990 to 1993, Schwarzenegger discovered a shocking lack of physical fitness in the youth of America's inner-cities. The experience led him to launch a Los Angeles-based organization called the Inner-City Games.

That organization morphed into Arnold's All Stars and, later, Afterschool All-Stars, as the demand for more comprehensive afterschool programs increased. With more than 70 percent of households headed by either a single parent or two parents who work, California led the nation in beginning to invest in afterschool programs.

Polling by Schwarzenegger's political consultants showed that expanding such programs was a popular notion. Demand for these programs greatly exceeded supply, creating an untenable situation in many communities. Arnold and his team shrewdly put together a bipartisan coalition of law enforcement and education and, in 2002, put Proposition 49—the After School Education and Safety (ASES) Act—on the ballot. If passed, Prop. 49 would increase the state's annual investment in afterschool programs from $138 million to $550 million. The major opposition came from fiscal conservatives, who challenged a spending increase amid the state's budget crisis in the wake of the dot-com bust. To address this, the act had a trigger that delayed implementation until the state's general fund revenue had reached $1.5 billion above its previous high-water mark in 2000.

In November 2002, California voters overwhelmingly passed Proposition 49 by a vote of 56.7 to 43.3 percent. Upon implementation, schools would be given grants based on the average daily attendance in afterschool programs at a rate of five dollars per student, per day. The initiative was designed to fund all K–8 schools in the state, with grants of $50,000 for an elementary school and $75,000 for a middle school, regardless of their sizes. Schools would be required to provide 50 cents in local matching funds for each state dollar provided. If the annual appropriation were insufficient to fund all grant applications, priority would be given to schools with more than one-half of their students eligible for the federal free or reduced-price lunch program.

It would take until 2006 for the state's general fund revenue benchmark to be exceeded, triggering implementation of Prop. 49. But because of the supply-demand imbalance, particularly in low-income communities across the state, the benefits Prop. 49 offered couldn't come soon enough.

The law enforcement perspective on afterschool programs was clear. The hours between 3 p.m. and 6 p.m. were times of trouble. Crime went up, and studies showed that drug use and teen sex were rampant in these unsupervised hours across all socioeconomic levels. Santa Ana's school superintendent, Dr. Al Mijares, shared with Randy the education perspective on why these programs are so important to low-income children or children of immigrants.

"Like it or not, schools today (2003) are like a manufacturing process. It starts with the raw material we put into that process," Al observed. "Our student most likely hasn't been to preschool or Head Start. His family didn't read to him. He's a monolingual Spanish speaker. We put that student into a half-day kindergarten in English and expect him to begin to read. Each day, he goes home to a crowded house where there are no books and no one speaks English. He falls behind grade-level expectations designed for middle-class students who speak English. As they go on, students attend school six hours per day, 180 days per year. With the long summers back in their bookless, Spanish-speaking households, they regress and fall further behind. By middle school, they check out, and by high school, they drop out."

"If you can build me a system, not just a one-off program, that extends the school day to 6 o'clock and provides a program in the summer that is rich in learning, we can begin to change this equation."

Randy received the message loud and clear.

As THINK Together grew from six sites to fourteen between 2000 and 2003, it learned its volunteer-driven formula wasn't scalable. Volunteers were great as a supplement, but programs needed the reliability of paid staff to provide consistent quality. THINK also learned that future growth would come through the school-based model, as opposed to the community site model on which it began. Prop. 49 funding, which would drive THINK in the future, was for school-based programs only.

In 2003, a couple of dramatic events occurred that, together, set Randy on a new path. First, NMC was sold. The new owners did not share Randy's vision to diversify NMC's document delivery business into a small parcel delivery business. Randy's view was that, as the Internet matured, most documents would eventually be delivered electronically, greatly diminishing the demand for physical deliveries. Meanwhile, demand was growing (and would later explode) for parcel delivery. Sitting on top of one of the most efficient delivery platforms in the nation's largest market, which NMC had, was a great opportunity. The new owners, however, were title insurance companies whose priority was to get their real estate-related documents delivered. In the white-hot real estate environment of the early 2000s, they shortsight-edly elected to focus the business on document delivery. Seeing a dim future, Randy left upon the sale of the company, although he consulted for the new owners as he pondered his next act.

Meanwhile, in August of 2003, THINK Together ran out of money. Still all privately funded at that point, the organization had an annual budget of about $1.5 million. It had a relatively narrow donor base, much of which was composed of the organizations that had funded it from the beginning. THINK Together learned the harsh lesson that companies and foundations like to spread their money around and don't stay with an organization forever. THINK Together was forced to lay off its executive director, reduce other staff and close two sites. After paying the terminated employees and the other expenses related to the site closures, THINK had just fifty-three dollars in the bank and nothing in the pipeline. Several board members stepped in with dona-tions, and key funders like Knott's Berry Farm heiress Marion Knott provided a combination of grants and loans to keep the organization afloat. Randy and Mary provided loans as well.

Absent an executive director, Randy agreed to step in part-time and without pay while he explored other career options. But THINK Together's work was his passion, so it became difficult for him to do it just part-time. Still, he had to search for a viable economic model or the organization wasn't going to be sustainable. Randy and his family were used to a substantial income and, at this point, they were subsi-dizing THINK Together.

Soon, Randy received a call from Nancy Lev in Tustin. Nancy had moved to a new school in a more affluent part of the district. Nancy told Randy that the school had a program where parents paid $350 per month for afterschool care, but it was mainly just babysitting. She wanted something more integrated and connected to the school like she'd had at Thorman. Randy asked how many kids were in the program, and Nancy said they had ninety students registered. Randy quickly crunched the numbers and calculated that the program had more than $300,000 in revenue for the regular school year. A THINK Together program that size typically cost about $100,000 per year.

Randy began to see a way forward. He believed that the Prop. 49 funds would start flowing one day, although many people had their doubts. With only $50,000 per school allocated for a program that costs closer to $100,000 to implement, the challenge to raise the local matching funds on a sizeable scale was significant. However, Randy thought that if THINK Together could get into the business of providing programs at schools like Nancy's new one, he could use the profits from the more affluent schools to provide the matching funds at the low-income schools. This was essentially what the YMCA was doing in many markets around the country, except they tended to subsidize their middle-class programs with their childcare earnings, at least in places like Orange County, where they served relatively few low-income kids. To Randy's way of thinking, the Y had already proven the financial model.

As the months went by with no income coming into their household, Mary was becoming concerned. She couldn't see how Randy could ever make much of an income from THINK Together. She was not a big spender, but she worried that one day they would need to help care for her aging parents, who were running out of resources. This was in addition to raising their own young family, with college and their own retirement on the horizon.

Yet, Randy was feeling more confident about the emerging plan at THINK Together. He'd tell himself, "If we sell our house and downsize our lifestyle a bit, I think we can do this." Randy also was becoming increasingly fulfilled by the work itself. Still, he was torn. He had hoped one day to accumulate enough savings to be able to run THINK Together for just a token salary, like one dollar per year. There was no question that if he could afford to, this is what he wanted to do with his life.

He was sharing his dilemma with a friend from St Andrew's, a mortgage company executive named Paul Schott. Paul told Randy, "You've just been working to support your THINK Together habit anyway—you might as well be all in." Paul's comments struck a chord. Soon after, Mary and Randy sold their house, downsized their lifestyle, and Randy went to work at THINK Together full-time. Now, he was all in.

Back in Santa Ana, Al Mijares approached Randy with an idea. THINK Together was operating at three schools there. The district had grown its afterschool programs to most of its other K–8 schools with grants that THINK Together had helped to write. But the district couldn't afford to run the programs on only five dollars per student per day. Al explained that the district received about forty dollars per student per day for the regular six- to 6.5- hour day. There was no way it could run the 3.5- to 4-hour program after school on the five dollars per day with the current cost structure. He explained that the district had a $2.5 million encroachment on the general fund, which took away from its other priorities.

There also was no consistent quality in the district's programs. The Boys & Girls Club ran its program at several schools, the YMCA at others. Teachers ran some sites, while non-certificated school personnel ran others. And THINK Together was running three sites. Through other community partnerships, there was karate at some schools, dance at others, science here and there. There were good things going on in some places but not much in others. In the end, there were no goals and no collective outcomes for students in the district. This was a fairly typical first-generation scenario for afterschool programs: Just keep the kids safe and off the street.

The district asked THINK Together to come into Lathrop Intermediate, as part of a school turnaround. The Orange County Register was running an expose on Lathrop as the worst performing middle school in the county. The school had had a new principal each year for five or six years running, and the school was a mess. There was a teacher leading the afterschool program, but there was no plan and no connection to the school day. One teacher was getting paid ninety dollars per hour to teach a calligraphy class because it was her hobby. Meanwhile, the kids were flunking out of school. Lucinda Pueblos was brought in as the turnaround principal, and THINK Together was brought in as part of the turnaround plan.

Lathrop quickly started to see changes, and Al Mijares, liked what he saw. He wanted to bring some consistency to the afterschool program across the district and connect it to the classroom. Al wanted both a consistent program model and a sustainable economic model. He turned to THINK Together. "What if we passed that money through to you, and you matched it with your philanthropy, and you guys run the program?" Al asked Randy. "It's your organization's focus and expertise, and the district can focus its energy and resources on the regular school day."

Randy, of course, loved the idea, but the existing stakeholders didn't. The people and organizations that were involved with the program lobbied Santa Ana's board of education heavily to block this idea. Al and Randy had met with board members privately to brief them and seek their support. Four members indicated they would support the new direction, while one would oppose.

The night came for the board to vote on this initiative. The boardroom was packed with existing stakeholders, parents, and community group leaders. Hours of public comments led up to a lengthy debate among the board members. Randy felt that the presentation itself was pretty sloppy. Al had one of the assistant superintendents make the presentation, and he was not on top of his facts. He couldn't handle many of the board's questions. Meanwhile, Randy, who was not part of the presentation, sat in the audience and stewed. Finally at 1 a.m. the board tabled the issue. One board member walked with Randy out to the parking lot after the meeting and told him, "This is too hot to handle right now. We will pick this up after the election in November." Never mind that school started in August, and contracts had to be signed and agreed to prior to that. A delay to November was akin to a death sentence.

Randy was furious. On the drive home, his cellphone rang. It was Al. He apologized that they couldn't get it over the finish line and encouraged Randy to hang in there. Randy vented his frustration. After an already long evening and listening patiently to Randy vent, Al finally issued Randy a challenge. "Look, this is what urban education is like. If you want to work with urban schools, you've got to decide if you've got the stomach for it. If not, get out now." Chastened, Randy took that message to heart.

Next door in Tustin, another opportunity emerged. Tustin's superintendent, Pete Gorman, approached Randy with a similar idea. Tustin however, didn't yet have the funds. Another organization had been working with several local principals to write grants to acquire the funding, but Pete didn't feel they had what it would take to be successful. He admired the work THINK Together was doing at Thorman and next door at Currie Middle School, and wanted to see that work expanded. And, though there were politics to navigate within the district and with the board, they paled in comparison to Santa Ana's. Together with the district and the other agency, a federal 21st Century Community Learning Centers grant was won, and THINK added nine schools beginning with the 2004–2005 school year.

Now that he was doing this work full-time, Randy had been carefully examining the broader out-of-school time landscape. His business and finance background helped him think about the economic underpinnings of this world a little differently than most of the players in it did. The California School Age Care Consortium (Cal SAC) put out a piece on workforce development for the industry that implied that, in 2004, in California alone, afterschool care was a six billion dollar industry, and that the state and federal subsidized child care was about $750 million per year. This was in addition to the $550 million that was coming in from Prop. 49 funds, and the $140 million or so that came to California from the federal 21st Century Community Learning Centers pot. Clearly, afterschool was big business in California, but few organizations thought about it that way.

Randy wanted to learn more, so he attended the National Afterschool Association conference. His jaw dropped as participants discussed issues about site safety and state licensure guidelines, things he hadn't really been focused on. Most of those in attendance were licensed child-care providers, not educators interested in extending academic learning or providing enrichment related to the school day.

To better understand the issues related to the work of his new peers, Randy went through the process to become a licensed child-care provider. He was shocked that there was so much focus on facilities: the need for small toilets, no electrical outlets that kids could stick their fingers into, and ensuring that chemicals were out of the children's reach. It seemed irrelevant for school-based programs where campuses already met these requirements. There was no focus on program quality. Together with the input he was getting from schools, the licensed child-care space seemed ripe for innovation.

On those points, THINK Together was way ahead of the curve. It had started at Shalimar and entered into Santa Ana and Tustin with the idea of improving achievement, not just providing child care. In fact, many of the schools THINK entered in Tustin already had licensed child-care programs. Low-income parents received subsidies to pay for the programs, which included coverage in the summer. When THINK Together came to their campuses, many parents wanted to get into the THINK program instead of the child-care program. But THINK didn't have summer funding, and parents needed the child-care coverage. Parents felt trapped by this dilemma caused by two separate funding streams arriving onto their campus and dividing the children into separate camps. To the parents, administrators, and the students themselves, it made no sense.

Randy learned a lot about this afterschool world over the next few years. As he became more involved in the field, he came to be viewed as a bit of a pariah by his colleagues at other organizations. Most of them had come out of child development or youth development backgrounds. They thought that kids were in school for enough time and that what students really needed was time to play. Randy didn't completely disagree, but with large swaths of the children flunking out of school or seriously underperforming, he believed that extending learning from the school day needed to be part of the mix. After all, he had seen it work for years at Shalimar, where some of THINK's early students were now starting to graduate from college.

This emboldened Randy's resolve and commitment to the academic piece of THINK's program. Randy also saw the customer differently from his colleagues. To Randy, the school was the customer—this is who THINK Together contracted with. Donors were also a customer. Most others in the field saw the children and their families as the customer. They, of course, were the recipient of the services, but it was the schools and the donors that provided the revenue that made the programs possible. Many organizations saw the regular school day as failing the children, and the school was, therefore, the enemy.

Another thing Randy learned was that there were a lot of impediments to quality programs. First, the economics were tough. Second, with the exception of LA's BEST, the first large-scale provider of afterschool programs, most of the organizations trying to deliver these programs were small and weak. Third, from Randy's point of view, a lot of the talented people in the field were working at intermediary organizations. These intermediaries provided training and technical assistance to programs, among other things, but Randy felt they were too far away from the kids to maximize their impact. Because the organizations delivering the programs were so small, they couldn't afford the best talent.

When Luan Mendel left THINK as director of program & operations, Randy hired one of those intermediary consultants to succeed her, Dr. Becky Newman. Becky had been a teacher for many years and worked in a variety of education posts in the public school system. While working on her doctorate at UC Irvine around 1998, she served as a site coordinator at one of the first federally funded afterschool programs at Madison Elementary in Santa Ana. She later worked at an intermediary and consulted with programs around the state.

When Randy hired Becky to come in-house at THINK Together, the lightbulb went on. With the exception of Lillian French and Nancy Lev, most principals didn't see the afterschool programs as educational partners. They saw them more as child-care providers. They saw that THINK's staff didn't look like the school day staff and looked down their noses at what they were capable of. When Becky came on board, principals saw her as one of them. Becky could talk to them in their language and had the same credentials. So while THINK's front-line staff was still the same, at least some of the schools became more open to the possibilities of the program.

In January 2006, then-Gov. Arnold Schwarzenegger announced that the Prop. 49 funding had been triggered. Months earlier, his aide, Bonnie Reiss, had begun to gather representatives from the field to discuss implementation. The field voiced a concern that, given the economics of five dollars per student per day and 50 percent local match, and that fact that it was a reimbursement program and that the state tended to be very slow reimbursing schools, there was only modest interest in the funding from schools and from program providers. In the months that followed, state Sens. Tom Torlakson and Roy Ashburn would co-author legislation to raise the grant formula to $7.50 per student and make it a direct grant with attendance performance targets rather than an ADA or expense reimbursement grant. With per-student and per-school funding levels increased, there wasn't enough money in the $550 million pot to fund all schools. So the new legislation targeted the funds to low-income schools. It later turned out the funding cutoff was at schools that had a student population of 50 percent or greater qualifying for free or reduced-price meals.

For Randy and THINK Together, this was a game changer. Randy started to do the math. If he could raise three to four million per year more in philanthropy, he could potentially leverage that tenfold in school district contracts. That would get THINK Together to two hundred sites or so, the scale Randy felt THINK Together needed to hire some intermediary talent and build a sustainable support system that could improve program quality at scale.

Randy began to make the case to his board of directors. When they began this discussion in the winter of 2006, THINK Together was a three million dollar organization with one hundred employees, serving four thousand students at twenty-five locations around Orange County. Under Becky's program leadership, THINK had documented its model and was organized enough that it felt that it could replicate and scale its work with fidelity. Randy believed that while a fast scale-up might be bumpy, programs would be stronger over time because they could finally afford to invest in the supportive structure that enables quality and consistency across the board.

Becky was considerably more cautious than Randy about this. But Randy's view was simple and straightforward: Schools could hire THINK Together, they could hire somebody else, or they could do it themselves. If the state was going to put all the money out at once in a big-bang implementation anyway, everyone was going to be in the same boat. In light of the alternatives, Becky agreed that THINK Together stood a better chance than most of getting it right.

The state put together a task force to help get the word out about the Prop. 49 opportunity and help think through the implementation issues. One of the members was Steve Amick from the San Diego County Office of Education. Steve was the regional lead, overseeing afterschool programs for Orange, San Diego, and Imperial counties. For advice, Randy turned to Steve, who had decades of experience in every level of afterschool service and administration. Randy learned that he was trying to help California pitch the idea of afterschool programming in districts that had none, many of which were in Riverside and San Bernardino counties. Most of the areas that had success in the early days of the five dollar per student per day formula were those where there was a strong local philanthropic community that could provide local match or where cities were willing and able to kick money in. The state was worried that districts without one of these factors wouldn't pursue the funding even at the $7.50 per student per day level. Few districts would be able to deliver quality with that level of funding. Steve had a list of schools he was contacting and told Randy, "If you're interested, I can give you the list. All of these districts are within an hour of your office." That became the target prospect list for THINK Together as it sought to bring high-quality programs to communities that might turn down the funding opportunity, even though they had students and families with great needs. As Randy and Steve talked through the list of potential matches, about six hundred schools emerged as prospects.

Not everyone was as convinced as Randy that Proposition 49

would make it to implementation. California, the land of the ballot initiative, had another law known as Proposition 98 that guaranteed that 39 percent of the state's budget would be spent on K–12 education. During the post-dot-com economic downturn, the state borrowed four billion from the Prop. 98 guarantees to help balance the budget. The California Teachers Association, the strongest political power in the state, was demanding that those funds be repaid prior to implementing Prop. 49. The Torlakson and Ashburn legislation was going nowhere until that issue got resolved. Yet Randy remained uniquely optimistic. He felt that Prop. 49 was a signature piece of Arnold Schwarzenegger's legacy, and with a re-election campaign looming, the governor would figure out some way to make it happen. Randy felt that this was a once-in-a lifetime chance to scale the organization, and he wasn't about to let naysayers slow THINK Together down.

As Randy began to reach out to the six hundred schools, he started with his old friend Lillian French. By then Lillian was the superintendent of a small district in southeastern Los Angeles County called Los Nietos. Lillian was excited about the prospect of getting support in her new neighborhood for her under-served student population. Randy told Lillian that he would need to get a critical mass of schools in that area to build a quality support system. He felt that clusters of forty to sixty schools would be ideal. Lillian suggested that THINK establish a pilot site in Los Nietos that they could use for a demonstration project. So, even though it wasn't in either of their budgets that year, Randy and Lillian figured out a way to make it happen.

Next, Lillian convened a meeting with her superintendent colleagues in the area to try to get them on board. "I want to introduce to you Randy Barth," she began. "He is a man with a vision. He is a man who read about a problem, not just in his backyard, and did more than say, 'Isn't that horrible?' Randy did something about it. He began an afterschool center in an apartment he rented. His program is called THINK Together. Now it's time for all of us to be a part of that vision."

A number of districts at the table were supportive. Soon after, Dr.

Sue Cornell from Ontario-Montclair, then the largest K–8 district in the state, expressed strong interest. Eventually, 180 of the 600 schools on the prospect list signed up.

Under California's top-end, income-tax-dependent revenue structure, a crazy quirk of fate occurred. A small handful of early Google investors cashed in their shares, creating a capital gains tax windfall for the state. The governor would now have the funds to pay back the Prop. 98 guarantees, which enabled him to cut a deal with the teachers union to support the Prop. 49 legislation.

It was obvious that Randy had set himself up for a major challenge. The governor signed the authorizing legislation authored by Sens. Torlakson and Ashburn in September 2006, and it required grant applications from the schools just six weeks later. If a district wanted a full year of funding, which it would need to garner the start-up funds necessary to pull off a big-bang implementation, it would need to open pilot programs just six weeks later, in mid-December, and open all program sites by February 4, 2007.

Under this timing structure, grants would not actually be awarded by the California Department of Education until January, so afterschool programs had to open in advance of knowing for sure whether they won an award. Then, the actual payments would not show up until May 2007. This gauntlet would prove too daunting for most organizations to navigate at any considerable scale. Later, Randy would be very surprised that other organizations didn't take the gamble, even though many were better-positioned to do so. Even Arnold Schwarzenegger's organization, Afterschool All-Stars, didn't take advantage. How many organizations did take the opportunity to scale up significantly? Only one: THINK Together.

To pull this off, THINK Together would need a combination of capacity-building grants and loans to provide cash flow for the expansion. The capacity-building grants were harder to come by than Randy ever imagined; longtime supporters Bill Podlich, real estate developer Ranney Draper, and Marion Knott were the only ones who came through. THINK Together would have to borrow the rest, so Randy went hunting for a bank. He would ask schools to contract with THINK Together and put in a clause that would let them out if they did not receive funding. Within one hundred days, THINK would need to hire one thousand people and serve 20,000 students at 180 new locations, with an annualized budget of twenty-six million. Randy would need bridge financing for the organization until the districts received payments from the state and could, in turn, pay THINK Together. THINK's net worth at the time was a mere $200,000.

In the early days, Randy; his wife, Mary; and, at times, a few board members served as THINK Together's bank by providing loans to fund growth or get the organization through the difficult periods. Randy and Mary had loaned up to $500,000 of their own money, which at times was all they had liquid. In late 2005, St. Joseph Health System provided a line of credit of $500,000 to replace the couple's financial role. But Randy and Mary were back in again as THINK needed to start hiring people en masse to hit the December and February opening targets.

Randy had been involved in his share of financings throughout his career, but this one was going to be a challenge. Ultimately, he figured THINK was going to need a line of credit of about six million on top of St. Joseph Health System's $500,000. The St. Joseph board had graciously agreed to subordinate its loan to the new loan that THINK would need. Randy began talking to a number of banks, including Comerica. Comerica stood out to Randy because its representative, Melissa Pollard, agreed to either meet with or call Randy every day at 4 p.m. and give a progress report until Comerica either said yes or no. Randy loved that. He was used to dealing with banks that asked for information and then went into a black hole for weeks at a time with little or no information or direction. It was hard to take their pulse without a dialogue. Despite the welcome communication, the pressure was building.

THINK needed to hire program staff so that it could open the required pilot sites by early December. Randy gave the recruiting staff the green light. THINK was supposed to get some other grants in mid- to late November that could help with cash flow until one of the banks came through. But Randy was now sweating—THINK was completely out of cash. Comerica had indicated that if it decided to do the loan, it would require one million in personal guarantees from board members. Randy didn't want to have to go to key stakeholders whom he was already asking for a loan guarantee to make an interim loan as well. THINK was getting pretty far out on a limb.

There was some welcome footing, though. Six THINK Together board members were willing to each guarantee $100,000 to Comerica. And the Orange County Community Foundation had a loan guarantee fund that now had additional capacity because an anticipated project fell through. Randy had a great relationship with Shelley Hoss, Judy Swayne's successor as CEO, and investors in that fund included Bill Podlich, Ranney Draper and Mark Van Ness. They agreed to put up the balance of the loan guarantee.

Even so, Comerica still hadn't given final approval, and the other banks were awfully quiet. Simply sustaining THINK's existing program was becoming burdensome. Two grants Randy expected hadn't shown up yet. THINK had a payroll to meet in November 2006, and it was $43,000 short. Patricia Tyson, THINK's part-time chief financial officer told Randy that she would tap her home equity line for $30,000. Randy put the last $13,000 on his Visa card, and THINK met payroll just in time to celebrate Thanksgiving.

In early December, relief finally arrived. Comerica approved the line of credit. The grants showed up. THINK Together, thanks to the willingness of its board to underwrite this risk, was now off and running. THINK hired the recruiters and dispatched them to Starbucks and makeshift offices furnished with picnic tables, plastic chairs, laptops, and cellphones. Despite the challenges, THINK managed to hire one thousand people over the next one hundred days. There was no time to sign leases for regional offices needed in Los Angeles, Riverside, and San Bernardino counties, so in those locations, the recently hired staff plugged ahead in temporary space. At the same time, THINK's offices in a modest 3,000-square-foot building were moved to a 12,000-square-foot suite across the street.

THINK Together got a pilot site open in each of the sixteen new school districts that had signed on. And on February 4, the day the state designated as "hard start day," THINK Together opened more than 120 program locations. It was an amazing accomplishment. The programs were a little rocky at the start, but not too bad considering the challenge. When Randy was selling this to the districts, he told them the same thing he'd told Becky Newman: "The state is going to do a big-bang implementation. If you want to take advantage of the opportunity for your students, it's going to be crazy. If you want to do this, you can do it with us, you can do it yourself, or you can do it with somebody else. I don't know what the programs will look like initially, but we have a framework and have designed a system of support—with both a program model and an economic model —that we believe will ensure high-quality programs within eighteen months."

This is what THINK Together sold, and that is largely what it delivered. Randy felt that probably 30 percent of the programs got to relatively high quality well ahead of schedule, and about 15 percent lagged. The majority of programs were pretty much right on target. In terms of revenue, employee count, and students served, THINK Together grew tenfold in one hundred days. And, astonishingly, it worked.

4

Little Lake

Under No Child Left Behind, students are divided into five categories based on their performance on standardized tests: "far below basic," "below basic," "basic," "proficient," and "advanced." As part of their school performance measures, districts are graded on how many students moved up or down between categories. In the fall of 2008, Randy was presented with some interesting data that examined how THINK Together students were performing for the 2007–2008 school year, THINK's first year at scale.

Across the eighteen school districts in which THINK Together worked during that year, THINK students moved up a category or more at twice the rate of non-THINK students in those same districts. But in the Little Lake City School District, THINK Together students were moving up at three to four times the rate of non-THINK Together students.

Little Lake City is a small district of just under 5,000 students in nine schools—seven elementary and two middle schools. The district covers the city of Santa Fe Springs and parts of Downey and Norwalk in southeastern Los Angeles County. The area, like much of the Los Angeles sprawl, is a formerly white working-class suburb that is now predominantly Latino and lower-middle class to poor. Little Lake's students are 89 percent Latino and 71 percent socioeconomically disadvantaged.

Their exceptional academic improvement piqued Randy's interest, so one day he made an unannounced visit to Jersey Avenue Elementary in Little Lake, to see firsthand what was going on. Jersey Principal Monica Johnson invited Randy in to her office to explain the unusual achievement.

Monica said Little Lake had developed a finely tuned Professional Learning Community (PLC) system. The principal and the teachers at each school worked closely with THINK staff to make sure that the program was aligned with what was going on in the school day and supporting the needs of the students. What's more, THINK Together site coordinators were included in the bi-weekly Data Reflection Sessions that were at the core of the system.

Those who aren't educators may not be bowled over by the techniques used in Little Lake because they might assume this would occur everywhere. It would seem obvious that principals, teachers, and others who care for kids in a school would regularly communicate about learning goals and challenges students may be facing, and even collaborate with the afterschool program about how some of those troublesome areas could be addressed. Wasn't this what Nancy Lev and Lillian French were doing when they were principals?

Indeed, they were, but in Little Lake, the concept had been taken to the district level and honed. After Dr. Phillip Pérez became superintendent, Little Lake put the Professional Learning Community model at the center of its strategy to improve learning. PLCs, in the school context, are often used to organize teachers into collaborative work groups. Richard Dufour, a nationally recognized expert in PLCs, finds that the most effective PLCs "focus on learning rather than teaching, work collaboratively, and hold themselves accountable for results." A lot of school districts operate the PLC model, but in many places, it is not solution-oriented, and often it simply becomes a place where teachers gather to gossip or gripe. However, Little Lake developed a structured protocol for the meetings in which administrators and teachers review individual student data and identify trends, as well as strengths and weaknesses, for individual students. Their approach has turned out to be highly effective. Teachers look at districtwide benchmarks and determine weak areas. THINK Together utilized this data to target its support for students.

The new strategy altered the trajectory of Little Lake's low performance in the early 2000s. Phil Pérez, who had come to the district after serving as an assistant superintendent in the Riverside Unified School District, said he sensed the problem immediately.

"Everything felt so fragmented. There were a lot of initiatives, but it seemed like there was no payoff. There was nothing to show for the work," Phil recalled.

Phil embraced the challenge to turn the district around. He had attended Little Lake schools himself, and he'd volunteered at the local elementary schools when he was a student at nearby Santa Fe High. While earning his bachelor's degree and teaching credential at California State University, Long Beach, he worked at Little Lake as an instructional assistant. He went on to become an elementary school teacher at ABC Unified in Cerritos and also served as a principal within the Anaheim City and the Monrovia Unified school districts. Education was in his blood. Now, after earning his doctorate in education from UCLA, he was back home in Little Lake as the head honcho. He wanted to make a difference. Making things right in his hometown school district meant culling best practices from other places. He took a number of his administrators to other cities to examine their schools, to conferences to learn about promising strategies including PLCs, to districts that had elevated low test scores, and to schools that had adapted practices he felt would best serve Little Lake. During a conference on PLCs, he sensed a collective "a-ha" moment. If Little Lake stuck to the PLC model, it would make a difference.

Phil stands by that today. "We need to be very conscientious and stay focused on our strategy. There isn't a silver bullet out there that is going to magically improve the performance of under-served students. It's just adopting research-based best practices and sticking with them. It's not sexy work. It's not going to get you on the front cover of Educational Leadership, but it makes a difference for kids."

Today, the district environment is quite different than when Phil first arrived. Witness this Data Reflection Session at Jersey Avenue Elementary: Principal Monica Johnson met with the teachers, including Veronica Camelo and Jessica Staine, and the THINK Together site coordinator, Ramona Kocharian. The meeting followed a strict protocol in which they discussed challenges and solutions.

Ramona is an anomaly among the THINK Together site coordinators. Most of THINK's site coordinators are young people out of first-rate universities, like Yale, Stanford, Notre Dame, USC or UC campuses including Berkeley, Los Angeles and Irvine. Ramona didn't attend any of those schools; she's a parent whose children attended Jersey. She had volunteered at the school for a number of years and later joined THINK Together as a part-time program leader. (Program Leader is the name THINK uses for the front line staff who work with students in a 20:1 ratio.) When THINK's original site coordinator moved up to a quality assurance coach position, Monica Johnson recommended Ramona for the job.

At this particular Data Reflection Session in 2012, it was clear that Ramona was a veteran and knew the drill. She connected well with the students and their families and remained permanently ebullient about her role at the school. No problem seems insurmountable, not even the case of a third-grader, Melanie, who has struggled every year since kindergarten.

"She pretty much eats anything in front of her," said her teacher, Veronica.

"She even ate her name tag," Ramona said, smiling.

"One day, she spent a very long time in the bathroom, and it wasn't because she was just wasting time in there. She was really using the facilities," added another teacher, Jessica.

"She just had an accident, wetting, last week," said Ramona. "I told Mom to bring extra clothes."

"I think," said the principal, "that it is time to call for an SST."

SST stands for Student Support Team, a state-recognized legal process providing help to students struggling in school. In the first step, Melanie's parents would meet with teachers and the principal to find solutions to help Melanie succeed. The principal invited THINK's Ramona to join in.

The women also discuss the third grade's disappointing results on the district's benchmark test, which was created so Little Lake educators could determine how students are faring. They lamented that only 72 percent of the students were proficient in the unit. That would be very high compared to students in similar schools across California, but far below what have come to be the high expectations in Little Lake. Tests of other units have shown as much as 90 percent proficiency. The subject was math, and the group looked further and discovered that the word problems involving questions requiring calculations with money were what most often stumped the students.

"I think it's because there were so many word problems," suggested Veronica.

"This was the hardest test this year. I had a couple of criers," added Jessica.

"Are you working on word problems after school?" the principal asked Ramona.

The four educators put their heads together to come up with ways to have THINK staff begin a money-related question review the following week. Ramona is used to this; she begins every week going over the concepts taught in the classroom. The spiral review, as it's called, ensures that students get reinforcement of the previous week's lessons. There's also a review of several questions from the California Standards Test. It's not just "put-your-pencil-to-the-paper" time that might give the supervising adult in the room a chance to read a book. It's actually the beginning of a process in which students are asked to complete sentences: This question is asking _____. I think the answer is _____ because _____. In addition, THINK is helping to foster critical thinking skills that are part of the new Common Core State Standards.

The students are then clustered in groups where they are instructed to discuss their answers. They are told to use certain phrases such as, "I agree because ...," or "That's true. I also think that ..." or "I disagree because ..." The process continues after school, five days a week. This collaboration, long the norm at Jersey, is another element of Common Core.

Almost immediately after the Data Reflection Session, Ramona instructed her staff to work on the money problems during the after-school program.

"We are always involved in our core standards," Ramona said. "After school has evolved. We are definitely more than day care. We have a very structured program. There's no free play to just run around."

"We play a huge role in giving our kids a voice and bringing them out of their shell. We get them involved in the leadership of the program, which helps them understand how to organize things and how to lead. We are giving them great opportunities to practice and learn in ways that augment the additional academic support they receive."

After enjoying a healthy snack, one hundred students in first through fifth grades line up and file back into a classroom. The school day is over, but their learning is not. Before getting down to business, Diego was asked to read the behavior agreements of THINK Together's afterschool program. The group repeated after him in chorus:

"Be safe"

"Be respectful."

"Be responsible."

"Have fun!"

Everything the students do fits into this positive behavioral framework. If students are misbehaving, or getting off task or distracting others, the student leaders or the THINK staff remind them what they had previously agreed to. It's a simple, but highly effective system.

After the review of the agreements, the students launched into their lesson. Julio pouted and put his hands in his pockets. His eyes scanned the page: "Shamika is saving money to buy a book. She has saved one five-dollar bill, three one-dollar bills, one quarter, three dimes, and four nickels. How much does she have so far?" Julio rested his chin on the words and numbers.

The THINK program leader noticed his body language, "What is the question asking you? Julio, read the problem out loud."

Julio did, then sat and stared. He wrote nothing on the page before being grouped with other kids his age. They were prompted to talk with each other about Shamika. Julio's classmate Janella beamed as she explained that the correct answer is $8.75. She explained that she added the bills first, then the coins, and then added the total of bills and coins together. Julio seemed to be catching on, yet the program leader, Darla Chavez, watched Julio's continuing struggle. He was having trouble adding 25 and 25.

"That was the hardest lesson," said Darla, the program leader and a university student herself, who is studying to be a teacher. "The kids are having a really tough time with money. My hunch is that they are having trouble with the addition, regrouping the numbers in the problems."

Time was up. The class would soon be headed to physical fitness. Janella, a third-grader wearing sequined high tops, a skirt, leggings, and a sparkly sweatshirt, announced to the class, "it's time for a debrief."

"Class," Janella continued, "what activity did we just do?"

Classmate Alejandro, referring to the series of problems that allow the kids to experience standardized test questions every afternoon, answered: "We did math, fun, fast, and furious."

The ever-optimistic Ramona was glad the students had further exposure to the money problems, but she made a note to talk to the teachers again. No one would just skip over the matter. Ramona started bringing out plastic coins and paper money. When they have completed their other enrichment activities, the THINK Together students would play with fake money, to practice their math some more.

Randy liked how integrated the THINK Together program was with the regular school day in Little Lake and was impressed with the data-driven approach of the district—and especially its results. He wanted to study the Little Lake work more formally and document what was going on there. Other schools needed to replicate this work so that more under-served students could benefit from this very solid approach to learning. The results could also help overcome the stereotypes about afterschool programs that Randy felt were holding the field back.

Until the mid-2000s, afterschool programs were viewed primarily as places where parents could leave their kids. Studies to evaluate afterschool programs looked at indicators such as safety, level of student engagement, and attendance. As the accountability targets established as part of No Child Left Behind rose inexorably in combination with the budget cuts that came with the national recession, educators began to look for more support from their afterschool programs. Enlightened schools saw that a well-run afterschool program aligned with the school day could be a real asset in their quest to boost student achievement.

In 2009, President Barack Obama joined a bipartisan group of leaders from government at all levels, educators, and the business community in calling for a longer school day and school year: "We can no longer afford an academic calendar designed when America was a nation of farmers who needed their children at home plowing the land at the end of each day," Obama declared. "That calendar may have once made sense, but today, it puts us at a competitive disadvantage. Our children spend over a month less in school than children in South Korea. That is no way to prepare them for a 21st century economy."

In the absence of any state or federal initiative to lengthen the school day and school year, focusing on fortifying learning through already-funded afterschool programs seems like a very good idea. Yet, in 2009 there was precious little data to support the idea that academic support in afterschool programs could actually make a difference. There was a 2007 UC Irvine study that has become widely cited among educators. It indicated positive impacts in math for students who attended such programs two to three days per week over two years and who were involved in other enrichment activities. Other studies focused on English learners, a significant portion of California's students.

California's K–12 public school system educates 1.5 million English learners, about one in every four students. A 2008 study by Corey Newhouse of the consulting firm Public Profit that examined the Central Valley's afterschool programs showed that 23 percent of English learners in an afterschool program were reclassified as fluent in English, compared to 7 percent for all counterparts who did not participate in an afterschool program. While empirical research on program outcomes was still emerging, most of it focused on factors such as active youth engagement, increased attendance, better grades, and the relationship between students and staff.

Randy wanted more. He was driven to produce an ever-better product. He saw the impact high-quality programs had on the youth at Shalimar. They were now going to college at six times the rate of their socioeconomic peer group. He knew that if these kids could do it, so could millions of others. As a numbers guy, he knew THINK Together needed to document its work in order to continue to refine the process and to grow its funding. He turned to Dr. Jenel Prenovost, THINK's director of evaluation, to discuss the best way to proceed. She advised that they approach UC Irvine to study THINK's programs. Founding Dean of UCI's School of Education Dr. Deborah Vandell was one of the premier researchers in the world of afterschool programs. UCI and THINK Together already had some crossover. Jenel had earned her doctorate from the university and had continued to work with the School of Education when she worked in Santa Ana Unified.

Jenel and Deborah Vandell cooked up an interesting idea: They proposed that THINK Together create a doctoral fellowship at UC Irvine. The fellowship would consist of an investment by THINK Together, including tuition and a monthly stipend. In return, the fellow would study THINK Together's work in conjunction with the broader out-of-school-time program universe.

Randy and the THINK Together board of directors agreed to

the idea, and Tracy Bennett was selected as the inaugural THINK Together Fellow. A native of nearby Upland and a graduate of UCI, Tracy had earned a master's degree in education policy at the University of Michigan and had been a program evaluator for both UCI and Santa Ana Unified. At the time she was toying with how to best use her degrees when she received this boost from THINK Together. Within five years, she would emerge as a leading figure in the field focused on afterschool research. But at that moment, Tracy had little clue how to begin.

"After school is still transitioning from being viewed as a safe place where you leave your kids to a place that can help extend learning. The field is not halfway there yet. After school is a place to be creative," Tracy said. "You can ask yourself: If I had three more hours with these kids and I was not bound by any regulations, what would I do to help them?"

Little Lake became a natural place to start poking around. Tracy liked what she saw: lots of communication between teachers, the principals and THINK Together staff. The district had created the space for collaboration by giving the teachers release time from the classroom. This is the time that teachers used to meet with the principals for their Data Reflection Sessions. The district created a system using permanent substitute teachers, where during this release time the students did art, music, and physical education. By having this consistent system, students are able to benefit from a high-quality enrichment program.

Even though THINK Together's staff members were not certificated teachers, they were invited to school site staff meetings, where their opinions were valued. Lesson plans included ways to incorporate THINK's resources, and vice versa. Tracy called this meeting of the minds between principals, teachers, and afterschool staff "alignment." While the term was also being used in business and academia in different ways, for Tracy it meant principals and afterschool site coordinators were in agreement about academic resources, communication, and intensive partnership with the after-school.

If you weren't in education, you might wonder, wouldn't every school want that? Wouldn't they change what they do to create these great relationships so their students would excel? With a bevy of issues creating roadblocks, including those related to low expectations, previous programs with disappointing results, use of classrooms, differences in instructional styles, and demands on time, it really wasn't as simple as it might sound.

Tracy stayed in the Little Lake School District an entire school year, from October 2009 to June 2010, to study its work. She sat in on Data Reflection Sessions, interviewed district officials, analyzed standardized test scores, surveyed principals and teachers, and conducted focus groups of THINK's site coordinators. She was hoping to learn from the best practices at Little Lake so they could be replicated elsewhere. She learned that the valuable Data Reflection Sessions were part of a larger Response to Intervention (RtI-S) system that included other intervention instructors who provided targeted support to students who were struggling and enrichment for those capable of bounding ahead. Everything Little Lake did was coordinated and disciplined.

Tracy admired the strategies that were clearly set forth every day. Meetings were conducted with protocols, support was offered to help facilitate communication with parents, and resources were made available. Teachers shared successful strategies with others teaching the same grade. Strategies were developed to help students of differing levels of ability. School personnel made a point of updating THINK Together staff with lesson plans and strategies to differentiate afterschool lessons.

The result was that teachers were becoming better prepared to effectively teach to the state standards and to use data to drive instruction-based decisions. THINK could now implement standards-based lessons that complemented school day instruction. As Common Core State Standards came along, that approach was a logical next step to what Little Lake had already been doing.

The other thing that was impressive about Little Lake was the collaboration at all levels. The district had a stable board that supported its leader and didn't try to micromanage the district. They had a focused and effective leader in Phil Pérez, who also provided consistency and stability in that position over time. Phil had an exceptional assistant superintendent of education services, Marty Maya (later succeeded by Maria Soto), and a superintendent's cabinet and strong principals. Even the classified staff was on board. All of this served to support the work that the teachers and students did in the classroom. The district's culture of being results- and solution-oriented and highly collaborative extended quite naturally to its partnerships and to the parents. In Little Lake, there was no "us versus them." Everything was "we."

Tracy spent much of the school year determining how THINK could replicate and scale the alignment model that had been so successful in Little Lake. While many schools might not have the infrastructure in place to foster collaboration in quite the same way, many districts had other assets to build on. THINK Together started convening group meetings with principals from its other school district partners. It held up the Little Lake results, and then began discussions in each district about what alignment might look like. A variety of strategies emerged depending on each district's starting point. No matter where a school was located, THINK was able to foster alignment wherever principal trust and support existed. The two key ingredients were the school principal and THINK's upstream support system, which helped to build the skills of THINK's young staff. With these ideas in hand, Randy Barth was off and running to find more school districts that could benefit from these strategies.

Randy and his THINK team were not the first explorers to "discover" Little Lake. Other educators had taken notice years before. In the 2000–2001 school year, the small southeastern Los Angeles County school district had been placed on a state watch list because of three underperforming schools, among them Jersey Elementary. Phil Pérez was brought in as the new superintendent to lead the turnaround of these schools. To avoid further sanctions, the Little Lake school board approved Phil's recommendation to contract with a boutique consulting group, the Principal's Exchange, which had a great track record in turning around schools. Together, they created and implemented many of the forward-thinking strategies in Little Lake admired by Tracy during her time there.

The Principal's Exchange was created by a small team around a system designed by Dr. Robin Avelar La Salle, a former teacher who spent years as a school district administrator with responsibility for curriculum, staff development, and assessment. She worked in research and consulting across California, focusing on advancing academic success for historically underperforming students. Her work in education is an outgrowth of her own personal journey. She grew up in the tough Echo Park neighborhood near downtown Los Angeles and graduated from Belmont High School. She received her bachelor's and master's degrees along with a teaching credential from Cal State LA. She later went on to earn a PhD in education from Stanford University with an emphasis on language, literacy, and culture.

After years in the schools, Robin teamed up with Estella Ramirez to form the consulting group. They felt that they could have a greater impact on student achievement by working across multiple school systems from the outside, rather than a single district from the inside. The year was 1996, before the accountability era was ushered in with the passage of No Child Left Behind in 2001. The launch also predated California's Public Schools Accountability Act of 1999 that created the Academic Performance Index.

What moved Robin and Estella more than any government-induced urgency was what Robin called the "inevitability assumption about low-income kids and students of color." They wanted to prove that just because certain districts were composed of a population from challenging circumstances, where money was tight and English-language skills were limited, these kids were just as capable as any other students, given access to a quality education. After all,

Robin and Estella were living proof. "We just wanted to share what we had found had worked from our years as teachers and administrators," Robin said.

The Principal's Exchange launched with a "coming out party" at the luxurious Ritz-Carlton Hotel. Dozens of Southern California school superintendents were present. There was a buzz about the previous success that Robin and Estella had had in helping English learners and underperforming students. The calls came in the next day. Their work began in a cluster of schools near Belmont High School, Robin's ailing alma mater in the Los Angeles Unified School District. The group quickly worked its way east to the Whittier area, where it helped build systemic change that could deliver consistently great results for students across multiple districts. Whittier is next door to Little Lake, so when Phil was looking for partners to support his turnaround work, the Principal's Exchange was a logical choice.

The Principal's Exchange approach begins with an in-depth assessment of what is working and what needs improvement in a district. These audits result in a short list of barriers to accelerated student success and identify priority focus areas. The process then moves to the development of a plan that strategically allocates to specific challenges, depending on the need. The Principal's Exchange calls this process RtI-S, or Response to Intervention for Systems, and focuses on promoting equity rather than equality. Equality means providing every student with the same level of support while equity involves providing every student what they need to succeed. This critical distinction is central to the mission of the Principal's Exchange.

This enables district leaders to target their efforts more effectively to get some early wins and build confidence that their teams are on the right track. As in the other districts, what Robin found in Little Lake was what she called a lack of "alignment." Robin uses the word differently than Tracy and THINK Together. Robin's use refers to the need for crystal clarity about what is to be taught and learned at each grade level as well as articulation between grade levels. This "alignment" helps create a coherent operating system for everyone.

This simple cartoon illustrates the difference between equity and equality. Equity means giving every child what they need to be successful and equality means giving every child the same thing. We need to build systems that can differentiate curriculum, pedagogy, and support systems so that every child has what they need to succeed.

Little Lake was suffering from a lack of clarity. "The teachers, principals, and administrators were all very able and dedicated educators but were not working together toward clearly defined common goals," Robin said. "Of course, they all wanted the best for the students. But, for example, there were a wide variety of approaches to teaching the third grade. Each third-grade teacher might emphasize different elements of California's sixty different language arts standards. Further, each teacher might assess students in their own way, making it difficult to compare how students are performing across classrooms. This made it difficult to determine which practices were most effective and limited the opportunity for teachers and principals to share best practices." Robin pointed out that this lack of articulation can grow exponentially across grade levels and schools, to the detriment of the students' ultimate ability to achieve.

By the time THINK Together arrived in Little Lake, Phil Pérez and his team, with support from the Principal's Exchange, were well on their way to building a coherent system. Together, they looked at how the classroom teachers could communicate with each other, how they could determine what to teach, and how to assess whether it was being taught.

"Key to building coherence is the creation of benchmark assessments, so you know what targets you are shooting for," Phil said. "This is followed by discussions about them at every level and the repeated development of solutions to keep up a momentum."

An example of this was seen in Ramona's Data Reflection Session at Jersey Avenue Elementary. Achievement on a lesson segment was tracked by placing students' names in quadrants on a large page. Teachers could then see which kinds of students, for example, English learners, were struggling with one particular area of learning.

"Everyone has PLCs," Robin explained. "But sometimes, these end up being meetings in search of a purpose. Sometimes data are not the focus, leading discussions to stray into topics that may not directly impact student achievement. Often, districts or schools don't allocate enough time to really review data, or there might not be an effective feedback loop to get the data in teachers' hands in a timely manner and in ways that are actionable. In some cases, the PLC meetings may not even exist, or they may lack effective protocols. Without an effective structure, meetings can tend to focus on problems and not solutions. There have to be steps toward solutions that every participant helps to create. This fosters teamwork and collaboration and results in high morale. This is the RtI-S system that we put in place."

"There is a tendency to look at things superficially," Robin continued. "On the surface, it may look as if all students are being adequately served. But the reality underneath the surface may tell a different story."

Robin and another colleague, Dr. Ruth Johnson, called this tendency "The Wallpaper Effect." Like wallpaper that can cover over cracks and crevices, schools and districts often implement layers of programs that do little more than cover up deep issues of access to optimal educational opportunities and equity in resources. In Little

Lake and other districts, the Principal's Exchange has been able to work with teachers and administrators to develop pathways for students that enable them to avoid these cracks and crevices so that they can reach their full potential.

However, Prop. 49 created some new challenges. "When the Proposition 49 funding opportunity came around, things became a little more complicated," Robin said. "A number of our district partners turned to us for advice."

In one district, some students had to choose either an afterschool intervention session provided by the district to help underperforming students or THINK Together. The concern at the Principal's Exchange was that an outside afterschool program would be more like a holding tank and could draw kids away from the targeted extra learning opportunity.

"What we were concerned about was that many of these programs offer homework support, but that help is not strategic, and most of the rest of the program is primarily recreational," she said. "We said, 'This is not OK,' and we were quite passionate about it. We have kids here who can't read. One hour of general homework support isn't going to help them.

"Our partner districts told their afterschool providers that their students needed targeted interventions after school that extended the learning time from the school day. There was a pushback from many of the groups, but there was one provider that was responsive. It was THINK Together.

"We learned that there would be full-time site coordinators on campus each day. We saw that as an asset we could really utilize. In addition, they told us, 'We will do whatever it takes, whatever you want us to do, provided it is within the guidelines of the funding stream. We like clarity and we want to support the students in the best way possible.' At Principal's Exchange we were pretty surprised. We liked it!"

Thus began the process of opening the doors to THINK Together, of including the staff in meetings that were generally meant for principals and teachers. THINK became regulars at the Data Reflection

Sessions. Robin is now very grateful for THINK's integration into the process.

"They took the best of our ideas, made them their own, and even used them in other school districts. That really warmed our heart because we are doing our work to help as many kids as can be helped," Robin said. "If they can use our strategies in other places to help more students, that makes us feel really proud."

Robin and Randy worked together indirectly for years, but had never met. They learned about each other's work through district administrators that they both supported.

"I thought, 'Who is this THINK Together guy?'" Robin recalled. "Whoever he is, I love him. We are not arm wrestling them for kids."

After more than six years of collaborating, Robin, Estella, and Randy did finally meet in person. "In time, we came to realize that Randy and THINK Together are committed to the same mission as we are,'" Robin said. "Like us, he wants to challenge the inevitability assumption."

What is clear is that Robin's concept of alignment has stretched into learning that occurs beyond the regular school day, and Randy's concept of what THINK Together can do to better support students has also expanded. With the groundwork laid by Robin and the research done by Tracy, THINK Together now has a more systematic way of handling many of the challenges their students face.

The hurdles to academic excellence have never alarmed Robin, Estella, or the Principal's Exchange team. They could see the successes. At Jersey Avenue Elementary, 75 percent of the third-graders were now proficient on the unit test involving money questions. Robin recalled that when her group began its partnership with Little Lake, proficiency levels cited at Data Reflection Sessions were often less than 20 percent.

"What matters is that a red flag is raised. The beautiful thing is that there is a systematic way to deal with student needs during the school day and after school as well. THINK Together knows which kids are struggling. The teachers know. They have a way to share feedback.

There is a system in place to deal with this so *every* child is given a *real* opportunity to achieve."

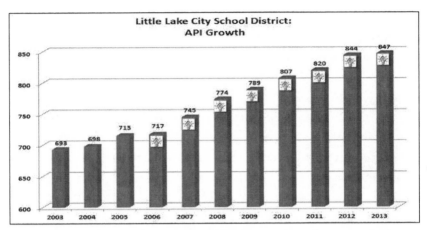

Growth in Little Lake City School District's Academic Performance Index. Little Lake is one of the highest achieving low-income school districts in California.

THINK Together jumped head-first into the concept of alignment. The concept was intuitive, yet it was clear the practice of it was not. Nor was it easy to walk into school districts and start barking orders.

Dr. Becky Newman, THINK's first chief program officer, taught Randy more than he expected about school district culture. Districts were more open to THINK Together because of Becky—because she was an insider. Dr. CynDee Zandes, who succeeded Becky when she retired, came from a similar background. She had taught every grade, served as a principal, and headed a district afterschool program. She now works with other THINK leaders with similar backgrounds. THINK Together leaders like these are able to help develop systems that better integrate with school systems because they have been on the other side.

For CynDee alignment is the key. "Is alignment just repeat, repeat,

repeat? Do we align everything or just certain things? Alignment is about being complementary and coherent with one another."

CynDee is continuously working with THINK's regional leaders to adjust the programs. "We try to have 70 percent of our program be consistent, so we can support it well to ensure high quality. But we also want about 30 percent to be the local adaptation so we meet the needs of particular schools and their strategies. As we mature and with the implementation of the Common Core, this may move more toward 50-50." She argues that the program should be so integrated into what the school is doing that the kids think the entire day is one piece, not two pieces: a school and an after-school. That does not mean that kids are doing the exact same thing as they do during school, it simply means that the work is tightly integrated.

In conceiving organizational strategy, CynDee believes that students must be engaged, and lessons must be relevant. Support can be of three types:

First, it can be front-loading students with concepts that will later be taught by teachers. An elementary geometry session the next week at school can be preceded by afterschool activities such as art, relevant playground sessions, or other hands-on, minds-on activities.

Second, support can be found through remediation. Afterschool program leaders can review concepts that teachers have presented and approach the concepts that students may have missed through different learning modalities and strategies.

Finally, support can be offered through side-by-side alliances among teachers and afterschool staff.

"Side-by-side alliances are frequently formed, but those are the trickiest," CynDee said. "The challenge is to get people to move out of the box. For years, we thought of teachers as a sage on the stage. There is so much knowledge now, this may not be true anymore. It's scary for us as educators to think that we do not know everything. Teachers are sometimes slow to adjust to this new reality. In regards to after school, there's more of an open environment, and we know we aren't supposed to be experts, so it's OK not to know. Instead, what we are promoting is the idea of looking things up. You can Google just about anything. It's the application of knowledge that becomes more important. But schools are definitely beginning to embrace new ways of learning."

In the fall of 2008, CynDee began facilitating discussions in each of the THINK Together districts and conducting principal meetings to share promising practices. CynDee shared the findings in Little Lake and led a discussion of what alignment might look like. Not everyone (or anyone) had the data-driven PLC model that Little Lake had, so the starting point for alignment needed to look different. In each district, there were principals who embraced the program and used it effectively and principals who didn't. CynDee asked principals who were using the program effectively to present their approach. There was also an opportunity to share concerns and problem-solve collectively in light of this new information.

These meetings became very popular and were repeated periodically. This data-driven collaboration combined with the sharing of successful practices and challenges planted the seed for how THINK Together's growing infrastructure could be leveraged across school districts to share promising ideas and even resources to help improve student achievement and reduce costs. The meetings also helped CynDee and the THINK Together team learn how to hone their own ideas.

CynDee and her program team are forever refining THINK's programs, even in simple ways. There are no more games of Battleship or dominos, for example, because the small pieces in the games became too expensive to constantly replace. Instead, there are paper and cardboard games to play, which makes a big difference in the bottom line.

"Everyone here is always learning. We want to see 'ah-ha' moments and learn about tweaks we can make to improve. We want to hear, 'Hey, that really is working,' or this approach isn't. We are always learning—everyone: students, program leaders, site coordinators, managers, everyone. It does not matter who you are," CynDee said. "We are constantly reading, updating, changing. If you can't create that culture in an organization, you will not succeed with the kids."

5

Santa Ana

The Grand Californian is the signature hotel of the Disneyland Resort and lives up to its name. It stands as an architectural tribute to the Arts and Crafts movement that produced the Craftsman homes found all over the state. In May of 2008, the ballroom of the Grand Californian was filled to capacity with an audience of business and civic leaders anticipating a big announcement. It was here that Randy and Mary spent a memorable evening with real estate pioneer and philanthropist Donald Bren and his dynamic wife, Brigitte, at a very special THINK Together celebration.

Steve Churm, an Orange County media leader, was the evening's emcee. He began by introducing the head of "one of the biggest and most influential enterprises in Orange County." This leader stepped onto the stage wearing a tasteful pink dress and a warm smile. A former elementary school teacher, Jane Russo had climbed her way up through the system to become the first female superintendent of the Santa Ana Unified School District. Churm, whose OC Metro magazine had named Jane one of Orange County's Women to Watch, told the audience that her district comprised 55,000 students, 63 schools, 6,000 employees, a $500-million budget, and billions in real estate holdings. He told the crowd that Jane "has the power to shape the lives of tens, if not hundreds of thousands of children over time."

Surprised, yet pleased, by the flattering introduction, Jane took the microphone. She was there to thank Donald Bren, chairman of the Irvine Company, for an astonishing gift, an $8.5 million donation to THINK Together. The private money would be used to extend the school day in Santa Ana, because public funds are just not enough to provide help for students like hers. Some 60 percent are still learning English, and 79 percent meet the federal poverty criterion.

Jane smiled at Donald, and then addressed the crowd of almost five hundred people. "Thank you, Mr. Bren, for your incredible compassion and generosity in this landmark commitment to our after-school program. ... I was once asked what I would wish for if I could do anything for our students. It didn't take long for me to respond. California has a short school day and a short school year. We do not have enough time with our students. I would ask for an extension of the school day. ... This partnership with THINK Together and this gift from Mr. Bren and the Irvine Company to extend our school day is a superintendent's dream."

Under the enlightened leadership of Donald Bren, the Irvine Company had long been a major investor in public education. The company's strategy to make great schools the center of its planned communities was a brilliant success. But this major investment in THINK Together marked a historic moment. Donald's backing was part of a plan to create a model urban, low-income school district, one that could be replicated in other communities across California.

Donald Bren became chairman of the Irvine Company in 1983. The company's major holding, the 185-square-mile Irvine Ranch, originated as several adjoining Mexican land grants accumulated by James Irvine and his partners back in the 1860s. The ranch covered one-sixth of Orange County, stretching from coastal mountains to the sea. As Southern California grew and the suburban sprawl moved south from Los Angeles, the ranch became too valuable to remain agricultural. In 1960, the Irvine Company became a pioneer in developing planned communities. Resisting pressure to sell off the land piece by piece, a long-range plan was put into place, redefining the entire concept of urban planning by creating model communities that offered a balanced mix of homes, business, shopping, parks, and open space. At its heart were a series of villages built around great schools. Over time, as the ranch became more fully developed, the Irvine Company began to expand into San Diego, Silicon Valley, Los Angeles, and Chicago.

As the company's fortunes grew, so did the charitable giving, with a focus on land preservation and conservation, research, and education. Not only has Donald Bren made significant contributions to public schools, he has endowed more than fifty chairs for distinguished faculty and researchers at universities and research institutions.

Known generally for being a private man, Donald made a unique public appearance in support of THINK Together and gallantly took the microphone. "We are thrilled with our investment ... a direct response to the governor's call for us to all be thinking about the importance of afterschool programming," Donald proclaimed. "Our investment today in THINK Together, and contributions from many of you, are making it possible for Randy and his staff to make a difference. ... The results that Randy and his team have achieved are simply astounding. We should be very proud of THINK's great progress to date."

The celebration at the Grand Californian capped months of discussions. Donald had long been interested in donating money to pilot some sort of education initiative. He knew that Gov. Arnold Schwarzenegger's Proposition 49 promoted public-private partnerships, which along with education, was something he embraced.

Donald Bren had once explained his philosophy in an interview with Forbes magazine: "In my opinion, education is the finest gift an individual can give a young person. And many of our public schools are falling short in successfully educating the youth of our country today. Gone are the days when state governments are fully able to fund our public schools. Future public education will require involvement and collaboration among various local, civic, private, and nonprofit entities, a concept I like to refer to as 'community entrepreneurship.' Over the past thirty years, I have sought to implement community entrepreneurship to benefit our local kindergarten through twelve grade schools, working in partnership with community leaders, local school districts, and well-run nonprofit organizations."

Santa Ana sits adjacent to the Irvine Ranch. It is the seat of Orange County's government and the heart of its urban core. Through the years as many of its wealthier citizens moved to the beach or to the southern part of the county, Latino immigrants replaced them. Because rents remained relatively high, multiple families crowded into homes and apartments in order to share the costs.

The massive migration and immigration from the 1980s to the early 2000s led to a period of upheaval in the city and its schools. By the early 2000s, Santa Ana was the fourth-densest city in the US. Its school district had seen its student population balloon from 40,000 in 1990 to 63,000 in 2003, before settling back to some 57,000 a few years later. What's more, its schools had the highest percentage of English learners of any large school district in America. Santa Ana was one of the youngest cities in the country, yet had one of the least-educated populations of parents. The Rockefeller Institute listed Santa Ana at Number 1 in its 2004 Urban Hardship Study, ahead of more visibly tough places such as Newark or Detroit.

By 2005, this turbulent period thankfully began to subside, and the city and its schools slowly stabilized. Yet, there was recognition, particularly among business owners, that the growing army of unskilled young people, some of whom struggled to fill out a job application even with a high school diploma under their belts, was not good for either Santa Ana or Orange County and their economies.

Around that time, former Santa Ana Mayor Dan Young became president of the community development division of the Irvine Company. The company had been working with California Business Roundtable, the California Teachers Association, and the governor's office on a set of education reform ideas. Part of the nascent plan included a series of public-private partnerships that could move some of these reforms ahead, while others would wend their way through the state legislature.

That led to Dan calling Randy one afternoon in the fall of 2007.

The two had met previously but didn't know each other very well. Dan asked Randy to organize an after-hours meeting at Randy's home and to invite Jane Russo along with Mike Metzler. Jane was then the relatively new schools chief, and Mike was the longtime Santa Ana Chamber of Commerce CEO and an old friend of Dan's. "Oh," Dan added, "have some good wine and hors d'oeuvres." The call caught Randy by surprise, but not entirely unprepared.

The four of them gathered at Randy and Mary's home a few weeks later. Randy pulled out a couple of his favorite wines, a Melville Inox Chardonnay and a Silver Oak Cabernet Sauvignon, while Mary prepared a platter of fresh fruit, imported cheeses, charcuterie, and prawns. After the usual get-acquainted chit chat, Dan got down to business. He outlined some of the conversations that had been occurring around the state on school reform and Donald Bren's support of what was happening. He mentioned that the company was interested in piloting some of these ideas in Santa Ana, which everybody in the room was excited about. Then he gestured to Randy, rather dramatically, and said, "And Mr. Bren wants to run it through this guy."

At the time, this was neither obvious, nor would it be easy. THINK Together was working in only 13 of Santa Ana's 47 K–8 schools. The discussions that evening included talk about early childhood education, school day pilots, extended learning for K–8, as well as high school programs. The chamber of commerce was deeply involved in a project called High School Inc., a partnership between Santa Ana Valley High School and the business community to better prepare high school grads for good paying jobs in the community.

In the weeks that followed Mike, Jane, and Randy all collaborated on various plans to present as options for the Irvine Company to consider. As the plans became more refined, the company indicated that it wanted to focus on younger students. The ideas were not competing with each other, but Randy's part of the proposal had the strongest data behind it.

One afternoon, driving back from a meeting in San Diego, Randy received another call from Dan Young. Dan announced that Mr. Bren had decided to make an $8.5 million investment, spread over several years, in Santa Ana through THINK Together to provide matching funds to the state Proposition 49 dollars at all of the city's elementary schools. The funding would both expand and enrich the afterschool programs, which Jane Russo had put at the top of her wish list. The investment was conditioned on creating a management structure whereby THINK Together would manage all of the afterschool programs districtwide.

This was something that Randy had worked on with both Al Mijares and, subsequently, Jane Russo since 2003. But, until now, they had never been able to get it over the finish line. Jane was excited about the prospect. The district had a lot of issues to focus on, and having a single point of contact for afterschool would enable her and her leadership team to focus on the regular school day. Jane told Randy that he needed to build a collaboration that included all of the existing stakeholders who wanted to stay in.

When Jane became superintendent the previous year, the district was emerging from a long turbulent time. She described her first years as wielding a Whack-a-Mole. Problems kept popping up everywhere. School board meetings were six to seven hours long, with everyone venting about problems that couldn't be solved: layoffs, problem teachers, union issues, and more. Jane began the process of creating districtwide systems to handle these problems. She also sought to establish some of the alignment principles, similar to those in Little Lake, so that teachers could have measurable benchmarks.

This prospective Irvine Company investment would potentially enable her to align what was going on after school with her overall goals for students and teachers in the district. But getting there was going to be a challenge. The same issues and politics that had plagued the program in 2003 were still alive in 2008.

While no doubt everyone was working hard, "the program just wasn't at the level we wanted," Jane recalled. "There wasn't a substantive curriculum, and we had supervisors who were taking on a program at 3 p.m. after working all day at school. We were grateful for a place for our kids to go that was safe, a place where they could do homework, but we knew we could do better."

With an eye toward improved instruction, Jane sought to extend the learning day through a more focused program. She was concerned that Santa Ana students didn't have enough exposure to English at home, that they were behind in their learning and needed additional instructional time. But Jane and Randy both knew that navigating the politics of change would be quite difficult.

"It was like sumo wrestling," Jane recalled. "But it was unconscionable to let the Irvine Company opportunity go. We had a responsibility to these children, and providing high-quality programs was even more important in Santa Ana than elsewhere. These kids don't have anyone to pay for private tutoring after school or buy them trombones or tennis skirts."

Besides, Jane had also become increasingly aware of administrative issues related to the afterschool program in her district. The state of California had ramped up accountability around these programs by including afterschool programs in a stringent Categorical Program Monitoring process. In Santa Ana, the preparation for this review highlighted to the board of education problems that the administration had long known about.

By having a coherent plan in place that aligned with other district goals, THINK Together and Santa Ana Unified were able to compete for additional funding to leverage the Irvine Company investment. This funding became even more critical as the state and national economy crumbled, beginning a five-year period of severe budget cuts for schools in California. The cratering of the economy would also completely wipe out Gov. Schwarzenegger's school reform plans.

First up, THINK Together and the district were able to win a $3.2 million per year federal 21st Century grant to expand the K–8 afterschool program and provide programming on non-school days. This came in just as the budget ax fell on traditional summer school, and as Jane approached Randy with a new idea for a next-generation summer learning program.

Jane was frustrated by the summer school program the district had run in recent years. The state funding that the district received for summer was targeted for students at risk of retention. Oftentimes, the last thing these kids wanted to do was go to school in the summer. To make things worse, unlike other districts, Santa Ana Unified had never negotiated a reduced rate for teachers for extra-duty pay. With seniority rules, the most senior teachers had first rights on the summer teaching slots. More often than not, these teachers were also burned out, but couldn't pass up the ninety dollars per hour for summer work. Because of the high rate of pay for teachers and the fixed reimbursement from the state, the class sizes were huge.

Taken together, you had burned-out teachers, unmotivated students, and large class sizes. It was awful. When the budget cuts came, Jane was glad for the opportunity to reimagine what summer could look like. There was a deep need for high-quality summer programming in Santa Ana. A Johns Hopkins University study showed that low-income students often regress in their learning by as much as two months over the summer. Cumulatively, the Johns Hopkins study makes the case that the entire achievement gap for low-income students could be attributed simply to summer learning loss. In Santa Ana, where students could go all summer without speaking or hearing a word of English, the problem was compounded.

Jane's deputy superintendent, Dr. Cathie Olsky, worked with the THINK Together team to redesign summer and to fund it with the 21ˢᵗ Century grant and local matching funds that THINK Together could bring through philanthropy. The teachers union agreed to a flat forty dollars per hour wage, which was in line with most other districts' extra-duty pay. The teachers would also work on the THINK Together payroll during the summer. The principals at each school got to recommend the teachers that they thought would be best-suited to teach the curriculum. The teachers would provide the academic lessons, and THINK Together would provide enrichment, both aligned around targeted learning goals. THINK Together would also offer physical education and create a fun, camp-like environment for these inner-city kids who weren't going to summer camp in the woods. On top of that, Santa Ana was able to double the number of students served, from 6,000 to more than 12,000.

This new approach to summer learning was a huge hit—especially with the students. Many spent the long summer waiting for school to begin. There was so little to do that they would literally count the days until they could return to their classrooms. Too often, after school, they would return to either apartments so crowded that there was no place to study or where there were no adults present. For students like these, summer learning programs provided an educational oasis.

At Pio Pico Elementary School, program leader Angie Lopez asked students to write about what summer meant to them.

Vanessa Sandoval wrote that without THINK Together, "I would not be doing anything but watching too much TV and being lazy every day."

And Yuliano Zapien wrote, "I enjoy THINK Together because we get to study in a quiet classroom where I can concentrate."

The other sentiments were similar:

Andreacancia Ordoñez. : "I enjoy THINK Together because I get to do fun science experiments."

Limni Peña: "I feel ready for my future in college because we have Kids to College day, and Mrs. Lopez tells us to try our best. If I did not have the opportunity to go to THINK Together, I would not be able to stay up with my regular school work."

Humberto Gomez : "When there is a problem, Mrs. Lopez helps us problem-solve with each other."

Jorge Viruel: "I know my program leader cares about me because if I fail, she tells me I'm OK."

Diamon Ambriz: "Mrs. Lopez tells us to do our best and never give up on our dreams. If I didn't have the chance to go to THINK Together, I would not have this much fun and learn a lot of things."

The following year, THINK Together and Santa Ana scored another coup. The partners were named as one of five US Department of Education National Demonstration Sites to build alignment between federally funded Supplemental Education Services (small group tutoring), federally funded afterschool programs, and the regular school day. This award provided funding for a third-party study of how things were going with these new systems.

Dr. Pilar O'Cadiz and Dr. Valerie Hall, under the direction of UCI's Dr. Deborah Vandell, found that students who participated in these programs had greater gains in both English language arts and math versus non-program participants. The study also showed that students who participated for multiple years and in multiple layers of programming (after school, summer, SES) had greater gains than those with a single treatment or who participated for a single year or less (see chart on the following page).

Others took notice. The National Summer Learning Association twice named Santa Ana and THINK Together a finalist for its National Summer Program of the Year Award. This particularly heartened Randy because THINK and Santa Ana Unified were able to deliver this program for cents on the dollar when compared to the other finalists. The THINK/Santa Ana program's daily cost was about $8.25 per student for a half-day program and about $16.50 for a full-day. This meant that they could provide a twenty-six day summer program for less than $500 per student—one-third to one-half of the cost of the other national models. This affordable cost structure meant that THINK could scale these programs and reach many more students.

Along the way, the Walmart Foundation partnered with the National Summer Learning Association to create the Smarter Summers initiative. NSLA chose THINK Together as its California partner to deliver programs in San Diego, Los Angeles County (Baldwin Park Unified and Mountain View School District in El Monte), and Sacramento (Elk Grove Unified). These programs were based on the Santa Ana model and targeted to middle school students. Once again, the results were very promising. Later, the David and Lucile Packard Foundation included THINK Together and Santa Ana as a featured program in its Summer Matters campaign that endeavored to build model summer programs that incorporated best practices and encourage the legislature and local school boards to prioritize summer funding.

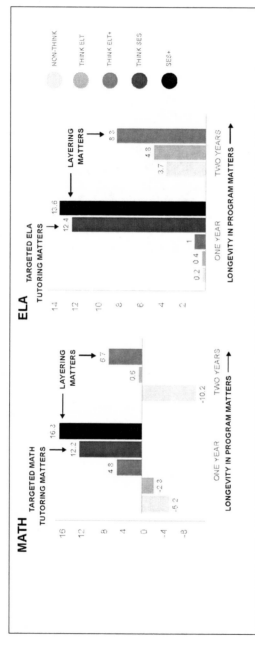

UC Irvine study showed that students in THINK Together afterschool, summer and small group tutoring programs outperformed students without those treatments in both math and English language arts. Students in the programs multiple years had greater gains than students in just one year.

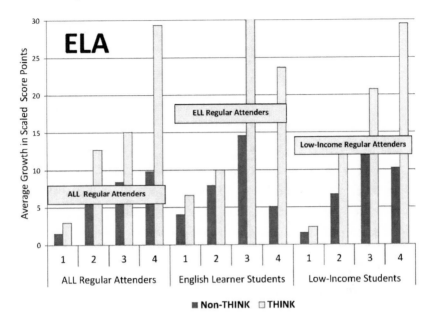

Students in grades three through eight, who regularly attended the programs for two, three, or four years, experienced statically significant higher growth rates on their 2012 CST in English language arts when compared to students who did not attend THINK Together.

All of this work served to support the great work that Jane, her leadership team, and teachers were doing to turn around Santa Ana's schools. They rebuilt the foundation and the systems of the district and moved student achievement forward dramatically. Jane was even able to garner support for a bond measure to build new schools and expand and modernize others so that students could have facilities that matched those in more affluent communities.

"The transformation occurred," she observed, "because it was all planned."

Jane took into account the whole state of the district: teaching skills, the district budget, and the socioeconomic level of the student population. She pinpointed goals. She enlisted everyone in the community: business, other educational institutions, health organizations, churches, elected officials, police, politicians, nonprofits, and youth.

"Then there were the parents, students, and the employee unions. Getting everyone on board is about the only way a large, clunky urban school district can improve itself," she said. "You need leadership with instructional chops, which informs how to get where you want to go. You need to get the right people on the bus, especially principals and the cabinet. In the first year or two that I led Santa Ana, we changed out about fifty administrators. Resources really weren't our largest issue. We had money, at least before the budget cuts, but nothing was happening. So we began to align everything we did around a common direction."

Teacher unions, particularly in large school districts, have often been vilified and blamed for bad student performance. The argument runs that the unions ensure teachers' job security even when student performance is poor, so there's little incentive for teachers to excel or to conceive innovative strategies for instruction. Critics also charge that the unions are heavy-handed, creating strict rules that prevent change. But in Santa Ana, the unions began to play ball. One major shift involved changing the protocols so that principals were allowed in the classrooms to observe teaching and become instructional coaches.

Jane established Principal Academies to build the capacity of principals to shift from the traditional "plant manager" role to "instructional leaders." The district tried to take as much bureaucratic work off the table as possible so principals could get into the classroom. At the same time, district administrators helped principals understand data, made them more familiar with new curriculum and pedagogy, and showed how to take guided walks through schools to encourage peer-to-peer learning. As these strategies were implemented, Santa Ana saw the competency of its teachers and principals steadily improve. Student achievement began to follow.

While Jane and her team focused on building the systems necessary to support student achievement during the school day, THINK Together was working to bring the afterschool programs in line with the school day goals. At first, it was uncomfortable for some of the parties involved. The union teachers were losing extra pay, and longtime programs were being asked to work under the management of a peer organization rather than reporting directly to the district. Yet, despite these tensions, there was collaboration, because everyone involved knew that Santa Ana students could benefit from more coherent programs that supported the district's goals.

One of the keys to the success was the upstream support infrastructure that THINK Together was able to build as a result of going to scale. A system of quality assurance coaches, one for every ten school sites, spend their days making sure the young frontline staff are successfully implementing curriculum and behavior management systems with fidelity so that there is consistent quality across all sites. These coaches are people like Natalie Bates, a UCI graduate who came up through the THINK Together system. In addition to curriculum and behavior management, she also helps the site staff with things like time management and student study habits. Natalie also works with the site coordinators to build relationships with their principals so that THINK knows what school leaders are looking for. Together, they work on setting goals, establishing benchmarks, and defining a work plan that is constantly refined and reviewed.

"Constant communication makes the program fit the needs of the school and the student," Natalie said.

But things weren't always so cohesive. When Natalie began her work with THINK Together as a volunteer in 2004, programs varied from school to school and city to city. Quality depended largely on the strength of the local site coordinator. Randy learned from Peter Drucker that if you build a system that depends on having a star in every position, you will never have great quality. At a certain point as you grow larger, your staff is going to be more average by definition. The key to success, Randy believes, is to build a support system that enables even average people to do great work.

"During the Prop. 49 implementation in 2007, we created a system so that so we could replicate and scale our work," Natalie said. "This allowed us to later scale districtwide in Santa Ana pretty seamlessly." The infrastructure that THINK Together had built that enabled it to go wide with its programs could also be leveraged to go deep in a community. This infrastructure could serve as the backbone for collective impact initiatives in troubled urban areas.

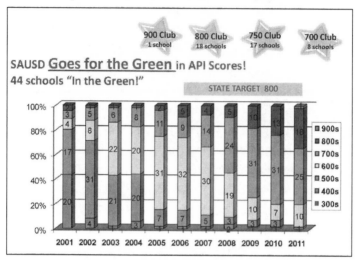

This graphic illustrates the progression of Santa Ana Unified schools toward the California Academic Performance Index target of 800 over a decade.

Each evening around 6 p.m. when parents would pick up their children from THINK Together's Extended Learning Time program, Snow Mendoza would have the chance to speak with them. Snow, a THINK Together site coordinator, is an American of Mexican descent. As trust built between the parents and Snow, their conversations expanded beyond school-related issues or student behavior and into the home. Snow became a resource for these parents, and they began seeking his advice on a variety of pressing subjects: how to do their taxes, how to complete forms in English, how to cope with cramped housing, how to deal with healthcare issues, how to deal with issues relating to immigration status, how to deal with landlord disputes, and finally—how to make ends meet.

Snow says the prevalent issue "is that children often live in a bedroom with their mother, father, and siblings." Usually, other families live in the other bedrooms of the house or apartment. "I wonder and worry about our kids. How can they even study? Where would they be without a place to study like THINK Together?" Snow worried that families had issues and challenges well beyond what he, his organization, or his school were equipped to respond to.

Randy had the same concerns. The issues that confronted Snow via these parents were the same ones that confronted nearly every THINK Together site coordinator since the early days on Shalimar Drive in 1994. Early on, Randy was confronted with a choice: Do he and his partners go deeper into a single neighborhood and attempt to meet the myriad needs that these families faced? Or, do they stay focused on providing academic support and spread that intervention more broadly? Go deep, or go wide?

Randy chose wide. He made this choice because he thought that education was the single best way out of poverty, and that by partnering with parents and schools, THINK Together could be part of a system that changed the trajectory of tens of thousands of students. Maybe even more.

But Randy was also keenly aware of the numerous challenges these families were facing. Now that THINK Together had achieved fairly significant scale, he wondered whether now might be the time to revisit the issue. There were a lot supports available in Santa Ana, but parents often didn't know about them. Programs and services too often operated in silos without links to one another. Randy wondered whether THINK Together's infrastructure could now be leveraged to go deep into a community as effectively as it was going broad across the region.

Over the years, Randy had continued to watch and learn from the work that Geoffrey Canada was doing in New York with the Harlem Children's Zone. As Linda Perlstein, writing in the New York Times, put it; "When assessing the state of America's children, people speak of the achievement gap between the middle class and the poor. But really there's an everything gap: a health gap, a safety gap, a technology gap, a conversational gap, a 'turning off the TV and going to the library' gap. Schools can help make up for some of these deficits, but they can't make up all the difference." Geoffrey Canada and his supporters chose to go deep in ninety-seven blocks of Harlem and take on all of these gaps.

California has a different landscape than Harlem—fiscally as well as geographically. Geoffrey Canada built the Harlem Children's Zone with mostly private money. California, the land of ballot initiatives, has several public funding streams that Randy thought might be woven together to create a comprehensive support system at scale. Philanthropy would be needed as well, but Randy didn't think that he or anybody else could raise the kind of private funding that Geoffrey and his board chair, Stan Druckenmiller, were raising in New York.

HCZ was a more comprehensive version of a community school model. This type of model was also difficult to replicate and scale. Randy preferred something he called a "school support ecosystem." The idea was similar to what the Irvine Company engineered into its planned communities: Place the school at the center of the community, and use it as a hub to integrate services for children and their families that were needed across the community. Most importantly, build it in a way that was replicable and scalable.

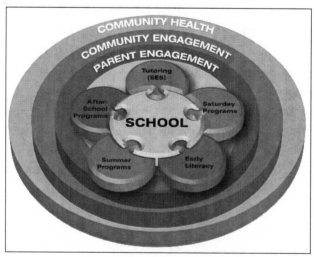

This is the scalable support system around schools that THINK Together is endeavoring to build across California.

In 1998, Californians passed Proposition 10, the Children and Families First Act. This was a tobacco tax that funded early childhood education and health programs for children up to age five. Under the implementation plan, each county created a local commission to decide how to invest these funds. Many places, this was called the First Five Commission, but in Orange County, it was known as the Children and Families Commission of Orange County.

In 2009, the commission was developing a new ten year strategic plan with the help of a nonprofit consulting firm called the Bridgespan Group. Bridgespan found that much of what the commission was doing in terms of health and school readiness was very effective. But in the area of early literacy, Bridgespan felt that the commission was trying to do too many things in too many places. They advised focusing on a few of the most effective, evidence-based strategies, and target those strategies in Anaheim, Garden Grove, and Santa Ana—the areas of greatest need in Orange County.

Mike Ruane, the entrepreneurial executive director of the commission, called Randy. He wanted to know if Randy would be interested in partnering to leverage the infrastructure THINK Together had built around Santa Ana schools to provide these early literacy supports. Randy jumped at the idea. Santa Ana had approximately 5,000 incoming kindergartners each year, and fewer than half of them had participated in preschool or Head Start programs. With the lack of support systems at home, this meant that many of the other 3,000 children were coming into school completely unprepared and behind their middle-class peers in other districts. This is exactly what Al Mijares had described to Randy years ago.

The partnership worked well. THINK Together was able to expand the early literacy programs in Santa Ana much more cost-affordably than the commission's previous efforts. Evaluation results indicated that the impact was equal to or better than before. Several years later, the commission approached THINK Together about taking over the day-to-day management of all of its early literacy and math efforts. THINK Together accepted and is now working with the Children and Families Commission, Orange County's United Way, and others to build a countywide early literacy effort. THINK Together's program management and data capacity enable it to serve as the backbone, while other partners can invest or provide content that can be spread to reach the gaps in children served across the county. THINK Together hopes to replicate this work in the other counties it serves across the state.

A few years later, a major foundation, the California Endowment, launched an initiative called Building Healthy Communities. The Endowment, a four billion health foundation, was also looking to have greater impact as part of its next-generation strategic plan. Similarly inspired by the Harlem Children's Zone, the Endowment selected neighborhoods in fourteen cities to launch place-based initiatives. THINK Together, the Children and Families Commission, and Santa Ana Unified were among the scores of players that joined together to accomplish ten ambitious goals over the following ten years. These goals can be summed up by the desire to create communities that are healthy, safe, and ready to learn.

All of these efforts together composed about a twenty million per year investment, spread over a community of 350,000 people with about 80,000 children under the age of eighteen. In Harlem, HCZ was investing approximately $100 million per year in 10,000 to 12,000 children. This is not exactly an apples-to-apples comparison because the HCZ budget includes its charter schools, and the twenty million in Santa Ana excludes the related school budget. Santa Ana has a long way to go to try and match the work in Harlem. But Randy feels it is crucial to continue to learn from the HCZ model and figure out how to replicate cost affordably as he has done with other pieces of the support system. He believes that there are existing investments from the state, philanthropy, and parents that can be knitted together in better ways to make it work like it has in Harlem.

Geoffrey Canada sought to improve lives in a 97-block patch of Harlem by creating an unbroken chain of support he called "the conveyor belt." He created programs for new parents, toddlers, and pre-kindergartners to pave the path to success. Baby College is a nine-week parenting class for expectant parents and parents with children up to three years old. The workshops promote reading and encourage verbal discipline over corporal punishment. Single Stop offers residents help accessing public benefits, advice on improving finances, debt relief counseling, and domestic crisis resolution. Other programs seek to help with asthma, a prevalent problem in Harlem, as well as obesity. The Harlem Children's Zone also runs elementary, middle and high schools, all of which boast impressive scores on standardized tests. But several things are different in Santa Ana.

Many Santa Ana parents have little understanding of the complexities of the education system. They hail from rural Mexico and have limited formal education. Most of them work in jobs that pay less than twelve dollars an hour, barely enough to pay the bills. Ask them what they hope for their children, and they will say, "*Que salgan adelante,*" that the children progress, or "*Que agarre una carrera,*" that they forge a career. The parents sadly know their good intentions alone may not be enough to produce that outcome. But they do know that there's helpful support in their local public schools. They have full faith in the teachers and the system. Whenever they are offered the chance for free afterschool programs, Saturday learning, or even parenting classes, they jump at it.

"It is very exciting to have the opportunity to learn after the school is technically closed," said Leticia, a single mother who has participated in several THINK programs. She lives with two young children in a bedroom she rents for $450 a month. "I am very optimistic for my children and their future, and I know that it will be all right because they listen to their teachers and study hard. Every time I see what my children do in school, I get so excited. I like to see any achievement. It feels like I have achieved something, too."

Leticia is not alone; other parents with children at Pio Pico Elementary agree. The school is just blocks away from downtown Santa Ana, an area that reminds some of a little Mexican city. The school's demographics also reflect downtown's cultural veneer: 86 percent of Pio Pico Elementary School students have "limited English proficiency," and 99 percent are Latino. What's more, 97 percent of the seven hundred students receive free or subsidized lunches.

Carolina, a mother of four with two at Pio Pico, stumbles in to visit the THINK site one morning, and it seems she's not really listening and her eyes are slowly closing. Then she explains why. She has not slept the night before. She works six days a week, twelve hours a day, for $8.50 an hour, barely above minimum wage. Working alongside her husband, she inspects packages of freeze-dried bricks of noodles in a giant factory. An aunt watches the children when the couple's shifts overlap. Carolina has been in the United States eleven years and has worked with English-speaking seniors as a caregiver, but she never learned enough English to feel confident to help her children with their schoolwork. After all, she barely finished nine years of schooling in back in Mexico City.

"When my older child was in kindergarten, I asked, I begged the principal to allow THINK Together to provide afterschool help for kindergarten students. She did not want to because she was afraid they could not participate in a program that is three hours long," Carolina said. "I tried to explain to her how important this was, and by the time my second child was in kindergarten, THINK offered the program to kindergarteners. This was very, very helpful because, it's embarrassing to say, but I could not help the children with their homework even in kindergarten. The work didn't look that hard, but I really could not understand the directions."

When a flier came home one day announcing an all-day summer program, Carolina's children were ecstatic, begging her, "Please let us go to school in the summer!"

Melody Gonzalez, a THINK Together family and community coordinator, has met many parents like Carolina at Monte Vista Elementary. At Monte Vista, 97 percent of the students are Latino, 94 percent qualify for subsidized lunches, and 78 percent are English learners. Melody's routine includes a Zumba class that promotes adult fitness, a nutritional snack, and then a morning circle, where parents can talk about their problems and where they listen to speakers on subjects including parenting strategies, discipline strategies, and accessing community resources. There are also opportunities for parents to receive one-on-one counseling. Even though she can't solve all the problems the parents face, Melody keeps focused on stabilizing the lives of the students so they can achieve their best. She realizes, for example, it would be nearly impossible to tackle the city's housing problems.

"What we want to create is a welcoming environment where parents can get the help that they need. Our goal is to strengthen families," explained Melody, a University of Notre Dame graduate with years of contact with vulnerable families in other communities.

The most common problems she hears among these families are struggles to pay the rent or afford school uniforms, or with disciplinary issues at school and in crowded homes. Exacerbating tensions in the community is the rivalry between nearby gangs.

"The school lies on the border of gang territories, and even elementary school children, who may know gang members and drug dealers who are relatives and friends, know that violence persists on the streets," Melody explained. "We see these kids struggle sometimes in school because they can't focus on learning. They have other things on their mind. It might be violence they witness on the streets or problems at home, and this has an effect on them."

During the parent sessions, they work on strategies to improve communication with their children and learn to express love to them.

"Before, I was doing things that were done in my house where I was raised in Mexico. It was a very aggressive environment. There was yelling and even hitting when there were frustrating times," said Hilda Ambrosio, a forty-year-old mother of three children aged fifteen, eight, and six. "I have learned how to cope better because of this program. If my kids throw a fit, I take my time to respond. I calm myself. I try to think of a resolution."

Hilda was one of hundreds of parents who joined Melody for an explanation of new Common Core Standards, which are being adapted by school districts around the state in accordance with a 2010 state law. Common Core State Standards identify the elements expected in classrooms: high-level, text-based discussions; focus on process, not just content; assignments with authentic purpose; making persuasive arguments instead of just talk. Students should learn critical thinking, problem-solving, communication, and collaboration skills.

To drive home Common Core, Melody and a few moms invited the Monte Vista parents to a gathering. They served tamales and *champurrado*, a thick, chocolate Mexican drink made with hominy flour, unrefined Mexican sugar, milk, and cinnamon. After eating, it was time for business.

Melody engaged the group in an exercise involving Bloom's Taxonomy of Questions, which range from lower to higher levels of cognitive thinking. She knows that parents are told to ask their children about what they read, but often they don't know that there are different types of questions that encourage critical thinking. To introduce the six levels, Melody organized an activity to let the parents practice developing questions according to each level. This way, they could know it in their heads, feel it in their hearts, and do it with their hands. She chose children's stories, "The Three Little Pigs,"(*Los Tres Cerditos*) and "Little Red Riding Hood" (*Caperucita Roja*) to talk about how parents could ask their children questions that would help them better analyze reading materials to, as Bloom said, "climb to higher thought."

Parents and children in the fourth and fifth grades also can participate in a six-week creative writing and book-making workshop run by Melody's husband, Hector Luis Rivera. The workshop was funded by a grant from the California Endowment to THINK Together. The adults and children write poems and create books in the *cartonera* form, a Latin American genre that encourages active community participation in the making of a book. The product is dozens of poems bound in thick cardboard, each hand-decorated.

On Page 9, student Heyra Careaga writes, "I am awesome like the Earth and like big mama, I am a joker. I am friendly with my BFFs, and lucky like a leprechaun. I am active like a monkey and strong like the Earth."

A poem from the heart of parent Maria Careaga is on Page 10: "I see the sun set and I feel the cold air that tastes like a sweet cookie and I hear bells ring and I see happiness."

Hilda culls a simple idea from the activities: She tracks her children's school assignments, has them read aloud, and asks them more questions about what they read. Hilda is one of fourteen children born into a family that grew peanuts, tomatos and corn in the Mexican countryside. She only made it through eight years of schooling when a godmother who had paid for the associated costs of "free" public education in Mexico told her that she could not afford to send her anymore. At twelve years old, she began working in the fields, rain or shine and whether she felt well or not.

Hilda knows she could have accomplished more in her life if she'd only had more education. When her own children faced problems in school, she was eager to find solutions. With the help of THINK programs, she learned that she could help as well, even though she speaks no English. For example, her son's reading skills were faltering, so she took him to the library and had him read Spanish books out loud, just to practice pronouncing words he could see on a page. At THINK Together, she participated in numerous training sessions that led to certificates. She framed every single one.

"These efforts help her children. The children see the recognition she gets. They see the certificates she receives, and it motivates them to success. Through this engagement, Hilda is setting an example," Melody noted.

Melody quickly saw Hilda's deep-seated desire to help her children. At the same time, an anti-gang initiative was forming in which schools would have parents greet families each morning. Melody was tapped to organize the effort and decided to ask Hilda to be president of the greeters. At first, parents eagerly signed up to become greeters, but slowly, interest waned. Hilda decided to step up her efforts to replenish the pool of volunteers, initiating a holiday boutique at the school to raise money for the project.

"It's worked wonderfully, and it is creating a warmer environment in the school," Melody said of the greeters. Even though Hilda has excelled in her new role, she was initially reticent. The day Melody picked her in front of all the other parents seated in the room, Hilda had to ask if she really had the ability to take it on.

"Do you think I can do it?" Hilda asked. "I don't know if I have the preparation."

"I think you can," Melody told her. "Actually, I know you can."

The applause was deafening at the Orange County Great Park one sunny afternoon in August 2012. Members of the Pacific Symphony, donning white tuxedo jackets, black pants, and bow ties bowed graciously. Alongside them was a group of unlikely musicians they had trained, more than 150 fourth- and fifth-graders who participated in "Summer Strings," a partnership with THINK Together and the Santa Ana Unified School District. Most, if not all, of the budding musicians, qualified for free lunches and hailed from homes where parents can't speak English.

"It was really special because students got the opportunity to be exposed to the violin," said Elizabeth Alvarez, a THINK Together site coordinator. "Some of them have never played any instrument, so it's really exciting for them."

Wearing stylish red T-shirts donated by the Symphony, the children moved their bows across their borrowed instruments in unison. Their smiles nearly eclipsed the solemn sound of their strings as they played "Twinkle Twinkle Little Star" to an appreciative audience.

"Today, what I am most looking forward to is just the success and pride that the kids are going to feel for having accomplished something, and that success and pride, we hope, will spill into other parts of instruction, their learning, life," declared Herman Mendez, assistant superintendent of elementary education for Santa Ana Unified.

This symphony of collaboration is a perfect metaphor for the possibilities we can create for children when partners come together with a common vision as opposed to working in silos and protecting their own turf. It has a lot to do with leadership and will.

––––––––––––

Approximately 40 students at Santa Ana Valley High School stood side-by-side in a "gratitude circle," each sharing one thing that they were thankful for. This exercise is a component of the "just keep livin" program founded by Oscar-winning actor Matthew McConaughey and his wife, Brazilian model and designer Camila Alves. Students in the circle were thankful for friends, for learning more about healthy eating, for getting into a regular exercise routine, for connecting with a mentor, for learning how to serve others, and for getting regular academic support.

Several of the students were thankful for Gloria Alday, the THINK Together site coordinator at Valley. Like the students she is charged with, Gloria grew up in Santa Ana in much the same circumstances. Gloria excelled in school and went off to Yale, where her world view was greatly expanded. Gloria was one of just a handful of Santa Ana students to graduate from an Ivy League college during the period from 1990 to 2010. Her passion was to return to Santa Ana and be part of a support system that would enable students like her to reach their full potential. She found a home at THINK Together, where she now oversees programs at six Santa Ana high schools.

Matthew and Camila launched the just keep livin foundation to help high school students learn to lead active lives and make healthy choices so that they could become great men and women. As their program developed, it came to include a wellness component that helped students connect mind and body, including speakers and the gratitude circle; a nutrition component, where students learn to make healthy eating choices, track what they eat, shop cost-effectively, and prepare healthy meals; a fitness component, where students get a cardio workout, set goals, track their progress, and measure results; and a service component, where students give back to their community through participation in service events and raising awareness around social issues.

Matthew and Camila became connected to THINK Together through Shannon Rotenberg and Brigitte Bren. Shannon is just keep livin's executive director, and when she met Brigitte, she was helping to grow its programs. Brigitte told her about THINK Together and suggested that the two organizations team up to help just keep livin reach more kids while at the same time enriching the experience students were having in THINK's high school programs.

Matthew confirmed that this approach is working. "Camila and I, through the work of our just keep living foundation, are dedicated to the work of helping young people live healthier, more self-reliant lives. We have a great partnership with THINK Together that enables us to reach more kids than we could on our own. We applaud the efforts of Randy and his team and challenge all of you to get involved and give back with the children and youth in your communities."

These kinds of partnerships help promising ideas go to scale and have greater impact. THINK Together has become a platform to help scale other organizations' programs. At the same time, THINK Together is exploring conversations with other organizations to leverage their platforms to extend THINK's reach. These kinds of strategic collaborations are great models for how people can work together to both deepen and scale the impact of their work.

6

Building a High-Performing Organization

Each July, national and world leaders, along with policymakers and the business and cultural elite gather in Colorado for the Aspen Ideas Festival. This annual conclave is hosted by the Aspen Institute, a highly regarded think tank led by former *Time Magazine* publisher Walter Isaacson. In 2011, the headliner was New York Times columnist and author Thomas L. Friedman. Under the great tent that serves as the grand hall on the campus of the Bauhaus-style hotel and conference center high in the Rocky Mountains, Isaacson interviewed Friedman about his book *That Used to Be Us—How America Fell Behind in the World It Invented and How We Can Come Back.*

In the book, Friedman and coauthor Michael Mandelbaum examine some of the challenges that lay before America: globalization, the revolution in information technology, the nation's chronic budget deficits, its pattern of energy consumption, and the need to improve our K–12 education system. At one point during the discussion with Isaacson, Friedman turned to the audience and said, "To all you NGO and nonprofit leaders out there, unless your organization has scale commensurate with the problem you are trying to address, you don't have a solution, you have a hobby."

Randy had been involved with some of the Aspen Institute's education reform gatherings but had never attended the Ideas Festival. He was, however, able to watch the video feed of Isaacson's conversation with Friedman a couple of days later at home in Santa Ana. Randy's heart raced as he heard Friedman articulate what he had come to believe about the need for scale to address the issue to which he had dedicated his life: closing the achievement gap in America between poor and middle-class students, and the global achievement gap between middle-class American students and their peers around the world.

Thomas Friedman's point was that policymakers and government officials had to be at the table. Private efforts alone could not reach the scale necessary for the kind of societal change needed to keep America on top in a world where two billion new competitors were suddenly unleashed at the end of the Cold War. He made the case why public-private partnerships were the solution to many of our great challenges. America needs to tap into the creativity, ingenuity, and drive that come from the private sector's social entrepreneurs and marry that with the resources of the public sector to address these challenges on a national level.

According to a 2003 study by the Bridgespan Group, since 1970 more than 200,000 nonprofits have opened in the US, but only 144 of them reached fifty million in annual revenue. In other words, less than one-half of 1 percent grew to what was defined as "scale." The study was subsequently updated to include the years 2003-2008, and the number of nonprofits hitting the fifty million mark grew to 201. A few years later THINK Together joined this elite group and accomplished it in a less than a decade, with 97 percent of that rapid growth occurring between 2007 and 2012. But Randy questioned such a limited definition of scale. For him, Walmart had scale, UPS had scale, Amazon had scale, Apple had scale, Google had scale.

K-12 public education in America is a $550 billion a year industry. In fact, it's the second largest industry in the United States after healthcare. In an arena that large, the College Board (the ubiquitous provider of SAT tests and AP class curriculum) with more than $700 million per year in revenue is a nonprofit with scale. If THINK Together is ever to realize its dream of playing a catalytic role in closing both achievement gaps, it will need, as Friedman suggested, scale commensurate with the problem it is trying to solve.

But is bigger really better? Some people in California hear the talk of scale and they think of the Los Angeles Unified School District, which with 640,000 students is the nation's second-largest. Many think LAUSD is too enormous to manage and should be broken apart—for those people, large scale too often means big, lumbering bureaucracy. But with the right leadership, culture, and structure, organizations with scale can make a real difference.

In an October 2010 *Harvard Business Review* article headlined "The Emerging Capital Market for Nonprofits," professors Robert S. Kaplan and Allen S. Grossman summed it up perfectly: "While small may be beautiful, size matters when it comes to having a substantial impact on society's pervasive problems. By leveraging economies of scale and management talent, large nonprofits can deliver services at lower cost. They can offer staff compensation and career opportunities. They have greater capacity to conduct experiments, assess innovations and share best practices across multiple locations. In an effective (philanthropic capital) system, innovative nonprofits with the best management and social change agendas would grow in scale and scope while less effective and efficient ones would diminish and eventually disappear."

Why don't more nonprofits reach scale? The truth is that most don't want to. There seems to be a bias against scale in the world of nonprofits. Somehow, if a leader's ambition is to build an organization with size commensurate with the social problem that he or she is trying to conquer, it's criticized as "too corporate" or "too aggressive." Americans prefer their nonprofit heroes to resemble Mother Teresa: humble and poor, serving the humble and poor. While Mother Teresa is widely admired, and deservedly so, there is little evidence to support that the sackcloth-and-ashes approach will solve America's greatest social challenges. To solve major challenges, you generally need money, and lots of it.

Jeffrey Bradach, cofounder and managing partner of the Bridgespan Group, wrote about what he termed "The Paradox of Success in the Nonprofit Sector" in a *Stanford Social Innovation Review* article in the spring of 2003. In it he wrote, "The failure to replicate innovative social programs is usually attributed to problems of strategy and management. Much of the time, it is simply a problem of money. The fact that dollars seldom follow success is one of the most vexing challenges nonprofit leaders face. At precisely the moment when large amounts of capital would flow to a proven idea in the for-profit sector, funders in the nonprofit sector frequently back away. There are many reasons for this—donor fatigue, a belief that equity requires spreading money around, hesitance to make big bets—but the consequence is that proven solutions to pressing problems do not spread."

Many nonprofits start in ways similar to Shalimar and THINK Together. They start with someone who sees a problem, organizes a few resources, and jumps in to try and help. Often, the founder of the organization is a "program person" who is leading the delivery of the program day to day. It is very rare that this kind of leader also has the skill set to replicate and scale their work.

Wendy Kopp started Teach for America (TFA), an education nonprofit dedicated to spreading educational opportunity, while an undergraduate at Princeton in 1989. Today, TFA has more than $250 million in revenue, which helps support over 11,000 current corps members in forty-eight high-need urban and rural communities. It is a member organization in the global network Teach For All, of which Wendy Kopp is a cofounder. Millard Fuller, a leader with business background, founded Habitat for Humanity, an organization devoted to building "simple, decent, and affordable housing for the needy" in 1976. Habitat now has annual revenues of more than $300 million. There are others, but examples are few and far between.

Founders that are program oriented are more inclined to fund direct program expenses rather than organizational capacity. Therefore, it's hard to build the infrastructure an organization needs to scale successfully. Let's examine how this played out at THINK Together.

Randy was somewhat unique as a founder because he wasn't directly involved in delivering the programs themselves. His focus was on raising the money, developing the relationships with key stakeholders, navigating the politics and, later, building the team and driving the strategy. From 1994 to 2003, Randy worked as a volunteer and later joined the staff as CEO. His background was especially suited to this role and to the way he managed it.

Right from the start Randy created an organization with a culture that was willing to take risks. He personally dove on the grenades that represented organization-killing threats at three critical junctures. The first was during the launch of the Shalimar Learning Center. Randy fought through the local politics and garnered the necessary resources to begin the program, and when at the last minute the sponsoring church shied away from the liability, he put the lease and utilities in his own name.

The second was when THINK Together ran out of money in 2003. Randy volunteered to serve for free as the part-time acting CEO. He and his wife, Mary, made grants and loans to the organization and got others to do the same, helping THINK survive that difficult time. Randy then helped design the public-private model that put the organization in position to replicate and scale.

The third was when the opportunity created by Proposition 49 arose. Randy and Mary once again loaned the organization money. Randy persuaded the board of directors and other stakeholders to personally guarantee the Comerica Bank loan that enabled THINK Together to fund the scale up required. Few nonprofits have leaders with the willingness or capacity to take the personal risk and the ability to persuade other volunteer board members to do the same. These traits were one key to THINK's success.

A second factor has been the dedication to the organization's vision and mission. All nonprofit organizations have a mission, and most have a vision statement. Sometimes those vision statements can seem a little hazy. THINK Together's looms large in the organization on a daily basis.

THINK's vision is simple and clear, "All children will receive the support they need from family, school, and community to enable them to reach their full potential and become productive adults and responsible, contributing members of the community." THINK's mission resides within that larger vision, "To provide high-quality academic support programs for students regardless of race, creed, or socioeconomic status."

So what does this mean, and how does it play out in THINK's daily work? To quote former Massachusetts Secretary of Education Paul Reville: "It is highly unlikely that we will be successful in closing the achievement gap until we build the kind of support systems for low-income children that children from upper-middle-class families benefit from."

THINK Together believes strongly that raising a child is similar to the equation: Strong family support + good schools + good community support = well developed young adult. This doesn't occur without a lot of blood, sweat, and tears, nor does it play out in every case, but THINK believes generally this equation establishes the conditions for success.

Randy reflected on his own family: "Mary and I were able to provide our two girls with a stable and loving household. They had high-quality healthcare from the beginning. We read to them, and talked to them, and they had a broad range of social, cultural, and extended family experiences."

The two girls attended a high-quality preschool and participated in ballet and gymnastics, later attending a top-notch K–8 school. In kindergarten and first grade, their learning was supplemented with a "Hooked on Phonics" reading program. Outside the classroom, they participated in Girl Scouts and soccer leagues.

Randy remembered, "Emily had voice and guitar lessons, and Katie continued to excel at soccer. They both were involved in musical theater and loved it. The girls participated in religious training, and when they hit algebra in eighth grade, they each had a private tutor."

In middle and high school, they participated in the National Charity League, where their mother, Mary, served as the local chapter president. Now 16 and 17, they both attend Orange County School of the Arts, an innovative charter high school in Santa Ana, and one of the highest performing schools in Orange County.

Naturally, the girls volunteer at THINK Together, serving as program assistants during the summer. They've also traveled fairly extensively and have been exposed to a wide variety of successful adult role models outside of school and family.

So when Randy and Mary examined their own children's equation, here is what they saw: The children had strong family support + good schools + good community support. They are hoping this will result in strong productive young adults.

In the national education discussion, there is often a debate about the relative importance of family versus teachers. School reformers say that if we are waiting for families to change and for poverty to go away, we will be waiting for a very long time. Their argument is that high-quality teaching can have the biggest impact on children. Leaders from the teachers unions say that teachers are doing the best they can with the children they are given. They say many parents are disengaged and not supportive, or don't know how to effectively support their children. THINK Together believes both are right to a point, but it really takes a village to raise well-educated, well-rounded healthy kids, no matter your socioeconomic status.

As mentioned previously, Californians have passed numerous ballot initiatives, which together with other state and federal funding streams have created an investment pool that will make a sizeable down payment on this strategy. Proposition 10 provides funding for early-childhood programs for kids up to age five, and now there's a sizeable investment in state preschool programming to augment federal Head Start services. Last year, California launched transitional kindergarten, which opened up the K–12 system to an additional 39,000 students. Because of Proposition 49 and the federal 21st Century Community Learning Center investment, California has nearly as much money for expanded learning time programs than the rest of the nation combined. In addition, there are large investments in subsidized childcare from both the state and federal governments.

Despite the increase in funding, Randy still believes that Californians are not getting the return on investment they could. Many of these programs operate in silos and are not integrated with each other or the school day in ways that would result in a coherent system. Also, program quality in many cases is marginal because organizations lack the capacity to deliver consistent results. There are simply too many small fragmented organizations delivering mediocre quality programs. For example, in the broader social service sector in Los Angeles County alone, there are 6,300 organizations delivering services to the needy. Too much money gets hung up at the administrative level, even when organizations are lean at the top. Fewer organizations could get the job done more effectively and for a lot less money.

THINK Together's vision is to take advantage of available state and federal resources and marry them with philanthropy to build an ecosystem of support around low-income schools, and do it statewide. This model is well under way districtwide in Santa Ana with promising results. Santa Ana is a perfect testing ground. It's the fourth-most densely populated place in America, with a school district about the size of Boston Public Schools. Here, THINK Together has partnered with the district and others to create an integrated educational ecosystem that works for everyone.

The third part of THINK Together's success lies in its people and its values. THINK is positively a values-driven organization. While many organizations have a set of values on a plaque in their lobby or on their website, few live them to the size and scale of THINK Together.

In a 2012 interview, Eric Chapman, principal at Harkness Elementary School in Sacramento said, "Mission just oozes from the THINK Together staff."

That's quite a statement from a relatively new school partner some five hundred miles away from THINK headquarters in Santa Ana. A strong sense of mission pervades the organization, with a set of values that define it all:

- Be accountable to our mission
- Service above self
- Treat others with dignity and respect
- Open and honest communication
- Collaborate internally and externally
- Honor our commitments
- Embrace diversity
- Be humble
- Persevere
- Learning is the work
- Enjoy the journey and have fun!

THINK Together hires leaders that exhibit these values. They are not embedded in just the leaders, but in people throughout the organization. Employee satisfaction surveys show that the number one factor in job satisfaction is how employees experience their direct supervisor. THINK Together now has more than 2,500 employees. If those employees are going to be satisfied with working at THINK Together (and surveys show they are), all of the supervisors must exhibit these values. A strong and healthy culture is a key building block for building a high-performing organization, and THINK Together has laid a strong foundation.

Randy has also built an excellent leadership team that has resulted in a deep well of talent throughout the organization. When he started working at THINK full-time, Randy began to attend regional and state meetings to better understand the field, and the talent he saw impressed him. But much of that talent resided in intermediary organizations. They provided training and technical assistance to the organizations that were doing the work. The problem Randy saw was that these organizations, including THINK Together at the time, were small and tended to have a lot of turnover of the frontline staff who are the ones doing the actual work with students. Therefore, many of the staff who went to the external trainings provided by these intermediaries were soon gone. Randy felt that organizations in the field needed to scale up so that they could afford to hire some of this intermediary level talent. In so doing, organizations could build their own internal systems, so when frontline turnover occurred, they could effectively train and support the new staff, resulting in more consistently high-quality programs.

The out-of-school-time field was suffering from one of the same maladies that school districts were suffering from. When staff members receive training, research shows that if there are not coaching and follow-up systems in place, participants retain less than 4 percent of what they learned. To address this challenge, Randy set out to build an organization that had the internal capacity to deliver reliable training and coaching, supported by data and evaluation.

In order to afford such a huge undertaking, Randy felt that THINK Together needed to scale up to at least two hundred program sites and to around thirty million in total revenue. This would enable the organization to spread the cost of the support system over enough students and program sites to be efficient. So, when the Proposition 49 funding came, THINK Together scaled up close to their target in one fell swoop. Together with some private philanthropy, this provided Randy with the resources to put a team in place that could deliver consistent quality on a much larger scale.

It worked. Since the initial scale-up in 2007, THINK has more than doubled in size again. This growth has been driven by its strong student achievement results and by its efficient financial model. THINK Together is taking over programs from smaller, weaker institutions or weak divisions of larger groups that lack the organizational capacity or culture of excellence necessary to deliver high-quality programs to students.

As Randy built the team, he wanted to keep a balance between business people and educators. When THINK was smaller, Randy ran the business side, and Dr. Becky Newman ran the program side. It worked, and Randy has remained focused on maintaining this dynamic balance. Here's what the leadership team looks like today:

On the business side, in addition to Randy, the team consists of

Mike Frobenius, chief financial officer. For ten years he served as director of finance for LA Chemical, a fast-growing high-volume/low-margin business that grew to $175 million in revenue before selling. Prior to that, Mike was a CPA with a regional accounting firm doing tax and audit work. Beccie Dawson is THINK Together's chief people officer. Beccie held senior human resources, staffing, and training roles in the software business, primarily at Sage Software, and WonderWare. Maria Reichel serves as chief of staff. Maria comes from a management consulting background, working for Mercer in Los Angeles and London before stepping off the fast track to raise her family.

Tim Shaw, chief development officer, and Steve Amick, director of policy and partnerships, have more traditional social sector backgrounds. Tim has served in a variety of leadership roles for organizations ranging from homeless services to Orange County's Great Park, but he really made his mark as CEO of the Irvine Public Schools Foundation. Steve came up through the YMCA, and then served as a regional administrator for afterschool programs for both the city of San Diego and the San Diego County Office of Education. He later founded a policy shop that served as the voice of the afterschool field in California in the early years of the Proposition 49 implementation.

The program side is led by Dr. CynDee Zandes, chief program officer, and Dr. Ken Giesick, chief educational services officer. CynDee had a thirty-nine-year career in public education, where she served as a teacher, principal, and district administrator. She was one of the intermediaries Randy met along the way, and many regard CynDee as one of the foremost experts in the US in out-of-school-time programing. Ken served as superintendent of a small school district in California's Central Valley after coming up through the public education system as a teacher and principal. CynDee oversees curriculum and staff development, while Ken oversees the field operations. Under Ken, a general manager who usually is a former school principal or district administrator leads each region of between thirty and one hundred schools.

The work in both sides of the house is driven by a strong data and research/evaluation effort led by Dr. Jenel Prenovost and Dr. Tracy Bennett. Jenel was a teacher while getting her doctorate in afterschool evaluation at UC Irvine. She subsequently oversaw the afterschool programs at Santa Ana Unified before moving to THINK Together. Tracy came up on the research side and earned her doctorate at UCI under noted afterschool researcher Dr. Deborah Vandell. Tracy's dissertation focused on the alignment between afterschool programs and regular school day. They are joined by Kara Johnson, who leads the organization's data collection and management efforts. THINK Together has over a dozen people on the data and evaluation team. Their capabilities in this area outstrip most nonprofits their size and most small and midsize school districts. This is a core competency that THINK Together uses to help drive performance.

Organization Structure

THINK Together is organized as a collaborative, matrixed organization. It has a strong set of centralized functions connected to seven regional hub offices, and there are soon to be more. The functions include the Program Office, which is responsible for curriculum development, training and staff development, e-learning, and program innovation, which currently is focused on STEM, digital learning and wellness. Human Capital is in charge of staffing, human resources, performance management, payroll and benefits, and volunteer recruiting management, which is vital to the mission. In addition to more than 2,500 paid employees, THINK Together has over 5,000 volunteers who work with the organization every year.

Other centralized functions include Finance & Administration, which is responsible for budgeting, reporting, banking, risk management, and facilities; the Development Office, which is responsible for fund development and marketing and communications; Strategic Planning, which is responsible for establishing annual performance objectives, creating and maintaining the dashboards that measure performance, and providing project management to large-scale project implementations across the organization. Recently, data and evaluation were moved from the Program Office and put under Strategic Planning as the organization looks to broaden its services with this as a core function. Finally, the CEO, in conjunction with the board of directors, leads the strategy discussions and new business development, with strong support from the chief of staff and director of policy and partnerships who also leads the organization's efforts as it relates to state and federal policy. These central office functions are currently staffed by sixty people and cost about 10 percent of the organization's sixty million in revenue. It's worth every penny.

The central office functions work in collaboration to support regional hub offices, which in turn support the field operations. In each region, Randy has sought to replicate the balance between the business side of the organization and the program delivery side. The regions are led by an executive director who is responsible for external relations and fund development, along with a general manager who is responsible for program quality, maintaining a strong and consistent culture, and maintaining relationships with the local school districts. These general manager positions are staffed by veteran school district administrators who understand deeply what the schools want and need. Each region supports between fifty and one hundred school sites, across as many as thirteen school districts. The hub staff includes hiring, human resources, a substitute coordinator, data management, and a quality assurance coach for every 10 schools. These coaches are a key link between the training and curriculum support and program implementation in the field. What's more, each program location is staffed with a full-time site coordinator who is integrated with the teaching and administrative staff at the school they serve, and is staffed on a 20:1 student-to-staff ratio.

We go into this level of detail for several reasons. This organization structure was developed intentionally to counteract the program quality issues afterschool programs in the field have encountered. In California, afterschool money flows from Sacramento to the school districts (or in some cases to cities or county offices of education) at the rate of $7.50 per student per day. To put this into context, the regular school day is funded at approximately fifty-three dollars per student per day, which is hardly enough. In fact, California funds schools at about half the level of a state like Massachusetts. And the funding picture diminishes sharply when the final bell rings. The afterschool programs have students for two-thirds of the length of the regular school day, but only have 15 percent of the funding. The challenge becomes, how to drive quality through a $7.50 per day framework? From a business perspective, Randy sees this as a high-volume, low-margin business. Organizations that run on high volume and low margin, like the FedEx or UPS, grocery stores or banks, all operate at scale.

Having a centralized support structure that can design programs and curriculum, and deliver training and coaching, helps make the frontline para-professional staff that much more effective. Organizations can't afford to pay teachers to deliver programs under this economic framework. Experience shows that even when teachers have been used to deliver program, it negatively impacts both their in-school work and afterschool work, because they lack the appropriate prep time for either one.

THINK Together has a site assessment tool that it hires, trains, and coaches against. This has resulted in very consistent program quality. It also uses a 70-30 framework in which 70 percent of the program is consistent from school to school, while 30 percent is flexible for local adaptation. This enables the schools to get access best-in-class practices from across the system while allowing enough flexibility to meet their local needs. But not every organization operates this way.

Many that have scaled have become chapter organizations, where there is a centralized national office and separately incorporated local chapters. The advantage of this model is that it helps to create stronger local buy-in, resulting in more local financial and political support. Randy studied a number of organizations that used this model and discovered that the advantages were offset by a lack of access to the efficiencies gained through economies of scale and inconsistent program quality. Randy felt that THINK Together could design an organization that felt local in each community not only by hiring locally but by creating neighborhood stakeholders through regional boards and leadership groups, while at the same time capturing the advantages of scale. Randy also felt that by building a large, high-quality delivery system, he could appeal to philanthropic funders who wanted to impact a large number of students through a single relationship.

To foster collaboration between the central office and the regions, a variety of systems have been established. These systems are anchored in what THINK Together calls its Strategic Leadership Group (SLG). The SLG is composed of the top thirty leaders throughout the organization. This group includes the top two or three people from each region along with the heads of each department in the home office. The SLG meets monthly to review performance via the organization dashboard, discuss new initiatives, and consider ways to manage growth including evolving systems and structures. Because THINK Together has fostered a culture of openness and transparency, the SLG creates a place to address problems and challenges within the organization so that local teams can be tasked with creating solutions to those problems.

Above the Strategic Leadership Group, there are two teams that run the organization at a senior level:

1. The Operating Committee oversees the internal functions of the organization and consists of the CEO, the chief program officer, the chief of field operations, the chief financial officer, the chief people officer, the chief development officer, and the director of strategic initiatives, who staffs the meeting, organizes the agendas (based on input from the team), and ensures that the team is tracking on the action items coming out of the meetings. Other leaders in the organization take part in the meeting periodically as dictated by the agenda. This meeting takes place weekly and is typically a three-hour working lunch.

2. The New Business & Fund Development Team is led by the chief development officer and includes the director of policy & partnerships, who drives business development with school

districts; the regional executive directors, who lead fund development in each THINK Together region; the rest of the fund development team; and marketing and communications. Randy, as CEO, joins this meeting monthly. The chief development officer sits on both committees and serves as the link between the two.

A fourth element of THINK Together's success has been its strategic plan. The plan has been able to keep the organization focused over a period of rapid growth, while enabling it to be open to opportunities. The plan rests on five major pillars that serve as its long-term framework: Program Quality, Measuring Results, Building the Platform, Leveraging the Platform, and Financial Sustainability.

The organization has created a dashboard that the Strategic Leadership Group and the board look at each month to gauge their performance. This is supported by deeper dives into performance data in each department, and annual engagement surveys to gauge employee satisfaction.

Ultimately all of this is held up against student data that is at the heart of THINK Together's mission. Everything the organization does is focused on delivering ever-improving program quality. Without this, Randy feels that there is no reason for the organization to exist.

THINK Together has a strong commitment to measuring results to help drive continuous improvement. As the organization grows, it is dedicated to investing in the people and systems that help support it so that it runs more efficiently and effectively.

THINK Together is always looking for more ways to provide services of value to its local partners, whether it's by delving deeper into a community through its school support ecosystem, by going wider and serving more schools in more regions, or as it looks to the future, by leveraging its unique positioning to offer school day assistance around the implementation of the Common Core State Standards, Blended Learning and Career Technical Education. Finally, like every nonprofit, THINK Together seeks to build a model that is financially sustainable over the long run so that these services can grow and continue. The real lesson of Shalimar is that one year of help or one summer of support is not where the real impact comes from. It can only come from having a reliable system in place for students and families, year in and year out.

The fifth element of THINK Together's success has been the active role of its board of directors. The organization was founded by Randy Barth and volunteers like the Irvine Company's Sat Tamaribuchi and Don Moe; St. Andrew's volunteers such as Bobbi Dauderman, Sam Anderson, and retired Western Digital President Kathy Braun-Lewis; and educators like Dr. Al Mijares. There also were volunteers who came through other churches and community partners like Glenn Howard, an attorney and CPA who has served the board as treasurer and its unofficial general counsel since the inception.

In recent years, the board has begun to evolve and has attracted business leaders who have scaled organizations and leaders with deep ties to the new communities that THINK Together is serving. These leaders include people like Eric Boden, retired chairman and CEO of HireRight; Doug Antone, retired CEO of Networks in Motion; Steve Bilt, CEO of Smile Bright; Fran Inman, senior vice president of Majestic Realty; Leona Aronoff-Sadacca, retired chair and CEO of Gate City Beverage; and entertainment lawyer, child advocate, and forward-thinker Brigitte Bren.

The strength of the board has been its willingness and ability to be entrepreneurial and opportunistic while remaining focused on results. The big difference from most boards has been its willingness to underwrite risk. This has enabled the organization to scale and to serve more students with more services and multiply the organization's impact manyfold.

There is no question that THINK Together has benefitted from a stellar board. But the scale of the problem is so large that even more is required. Compared to organizations like the Harlem Children's Zone (HCZ), Teach for America, or City Year, with similar operating budgets as THINK Together, it becomes apparent that

THINK still needs to attract more A-list board leadership to have future large-scale impact.

One of THINK Together's current challenges is to build on the strength of its board of directors and expand it into one that can effectively help the organization reach its full potential to impact education on a scale, as Thomas Friedman challenged, commensurate with the problem it is working on.

The three Shalimar moms who organized to take the neighborhood back from the gang. Eva Marin (front left), Paty Madueño (front right), and Maria Alvarez (top right). Photo Credit: Orange County Register.

Randy Barth as a Vice President with Smith Barney in 1994 in his penthouse office in Newport Beach. Pictured in front of the window that provided Paty Madueño a view into the world beyond Shalimar. Photo credit: Orange County Register.

Retired executive Sam Anderson tutoring a Shalimar teen. Sam was a tutor and life-changing mentor to scores of teens including Javier Diaz and Nadia Flores.

A corporate volunteer from money management giant PIMCO reads to a student in Santa Ana, making connections that enrich both of their lives.

THINK Together students engaged in learning after the school bell rings.

THINK Together kids enjoying themselves before a musical performance.

THINK Together student on a summer learning field trip to the Exploratorium in San Francisco. These kinds of opportunities help to expand the horizons of kids trapped in poor neighborhoods and create hope for a better future.

Dr. Phillip Perez, the superintendent of the Little Lake City School District, one of California's highest performing low-income school districts. He is pictured here interacting with students.

Grade level teachers and the principal at Lakeview Elementary in the Little Lake City School District during a data reflection session that helps them target their teaching and support system to provide kids what they need in a more strategic manner.

Donald and Brigitte Bren attend the THINK Together gala in 2008, announcing their landmark $8.5 million donation to provide matching funds to build an expanded learning platform for 10,000 students in Santa Ana.

Jane Russo, the pragmatic superintendent that led a turnaround in Santa Ana Unified after a stormy period that was partially the result of the massive wave of immigration that crashed into Southern California in the 1990s and early-to-mid 2000s.

Harlem Children's Zone CEO Geoffrey Canada and actor Matthew McCo-
naughey share a laugh at a press conference announcing JK Livin's part-
nership with THINK Together. Photo credit: Orange County Register.

Robin Avelar La Salle, the girl from a tough LA neighborhood who went
on to earn a PhD at Stanford. She later became the cofounder and CEO
of the Principal's Exchange and developed the Response to Intervention
for Systems methodology that is driving high performance in low-income
schools.

Randy Barth and THINK Together staffer Mia Castillo attend THINK alum Paolo Leon's graduation from the USC School of Architecture.

THINK Together alumna Nadia Flores with her preschool charges when she led the organization's early childhood efforts.

Randy Barth speaking to more than five hundred supporters at the THINK Together gala in 2012.

7

The Education
Gauntlet

In the past few years, the debate about how to improve education in America has become a false polarization between one side that says we need more money to solve our educational challenges and another that says we need more choice, competition, and accountability. It often resides within the framework of a larger conversation about the role of the federal government in public education versus local control. While these debates and their derivatives drone on, other countries are kicking our collective butts. In the meantime, our students don't achieve their full potential, and their shortfall reduces our economic growth. And on a personal level, it's a tragedy for both the students and their families. But there is some good news. There are enough examples of high-performing schools and school districts across the socioeconomic spectrum that we now know what works, and there's data to prove it. The conversation we need to be having today is how do we replicate at scale what we continue to see work?

Public education *is* a complex topic. Because it's public, and therefore governed under a combination of federal and state law and a local school board, public education is also very political. Because of that, leaders (elected, appointed, philanthropists, or educational) who want to create a major impact on their watch, seem to be in a perpetual search for the silver bullet that will cut through the complexity and effect the biggest change in the shortest amount of time.

What we have learned in the thirty years since President Ronald Reagan's National Commission on Excellence in Education published "A Nation at Risk," which warned that American public education was "a rising tide of mediocrity" that threatened the viability of our nation, is this: There are no silver bullets.

Jal Mehta, an associate professor at the Harvard Graduate School of Education, in a *New York Times* op-ed piece, put it this way: "The alarm it ("A Nation at Risk") sounded about declining competitiveness touched off a tidal wave of reforms: state standards, charter schools, alternative teacher-certification programs, more money, more data-based accountability, and, since 2001, two big federal programs, No Child Left Behind and Race to the Top."

Mehta continued, "But while there have been pockets of improvement, particularly among children in elementary school, America's overall performance in K–12 education remains stubbornly mediocre. In 2009, the Program for International Student Assessment (PISA), which compares student performance across advanced industrialized countries, ranked American fifteen-year-olds fourteenth in reading, seventeenth in science, and twenty-fifth in math—trailing their counterparts in Belgium, Estonia, and Poland. One-third of entering college students need remedial education. Huge gaps by race and class persist: The average black high school senior's reading scores on the National Assessment of Educational Progress continues to be at the level of the average white eighth-grader. Seventeen-year-olds score the same in reading as they did in 1971." The subsequent 2013 PISA scores were about the same.

Education reform scholar Charles M. Payne of the University of Chicago sums it all up in six words: "So much reform, so little change."

When you disaggregate the data, a somewhat different story emerges, but it also highlights the gaps by class. As part of its series on restoring American economic competitiveness, in June 2013 the

Council on Foreign Relations published a report titled, "Remedial Education: Federal Education Policy" that pointed out two very different education stories in America: "The children of the wealthiest 10 percent or so receive some of the best education in the world, and the quality keeps getting better. For most everyone else this not the case. America's average standing has tumbled—not because everyone is falling, but because of the country's deep, still-widening gaps between socioeconomic groups."

The report goes on to point out, "The wealthy inhabit an educational realm very different from what the national averages suggest. Consider these examples. If ranked internationally as nations, low-poverty Massachusetts and Minnesota would be among the top six performers worldwide in fourth grade math and science. Among fifteen-year-olds, Asian Americans, who also tend to be more affluent, are the world's best readers, and white Americans are third only to Fins and New Zealanders." The report concludes that these gaps persist because these children are the beneficiaries of more education spending and more two-parent families. The education spending for the wealthiest 10 percent, from preschool through college, includes what parents personally spend and what the schools are able to spend because of higher property taxes or, in the case of private schools, tuition.

There is consensus regarding the core elements of the superior education the wealthiest receive: High-quality teaching and rigorous curriculum, together with engaged students and supported by strong parents and good communities. This is what works. While these elements occur most frequently in wealthy suburban schools, there are also a few examples in urban public schools like Little Lake, in the best charter schools, as well as in the best private schools, both urban and suburban. High-performing school systems should provide the environment and the platform for this set of circumstances to occur. Yet, most of the reforms seen to date don't get at this systems-level approach.

Further, creating those conditions requires navigating a complex series of challenges. In *Waiting for "Superman,"* documentary filmmaker Davis Guggenheim called it "the blob." Randy prefers "gauntlet." Many good ideas in education never survive these challenges. To introduce reforms into the education system that will be effective and scalable, we need to think about how to navigate this gauntlet. To truly transform the system, we probably need to blow up the gauntlet—though Randy's not holding his breath on that happening anytime soon. So what exactly is this great and powerful gauntlet?

The Education Gauntlet

The e
ducation gauntlet is composed of the following elements:

- Federal and state education policy and funding systems
- Colleges and universities that prepare teachers and administrators
- Local school boards
- District superintendents and administration
- Employee unions
- Schools – principals and teachers (curriculum and instruction)
- Parents and the community

Federal and State Education Policy and Funding Systems

Unlike the rest of the world, education has been primarily a state and local responsibility in America. Though the federal government has been involved in education since 1867, the Department of Education didn't exist until 1979, when it was established as a cabinet-level department under President Jimmy Carter. During this restructuring, education functions that previously resided in the departments of Defense, Justice, Housing and Urban Development, and Agriculture were consolidated, with the exception of the Department of Health and Human Services' Head Start program for preschool-age students, the Department of Agriculture's school lunch and nutrition programs, the Department of the Interior's Indian education programs, and the Department of Labor's education and training programs.

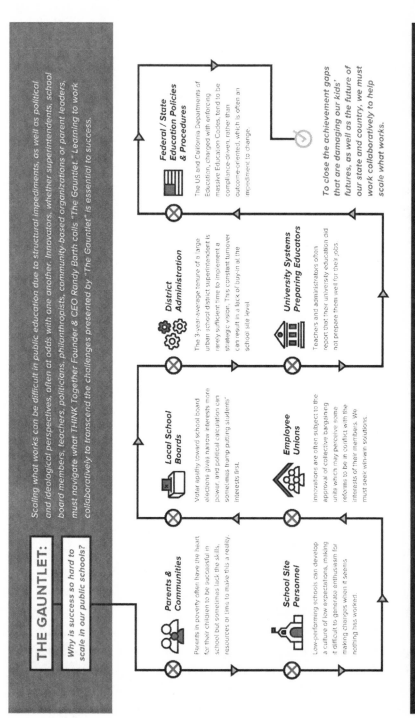

THE GAUNTLET:

Why is success so hard to scale in our public schools?

Scaling what works can be difficult in public education due to structural impediments, as well as political and ideological perspectives, often at odds with one another. Innovators, whether superintendents, school board members, teachers, politicians, philanthropists, community-based organizations or parent leaders, must navigate what THINK Together Founder & CEO Randy Barth calls "The Gauntlet." Learning to work collaboratively to transcend the challenges presented by "The Gauntlet" is essential to success.

Parents & Communities

Parents in poverty often have the heart for their children to be successful in school but sometimes lack the skills, resources or time to make this a reality.

School Site Personnel

Low-performing schools can develop a culture of low expectations, making it difficult to generate enthusiasm for making changes when it seems nothing has worked.

Local School Boards

Voter apathy toward school board elections gives narrow interests more power and political calculation can sometimes trump putting students' interests first.

Employee Unions

Innovations are often subject to the approval of collective bargaining units which may perceive some reforms to be in conflict with the interests of their members. We must seek win-win solutions.

District Administration

The 3-year-average tenure of a large urban school district superintendent is rarely sufficient time to implement a strategic vision. This constant turnover can result in a lack of buy-in at the school site level.

University Systems Preparing Educators

Teachers and administrators often report that their university education did not prepare them well for their jobs.

Federal / State Education Policies & Procedures

The US and California Departments of Education, charged with enforcing massive Education Codes, tend to be compliance-driven, rather than outcome-oriented, which is often an impediment to change.

To close the achievement gaps that are damaging our kids' futures, as well as the future of our state and country, we must work collaboratively to help scale what works.

THINK Together

www.thinktogether.org

But the federal restructuring was not without its opponents. Many conservatives saw the newly formed Department of Education as unconstitutional, arguing that it was an illegal federal intrusion into local affairs. Though the constitution does not specifically mention education, supporters argued that the establishment was allowed under the Commerce Clause, and that funding was covered by the Taxing and Spending Clause. Pragmatically, the federal government was already involved in education, so the consolidation seemed to make sense for most.

States and local communities, as well as public and private organizations, establish schools, develop curricula, and determine requirements for enrollment and graduation. The structure of education finance in America reflects this predominant state and local role. Of an estimated $1.15 trillion being spent nationwide on education from pre-K through college for school year 2011–2012, a substantial majority will come from state, local, and private sources. This is especially true at the elementary and secondary level, where about 87.7 percent of the funds will come from non-federal sources. This means the federal contribution to elementary and secondary education is about 10.8 percent; this includes all of the programs both inside and outside of the Department of Education.

The federal role in education is to promote student achievement and preparation for global competitiveness by fostering educational excellence and ensuring equal access. After World War II, access came in the form of the GI Bill, which made college possible for returning troops and gave the US a massive human capital advantage over our economic competitors for nearly fifty years, an advantage that we have now squandered.

In the 1960s and '70s, access played out differently, with a focus born out of civil-rights and anti-poverty legislation. The three big anchors of federal equal access funding are Title I, which provides aid to poor urban and rural schools to try to level the playing field, IDEA funding—Individuals with Disabilities Education Act (aka special education), and Pell grants for low-income college students.

One of the canards in the education discussion is that over the past fifty years, we've seen a massive increase in education spending with precious few results to show for it. This is a true statement on the surface, but when you dig a little deeper and think about future policy implications, the story becomes more complex. First, fully one-third of the increase in education funding is in the area of special education. And though the US mandates this spending, the federal government has never fully funded it, creating a massive funding burden at the state and local level. If we are honest with ourselves, this is not the type of investment that is going produce results that will enable our country to compete globally. Morally, it is absolutely the right thing for the richest nation on Earth to do. But when you analyze the return on investment from our educational spending through the lens of international test scores, this investment needs to be discounted.

Another thing that needs to be considered is the baseline for teacher pay. Before the glass ceiling started to crack, professional women in the workforce were primarily teachers and nurses. Other avenues simply weren't open to them. In the late 1960s, things started to change. Now, the best and brightest female college graduates are in business, finance, the law, medicine (as doctors, not just nurses), engineering, as well as education. The previous lack of mobility artificially depressed wages. As a result, teachers were exploited, which spawned the launch of teachers unions in the 1960s and '70s. Al Shanker, whom most regard as the founder of the teachers union movement, famously pointed out that in the late 1950s parking attendants in New York City were paid more than teachers. The simultaneous shattering of the glass ceiling and raising of wages both increased the cost of teachers (and other employees in the education system) while diluting the quality as many women fled to greener pastures (approximately 76 percent of the K–12 workforce is female). Again, when the growth in education spending is analyzed, we need to recognize that the starting point that is often used is an artificially constrained base.

The third major area of growth in education spending is around supports for low-income students. While different states and local communities have different ways they fund public schools, the primary base for funding is local property taxes. Affluent communities have higher property valuations and, therefore, higher tax bases, thus, their schools tend to be more richly funded. Federal Title I funds are designed to help offset this disadvantage for poorer communities. This is an area that does need improvement—we have not seen the return on investment that we need to.

There is the added challenge in California, where if 10 to 40 percent of the students in your district come from low-income families, the district does not qualify for much in the way of additional resources to support these students. Adequate resources only kick in when the percentage exceeds 50 percent. If there were a system at both the federal and state level where the extra support followed the individual student, the system would be far more equitable.

The other big areas of growth in education spending are Pell grants for low-income college students and the growth that comes with the increase in the student population served.

Standards

Conservatives in Washington, DC, believe that the federal government cannot and should not try to serve as the national school board. It's not flexible enough or nimble enough. On that point there is broad agreement. We can spend time trying to decipher what the framers of the constitution intended, and probably never agree. The constitution, timeless as it may appear, was written almost 250 years ago during an agrarian era, when trade and travel were not only arduous and slow, but education was limited primarily to rich white males.

Today, we have a twenty-first century global economy where knowledge rather than labor is valued at a premium. Most nations in the world have national standards. Conservatives see national standards as an unnecessary intrusion into a state and local issue. After all, state and local governments put up 87 percent of the money, shouldn't they set the standards?

No Child Left Behind attempted to thread the needle on this. It set targets for all schools to make "adequate yearly progress" toward the goal that all students would score at "proficient" or "advanced" on standardized tests by 2014. This has turned out to be a lofty but unattainable target with serious consequences. Falling short meant that schools and school districts would suffer a series of sanctions.

No Child Left Behind left it up to the states to determine the standards. Many states reacted—pragmatically or cynically, depending on your view—by *lowering* their standards. This may have been an effective way to game the sanctions, but it did nothing for the students, and it misled their parents. When these students moved on to college or into the workforce and had to compete with graduates from a higher-standards state or overseas, they often found themselves at a disadvantage. By dumbing down the standards, did we really do the right thing to prepare each student to compete in a global economy? Employers across the board are answering a resounding, "No."

In 2009, the National Governors Association hired Student Achievement, led by David Coleman, to create curriculum standards, to be known as Common Core, in literacy and mathematics instruction. The initiative's stated purpose was to "provide a consistent, clear understanding of what students are expected to learn, so teachers and parents know what they need to do to help them." Additionally, "The standards are designed to be robust and relevant to the real world, reflecting the knowledge and skills that our young people need for success in college and careers," which will place American students in a position in which they can compete in a global economy. Forty-five of the fifty states are members of the initiative, with the exception of Texas, Virginia, Alaska, Nebraska, and Minnesota, which adopted the English language arts standards but not mathematics.

States were given an incentive to adopt the Common Core Standards through competitive federal Race to the Top grants. President Obama and his secretary of Education, Arne Duncan, announced the grants on July 24, 2009. To be eligible, states had to adopt "internationally benchmarked standards and assessments that prepare students for success in college and the workplace—in other words, Common Core State Standards or a similar career- and college-readiness curriculum.

Randy believes that the Common Core State Standards are a giant step in the right direction for creating a framework for learning that will ensure that American students will be prepared to be effective citizens with the skills to compete in the 21st century global economy. He also believes that Common Core will have challenges (which we are now seeing in spades) as it attempts to run the gauntlet in the move toward implementation.

Choice

Another debate at the federal and state level is over school choice and injecting competition into the public education arena. The argument in favor is that public education is a stale or bloated government monopoly. It's unable to change and improve at the rate our society requires. At the same time, we have a university system that is not only open to competition but is the envy of the world. If we were to inject competition into public education, the argument goes, the market will solve the problem and improve the quality of education across the board while keeping costs low. In its purest form, the method to accomplish this would be to give students a voucher and let them select the school of their choice. Short of that, the strategy has been to liberalize the availability of charter schools so that parents have more options for their children. The injection of competition into the system seems like a good idea on the surface, but Randy believes it's probably not the silver bullet many supporters think it is.

Let's take a closer look. First, from a supply and demand perspective, about 10 percent of students in America attend private schools, and another 3 percent attend charter schools. Therefore, about 87 percent attend traditional public schools. So even if the floodgates were opened, the limited supply of private and charter schools is an extraordinarily long way from making a real difference.

Further, it's not at all clear if there is in fact the demand. Public education is kind of like Congress. Polls show people hate Congress but like their local representative. Polls show people are unhappy with public education generally, but most are happy with their local school.

A glaring example of this dynamic occurred several years ago in San Bernardino, California.

San Bernardino is an economically depressed city sixty miles east of Los Angeles. In 2009, twenty-nine of their schools were ranked in the bottom 10 percent when compared to schools of similar demographics and socioeconomic status. When the US Department of Education asked each state to identify the lowest-achieving 5 percent of schools and to target those schools with assistance through large School Improvement Grants, San Bernardino had eleven schools included. This was the largest per-capita percentage of schools of any district in California. Shortly after these results were made public, the *San Bernardino Sun* conducted a poll to see how local residents felt. Surprisingly, 53 percent of residents said they were happy with their schools! It is far from clear that the parents there are ready to demand change or take advantage of choice. Randy's experience across more than forty similar school districts in California suggests that the San Bernardino example is more the norm, rather than the exception.

Arne Duncan echoed this during an interview with education-reform advocate Laurene Powell Jobs at the 2013 Aspen Institute-New Schools Venture Fund Summit in Silicon Valley: "I wish we had a lot more parents demanding a world-class education for our kids. You watch the presidential debates, education was not a big issue. ... When you poll the American public, everyone says that their school is OK, but the rest of the country's schools aren't. That is physically impossible."

Early in the George W. Bush presidency, No Child Left Behind was debated and ultimately passed. Voucher advocates wanted very badly for choice to be a central part of that legislation. That wasn't going to fly. As a compromise, a portion of Title I was carved out for what was called Supplemental Educational Services, or SES. The idea was that for students trapped in failing or underperforming schools, parents could receive a voucher for their student's pro-rata portion of their Title I dollars and use it to purchase private tutoring. It seemed like a promising way to inject some parent choice into the system. Unfortunately, that promise was short-lived.

SES, by most accounts, has been a disaster. In large or midsize districts, there could be more than sixty SES providers offering services to parents. The parents, sadly, often fell prey to firms with the most attractive giveaways. In recent years, these were often refurbished computers with no connectivity and little or no software. So, for a $1,500 voucher, a student might typically receive twenty hours of tutoring and a computer that would likely see more use as a doorstop than a tool to help cross the digital divide. To put this into context, a daily THINK Together Extended Learning Time program would offer more than 600 hours of program (albeit at a 20:1 ratio) funded by a $1,300 state grant and some private matching funds. In its own SES offering, THINK offered forty hours of tutoring and achieved very good results. But parents more often chose the twenty-hour alternative with the "free" giveaway.

Most of the smart players like Sylvan Learning and Michael Milken's Knowledge Universe left the SES game early on. The hyper-competition meant that providers were forced to spend too much of the voucher reimbursement on marketing and client acquisition, at the expense of actual hours spent tutoring students. The results, therefore, were very spotty. There are ways to clean up SES and make it more effective by offering limited choice, but as reauthorization of the Elementary and Secondary Education Act stalled and the Obama administration grants waivers to states from No Child Left Behind, SES is largely fading from the scene.

The SES experiment, in many ways, echoes the experience of the for-profit college sector. One of the favorite arguments of the school-choice crowd is that public schools are run by bloated bureaucracies and that not enough of the education dollar makes its way into the classroom. But if we move to a true market-based solution, organizations will need to compete for students by marketing themselves. In the school districts in which THINK Together operates, the overhead runs at about 15 percent. Contrast this with the for-profit college sector, which is subject to intense competition. Many of the for-profit colleges are public companies, so we can get a peek into their financial statements. Apollo Group, which operates the University of

Phoenix, spends about 34 percent of revenue on sales and general and administrative expense (SG&A). Corinthian Colleges spends about 36 percent on SG&A, and Universal Technical Institute spends about 42 percent. A company like Microsoft spends about 27 percent. Most private companies in highly competitive markets spend in this range. Couple this with the SES experiment in which customer acquisition costs eroded the amount of tutoring hours students received, and it is hard to see how a free market in K–12 education would deliver more dollars to the classroom for students.

At the same Aspen Institute-NSVF Summit at which Arne Duncan appeared, Randy had an exchange with Tom Friedman about competition and choice in the education system. Friedman, in a discussion with NSVF CEO Ted Mitchell, pointed out that there now are websites that let you compare the performance of any school in the world. So, if a parent from a place like Palo Alto or Irvine wanted to compare their student's school to, say, a top-performing school in Shanghai, they can now do it. If the Shanghai school was preparing its students better than the Palo Alto or Irvine school, Tom feels that the Palo Alto or Irvine parents would be down at the school board, demanding changes. This kind of transparency and potential response will create competition that can boost performance. In another portion of his presentation, though, Friedman talked about the challenges for the children of immigrant parents who don't know how to navigate our systems. Randy asked Friedman, given these two disparate parent groups, how he sees choice and competition working. Friedman admitted he hadn't thought about it in that light. Using the San Bernardino example, parents are very unlikely to drive change in the places that need it the most.

Randy has another concern about letting the market alone solve the problems inherent in public education. If you drive around the ghettos and barrios that contain some of our lowest performing schools, here is what you are likely to see: Check-cashing businesses that charge an arm and a leg to cash a weekly paycheck—not banks. Convenience stores with unhealthy prepackaged food—not supermarkets. A paucity of hospitals and healthcare options. These are the neighborhoods occupied by the losers in the market-based system of competition. There is very little evidence that these same neighborhoods will turn around and attract winners if we move to a similar system of public education. Market-based solutions look very different from ivory towers rooted in upscale settings than they do on the hardscrabble streets in underserved communities.

.300 Hitters

School-reform advocates point to the relative handful of charter schools that outperform public schools to show things can be different. And certainly education can and must be better. But many of these models are much like .300 hitters in baseball; they are fairly rare. These schools are usually composed of the most motivated teachers, parents, and students in tough urban areas. They set very high standards, they often exclude special-needs students (especially the extremely needy who wind up in traditional public schools), and the top 20 percent get great results.

These dynamics and results don't only occur in the top charter schools. Santa Ana has a handful of "fundamental" elementary schools, three fundamental middle schools, and two fundamental high schools. There is a lottery to get into these schools, which have higher standards for student behavior and parental involvement. These schools also are able to drop students who don't comply. Their results are just as impressive as the top charter schools serving similar populations. These schools are all award-winners, many of them National Blue Ribbon and California Distinguished Schools.

These pockets of excellence are like magnets that attract the most motivated parents and students. Because of this, they also attract the most motivated teachers. Randy's children attend a charter school in Santa Ana, the prestigious Orange County School for the Arts (OCSA, pronounced Oh-sha). As an arts school, students have to audition into one of thirteen conservatories in order to get selected.

The year Randy's two girls were accepted, 4,000 students applied for four hundred slots. Students come from one hundred different cities across Southern California to attend.

As Jim Blaylock, director of the Creative Writing Conservatory that Randy's daughter Emily attends, told parents, "This is heaven for a teacher. We have the most motivated and talented students here. These are not like the kids smoking pot behind the liquor store on the way to school. If you want to teach, this a great place to do it, therefore, we attract great teachers."

These are the .300 hitters. They are out there, but they are rare. So what can we learn here? First, charter schools were designed free schools to create pockets of innovation that public schools could learn from. Randy spends a lot of time with school administrators talking about how to improve education, but rarely does an administrator ask, "What can we learn from these successful school models, charter or otherwise?" The conversation usually revolves around how charters are "creaming kids," leaving the less-motivated students and parents for traditional public schools and sometimes the least-motivated teachers, too. So, even if these successful schools do have some of the most motivated kids and parents, there are things to be learned from them in terms of culture and climate, student engagement, school structure (including longer days/years), blended learning (bringing technology into traditional classroom settings in a meaningful way), parent engagement, and setting high expectations for parents.

Merit Pay

One of the other big debates in the school reform discussions is over merit pay. Teachers are generally paid in what is called a step-and-column system: They start out with a base pay, and as they add seniority, their pay automatically increases. It also moves up for graduate degrees. This system essentially treats all teachers as equals, regardless of performance.

One idea that has been experimented with is paying teachers for results, rather than for years of service and levels of education. In its crudest form, this means providing bonuses to teachers based on improved student performance, most easily measured by test scores. This is another idea that is initially appealing to a private sector guy like Randy, but again becomes problematic when looked at more closely. However, there might be more effective ways to apply the idea, which do have some, for lack of a better word, merit.

First, let's take a look at teacher pay levels. Using Santa Ana again as an example, beginning teachers start out at $48,660 for a 183-day contract. On top of that, they receive stipends for holding their credential and also for going to certain meetings. If they coach sports, tutor after school, or work in the summer, they receive extra duty pay. Their straight base pay plus the stipend equates to about $273 per day. This is in line with starting engineers (the highest-paid college grads out of the gate), who average around $66,000 for a 240-day work year, which equates to $275 per day. Add to the teacher's pay the much richer health and pension benefits that public sector employees enjoy when compared against the private sector, and you get the picture that starting pay is not a big problem in attracting talent.

The major difference is pay stays pretty flat unless you add additional education units. A year-10 teacher with a master's degree is at $74,308 plus stipends and extra duty pay, plus the richer public benefits for a 183-day contract. This salary equates to close to $100,000 for a 240-day private sector worker. At the top end of the range, a 26-year teacher with a master's tops out at $94,284 plus benefits, for a $125,618 240-day equivalent. With the stipends and extra-duty pay available, the time to do the extra work given the 6.5-hour day (not including grading papers and prep), and a 183-day year, fully one-third of Santa Ana teachers make over $100,000 per year in W-2 income plus benefits.

California is an expensive place to live, so teacher pay, while not at the very top, is above the national averages. One point is that published salary schedules tend to substantially understate a teacher's W-2 income. The second point is that while California is in the bottom few states in funding schools on a per-student basis, it is near the top in teacher pay. What gets squeezed in the middle are many things teachers complain about—larger class sizes, fewer books and supplies, outdated technology—and less of that bogeyman, "bloated administration," that people love to complain about but often can't actually pin down.

Now that we've established a salary baseline, let's talk about merit pay. Schools basically have flat revenue. Unlike a business, if you outperform your competition, you don't drive revenue growth. On the chance that you do, by drawing in students from neighboring districts perhaps, you don't increase revenue per student, so there is little in the way of margin growth. So if a school district is essentially a zero sum game in terms of revenue growth, then bonuses based on improved test scores pit teachers against one another in competition. If you come from a sales-driven environment in a mature industry you might say, "Welcome to my world." However, what we see in high-performing schools is actually collaboration and sharing best practices (again, remember Little Lake). So, in this case, the incentives actually undermine those best practices.

In a similar vein, Daniel Pink's work articulated in the book *Drive*, makes a strong case that the carrot-and-stick approach that worked well in the twentieth century is precisely the wrong way to motivate people for today's challenges. *Drive* makes a persuasive case that the carrot-and-stick approach works well for manual tasks, but for cognitive work it actually backfires. His work is grounded in studies by some of the leading economic researchers from MIT, Carnegie-Mellon, and the University of Chicago that were funded by the Federal Reserve. That is not to say pay is not important. A certain level of pay needs to be in place so that it becomes a nonissue. What works, Pink says, is giving people a challenge, providing them an opportunity for mastery, and connecting their work to a larger purpose.

THINK Together is an interesting example. Starting pay for full-time site coordinators is $33,400 for a 12-month (240-day) position. On a daily rate basis, it is half of what a starting teacher in Santa Ana makes. Yet, THINK attracts great people, often some of the best and brightest young college graduates from the communities it serves. THINK site coordinators hail from Stanford, Yale, UC Berkeley, USC, UCLA, UC Irvine, Notre Dame, and other top schools. They have a great challenge, and THINK Together has done a good job of connecting them to their higher purpose—closing the achievement gap. They are often serving children just like themselves, so they are role models for these kids and very motivated to make a difference in their community.

The opportunity for increased pay at THINK Together comes from taking on larger program sites or moving up in the organization. One model that THINK Together has used that might be transferable to the public sector is what it calls a complexity grid. Take, for example, a group of people in the same position in the organization but with different challenges. They all have roughly the same base pay, but THINK has created a point system that relates to the challenges a person might face within a position. So, a quality assurance coach might be supporting program quality at more schools than a colleague, or larger programs, or across multiple school districts, or middle school versus elementary, or may be working with a more dysfunctional school partner, or deeper poverty, etc.

In a school system setting, you might transition from step-and-column to a performance-based model linked to a complexity grid type of system. Since base pay starts fairly high but is relatively flat, it seems school districts could move to a system where people start at the same base pay. Then perhaps their base pay moves up tied to a multi-year evaluation system based on a combination of student performance and principal/administrative observation. This could be augmented by a complexity grid that could pay extra for things like math or science expertise, or teaching at the toughest schools. Mastery would surface through long-term student performance, not simply test scores on the one hand or higher levels of education on the other. Leadership would have some of the levers (incentives) they might need to get their best teachers to take the toughest assignments. By doing so, you could get to a pay system that is research-based, equitable and also pays for performance—but in ways that might be more productive than pitting teachers against each other in a zero sum game. It's also a system that may stand a chance of making it through the gauntlet, though not without some blows.

Data and Accountability

With the evolution of computing, the world has changed dramatically over the last twenty years. It has revolutionized the way we manage businesses. It is a truism that what we measure, we often improve the performance of. This is especially true if we allocate resources in such a way as to provide adequate support for the tasks we are measuring. No Child Left Behind ushered in the era of accountability for schools. Most teachers and a lot of administrators hate the side effects having to do with sanctions relating to the unrealistic target of having *all* students (including special-needs students) be "proficient" or "advanced" by 2014. They also complain, deservedly so in some cases, that adequate resources were not supplied to support the task at hand.

Teachers also complain of having to "teach to the test." In California, this was exacerbated by having standards that were very high and far too many. Educators will say that the standards were a mile wide and an inch deep. Then high-stakes tests were used to measure those standards. Many teachers raced through the material, forcing students to memorize lots of facts to regurgitate on tests, which they quickly forgot. This is not what the best teachers did or what the high-performing schools do, but it is what has proliferated in most schools over the last ten years. Common Core is a great evolutionary response to this state of affairs and mirrors what the high performers were doing all along: focusing on the most important standards and concepts, then creating mastery around them. It turns out that if you do that well, your students will do just fine on the high-stakes tests.

But for all the uproar over No Child Left Behind, it was good for poor kids. Ten years ago at low-income schools, THINK Together witnessed a lot of what viewers might have seen in *Waiting for "Superman"*: checked-out teachers showing a movie or reading the newspaper, while bored students slept or fooled around. Low expectations, low engagement, menial work. No Child Left Behind and its accountability shined a light into these schools. As a result, in most places, the schools have perked up. There is still a long way to go, as PISA scores and dropout rates indicate, but at least people are now paying attention. George W. Bush got it right when he talked about the "soft bigotry of low expectations" impacting our schools. Today, those expectations have been raised, although there is more work to do—including with parents.

Some of the other side effects have to do with cheating and gaming or managing the accountability systems. Cheating scandals have occurred on a small scale in individual schools, where some of the mom-and-pop charter outfits have been especially susceptible to this temptation, and on a large scale, including a recent case in Atlanta, where investigators found evidence that forty-four out of fifty-six schools altered students' answers on tests systematically. The scandal led to the indictments of thirty-five Atlanta Public Schools officials, including the superintendent.

More subtly, other unintended side effects occur as well. In California, the Academic Performance Index (API) system gives greater weight to moving students from category to category rather than for improvement on raw or scaled scores. Schools get more credit for moving students from "far below basic," to "below basic," and then to "basic," "proficient," and "advanced," than they do from moving up within the same band. For instance, a bubble student one point below the next band can move two points and land in the next band. This two-point move into the next band is worth more "credit" to a school than an 18-point move for a student from bottom to top within the same band.

This dynamic has encouraged schools and districts to focus their resources at the margins, on bubble kids that help drive their API scores. Now, in 2014, the target year for having all students become "proficient," there has also been a tendency to focus resources on "basic" students so that they can be moved up to that level. This has the unintended effect of leaving the "far below basic" and "below basic" students farther behind. Districts that have become particularly adept at managing the data game can often have rising API scores that help make "adequate yearly progress" under NCLB, while actually having declining student scaled scores overall. Starting from where we did in 2001 with No Child Left Behind, there was no way to design a perfect system. That is why it is so important to continue to refine these measures so that we really do improve performance for all students.

Recently, Randy attended a leadership summit in Santa Ana hosted by the Chamber of Commerce. Parker Kennedy, the longtime CEO and now executive chairman of First American Financial, a Fortune 500 company, talked about the impact computers and data have had on the firm's business. First American started as a title insurance company back in 1880, focused on Orange County. Title insurance companies, until very recently, tended to be local, county-based establishments. From the 1960s through the 1990s First American, led by Parker's father, Donald Kennedy, acquired county title operations all over the country and organized them under the First American corporate umbrella. But these companies remained separately incorporated and often ran fairly independently. What tied them together was that First American underwrote the title insurance they all sold.

With sophisticated computerized data and management systems, First American is now much more centrally managed. The customer interface is still local, and that's where relationships are fostered and sales are made. But the back office operations are more consolidated, and the company is far more effective and efficient. The local folks didn't like the transition very much, but the results for their customers were better, and the results for First American's shareholders were better, too. Fidelity National Title and Chicago Title (which subsequently merged) went through a similar transition. Had First American not made the move, their competitors would have killed them in the market.

First American's efforts to improve its proficiency around data to drive performance grew over time. In fact, it became so proficient at data analysis it developed a separate company it later spun off as Core Logic, a Fortune 500 company in its own right.

We are now in the era of "big data." The term refers to massive amounts of data measured in terabytes and petabytes that can used to enable greater insight, foster greater understanding, and drive constant improvement in everything from spotting business trends, to determining the quality of research, to preventing crime, to preventing diseases, and determining real-time road conditions. Yet the student data systems in most states range from archaic to nonexistent. This is shameful. The very aspect of our society from which knowledge flows should be at the forefront of managing and utilizing data, and yet the ability to grab data at the state level—forget the national level—is extremely limited. With the sophistication that the American private sector has in this area, there is no reason that public/private partnerships could not be created to address this fundamental building block.

One of the major problems with both the US and the state departments of education is that they are essentially compliance officers rather than drivers of outcomes and change. Arne Duncan has acknowledged this and set out to change these cultures through Race to the Top and Investing in Innovation (i3) grants. But change at this level comes grudgingly, and it comes hard. State and federal education departments are bureaucracies. Bureaucracies occur as organizations mature. Over time, they've seen lots of problems, so they create a rule for every problem that has ever occurred and a guideline for those that might occur in the future.

The California Education Code, for example, has sixty-nine parts, each with anywhere from one to twelve chapters, with each chapter having a number of subsequent articles. The type of people that go to work in places like the Department of Education are often risk-averse. They like the protections afforded to civil servants. These are the people that enforce compliance with the Ed Code. Since there is a rule or guideline for nearly everything, it is very difficult to make change. That's why these bureaucracies and local school districts too often become the "purveyors of the status quo." The system is set up to continue to do what it has previously done. And even if elected officials want to drive change, the civil servants charged with enforcing the Ed Code are often at odds with these changes. That does not mean they are necessarily acting capriciously, although that does occur sometimes when they bump up against people trying to drive change. It's human nature. Unfortunately, who they are personally and what their job entails are often at odds with changing the system in ways that support better outcomes for students. If we are going to truly transform our education systems, the Education Code needs to be slimmed down by about 90 percent, and we need to move toward an outcomes-based system.

Colleges, Universities, and Human Capital

Let's return to our discussion of competition as the way to drive improvement in public schools. Part of that argument rests on the assumption that competition works well for colleges and universities and has made American universities the envy of the world and a key competitive advantage for our economy. Even this assumption doesn't look quite as good when held up to scrutiny.

The Council on Foreign Relations' "Remedial Education" report observes:

> Educational excellence is increasingly the preserve of the rich. Everyone—black, white, rich, middle class, and poor—is testing better and enrolling more in college than the previous generation. But rich students, and particularly rich girls, are making bigger gains than everyone else. Strikingly, these achievement gaps exist when children first begin elementary school and are locked in place all the way through to college.
>
> Wealthy Americans have an advantage in the admission process for elite colleges, and despite the few who may slip in on family legacy, the advantage is largely based on academic merit. Students from families in the highest income quintile are now eight times more likely than students in the bottom quintile to enroll in a "highly selective" college, one that requires a high school transcript filled with A's in advanced

placement courses, SAT scores in the seven hundreds, and a range of enriching extracurricular activities.

Those who get in are doing better than ever. The best colleges are seeing their dropout rates fall to near-zero levels, especially for women. The education they offer is generally better than what students get at less-selective schools, too. One very revealing fact is that even for equally qualified students, academic outcomes at selective colleges are better across the board, and their graduates earn more and are more likely to progress toward an advanced degree.

The real quality crisis in American higher education—where the dropout rate is sky high and climbing—is in community colleges and lower-tier public universities. They have also absorbed most of the historic increase in college enrollment and disproportionately serve minority and low-income students. Money is a big reason for their worse performance.

At the college level, the divergence in per-pupil spending is staggering. Since the 1960s, annual per-pupil spending at the most-selective public and private colleges has increased at twice the rate of the least-selective colleges. By 2006, the funding chasm in spending per student between the most- and the least- selective colleges was six times larger than in the late 1960s.

In short, more money is being spent on wealthy students who have never been more prepared to excel in college. Meanwhile, poorer students who are less prepared—those who a generation ago would not have even enrolled in college—are getting a smaller slice of higher education spending. According to a study by the demographer John Bound and his colleagues, lack of institutional resources explains up to two-thirds of the increase in dropout rates at lower-tier colleges.

Over the last twenty years in particular, college costs have skyrocketed, growing at more than twice the rate of inflation. Competition has not done much to help control costs in this setting. And, you could argue looking at the "Remedial Education" report, it hasn't done much for quality across the board, either. Where you have cultures of excellence, with bright, hardworking students driven by successful and demanding parents, the colleges are great. Absent that, they are not so great. Sounds a lot like K–12 education but with much higher costs.

Let's take a look at the education schools within these colleges and universities. Over the last thirty years or so, education schools have been populated by the lower third of students at their respective institutions. Often, the education programs are considered the least rigorous department in the university. So, the bulk of the today's 3.2 million teachers, and the thousands of administrators running the systems that support them, come from the bottom portion of our higher education system.

A few years ago at a Wallace Foundation conference in Washington, DC, Randy asked Cincinnati Public Schools Superintendent Mary A. Ronan a question about the district's well-regarded collective impact strategy called STRIVE. "You know what my favorite part about STRIVE is?" Ronan responded. "The university is always in the media criticizing the public schools for sending them students that they have to remediate. Our quarterly STRIVE meetings give me the opportunity sit across from the university president and say, 'When you stop sending ill-prepared teachers, I'll stop sending you ill-prepared students.'" Again, there are no silver bullets, but there are a lot of aspects to the gauntlet that need to be addressed.

People point to places like Finland and South Korea with high-performing education systems. These countries tend to attract the top performers from their university systems into the teaching profession instead of the bottom third. Given the opportunities in the American economy coupled with the freedom women have here, it is not likely that we are going to attract and retain top talent overnight. Pay is an issue, but only partially. Prestige is an issue, too. But the culture of the profession is also key.

Meanwhile, the public universities are not likely to change overnight. They are bureaucracies themselves with their own tenure issues.

They need to change, and hopefully will, but the impact of those changes will be felt many years down the road. In the meantime, stronger professional development systems and leveraging technology through blended learning can help improve teaching and learning today. There are wonderful examples of where this is succeeding, including in Little Lake and East Whittier. Long Beach and Fresno unified school districts have also done some particularly compelling work for large urban districts that can serve as a model for others.

Local School Boards

If you are a citizen and a taxpayer and don't know what's going on in your local school district (whether you have children there or not), and you don't vote in the school board elections, you are part of the problem—a large part. Chances are, wherever you live, the school district is the biggest business in town. It is owned by the taxpayers—that means you—and yet, most people know little, if anything, about what's going on.

Is the school district really the biggest business in town? You probably never thought of it that way. Take the example of Santa Ana Unified. It has sixty-one schools with an average campus size of ten to twenty acres. Local real estate sells for about two million per acre. Assuming the low end of campus size, the district owns more than one billion worth of real estate. The district has 4,654 employees: 2,761 teachers, 1,715 non-teaching support staff, and 189 management personnel including principals and assistant principals. Santa Ana Unified has approximately 56,000 students and serves more meals than any restaurant chain in Orange County. It has a large IT infrastructure, and it provides transportation to thousands of students each day. Many school districts also run preschools and adult schools, and can even partner to colocate health clinics and other services. Districts employ nurses and counselors, and in Santa Ana and many other urban districts, they have their own school police force. All of this operates on a budget of around $500 million per year.

Running one of these districts is a big deal. This business produces arguably the most important product of any business in town. It is the key economic driver of your community. If you have great schools, you have higher property values. If you have great schools, you have a more educated workforce. This means your community will be more competitive when it comes to attracting and retaining good businesses, therefore producing more and better jobs and generating more tax revenues in a virtuous cycle.

So all of the citizens in your community treat the school district as your community's most precious asset, right? Not likely. Santa Ana is a city of about 350,000 people. The top vote-getter in the 2012 school board election received about 2,300 votes. It took about 1,800 votes to get a seat on the board. And that election coincided with a presidential election. About 18 percent of registered voters decide on school board races in a presidential election year in California, and the turnout is about half that in other years. In 2013, a recall election that removed two school board members in Fontana Unified, California's twelfth largest district, drew a paltry 7 percent voter turnout.

Who votes in these elections? Often, it's special interests. Who sits on these school boards? Often, it's people who represent those special interests. Is that the special interests' fault? No, it's your fault, because you didn't get informed and vote. There are good people on school boards, of course, lots of them. But when you look at their backgrounds, as a whole they are generally an unsophisticated lot. They have been entrusted by the voters of their respective communities to govern one of the largest and most important businesses in town. And many on these boards are there as a stepping stone to higher office. The progression often goes like this: school board, city council, state assembly, state senate, and then either congress or the county board of supervisors. So, while on the school board, members' primary interest is not the students but their own career. That means the goal is to deliver for the constituent group that can be most helpful in moving them up the ladder.

Netflix CEO Reed Hastings has an interesting perspective on this issue. Hastings has been involved in education since teaching math in the Peace Corps right after college. When he sold his first company, Pure Software, and made his first fortune, Hastings got deeply involved in school reform. He wound up serving a somewhat controversial stint on the California State School Board. He is also an avid supporter of charter schools, primarily as a vehicle to address governance issues. Hastings makes the case that school boards are one the biggest stumbling blocks to improving education.

Hastings shared his views on school boards at the 2011 Aspen Institute-NSVF Summit: "I have a dermatologist friend, and he likes telling stories about 'the rash.' He says most people just put cortisone cream on the rash, and some of the time, the symptoms go away. But what gets interesting is when the rash doesn't go away." Then you have to address the underlying issue.

Hastings went on to point out that really substantial progress was made more than a decade ago in urban districts such as Oakland, LA under Roy Romer, and Houston under Rod Paige, and then it all went away. "What we see is school districts oscillate up and down over a decade. It's a long enough period of time, that is, if you're not in the game for a long time, you can mistake this motion for real progress. There are fifty to one hundred large urban school districts. At any one point in time there's a half dozen that are doing really great work. The problem is, you can't find any large district that done really great work for thirty years in a row. It just oscillates."

"The problem is elected governance … an elected school board or elected mayor controlling the system." Because of that, Hastings observed, "They are doomed to a cycle of change."

People think of other things in education as "the big problem," and today it is the teachers unions. Again Hastings counters, "This doesn't make sense to me. Because the low union states like Arkansas, Mississippi, Tennessee, and Texas, they're not kicking butt. So how can the union be *the* problem?" In fact, strong union states like Massachusetts and New Jersey are top performers.

But Hastings is not blind to the problems with unions. "I'm not saying the unions are not a rash. It's scratchy as hell, and it itches. But, it's just not the fundamental issue."

Hastings believes we're looking for solutions in the wrong place.

"If you're a teacher, one in three superintendents you work for are great, and two out of three suck. And so, if you work in that system, you want a union, too. The union is a symptom, not a cause. It's a manifestation of protection because the management is not very good on average."

Why is that? "Because of the elected boards," Hastings said. "Take a great company like General Electric. They have been around 150 years, incredible innovation. What if their board of directors was elected by the general public? Would that continuity of success have occurred if the place was governed by people who wanted to but couldn't get into Congress and got elected every two years? Well, when you get elected like that, you have chaos, because there is no continuity of vision."

Hastings thinks this is why organizations such as nonprofits, churches, and the military have outperformed school districts, on average, over the last thirty years. These disparate organizations have a paradigm of self-perpetuating leadership and governance. It doesn't guarantee excellence, but it enables the possibility. Real excellence takes multiple decades and requires sustained leadership.

These ideas square perfectly with the observations of Randy and the team at THINK Together. There are some examples of school districts with strong cultures that are sustained from the board through administrative leadership. Elk Grove, the fifth-largest district in California, has had a very stable board historically and has had only five superintendents since the district was established in 1957. So it has had continuity and, by and large, good results. Little Lake has had the same leadership over the last ten years. Large urban districts like Long Beach and Garden Grove are also prime examples of sustained vision. But the list is a pretty short one for low-income communities. We might also point out that Elk Grove is not primarily low-income, so from a governance perspective, it may have more in common with more affluent communities where continuity of excellence is more common.

Administration and Leadership

Effective leadership starts with trust. One of the challenges of building a high-performing organization amid the education gauntlet is trust. A superintendent has, at best, well-meaning members of the community who typically have never run anything and often-adversarial unions as a workforce. If you run an urban school district, you operate in a socioeconomic nightmare and are charged with providing students the tools they need to escape that nightmare or to stay and help fix it. Because you operate the biggest business in town, because the schools touch so many different parts of the community, and because everyone has attended school, *everyone* has advice to give on how you could better do your job.

Teachers think you are a glorified version of them (or maybe a glorified principal), and therefore your pay ought to be just a little above theirs. Meanwhile CEOs of much smaller organizations make several-fold what you make (save for the pension). In Randy's view, there are two major differences between running a school district and running a company. The private company CEO has to drive revenue. Therefore, marketing, sales, and related activities are a large part of the job. The public school superintendent doesn't have that challenge. Theirs is actually more difficult. They must drive performance through the education gauntlet. Superintendent after superintendent has told Randy that the college and university training they received with their advanced degrees did little to prepare them for this confusing and gargantuan task. And, there are few opportunities to collaborate in meaningful ways with their peers—other superintendents—to help them learn, grow, and be more effective.

Randy thinks Reed Hastings' assessment that two out of three superintendents aren't very good is a little bit harsh. Randy's experience is that two out of three are actually pretty good. The larger problem that Randy sees is the lack of talent or preparation the next level down, in the assistant superintendent teams. A typical school district, except for the very small ones, has what is referred to as the superintendent's cabinet. These are the assistant superintendents that oversee the various aspects of the organization. For example, midsize to large districts usually have an assistant superintendent of elementary education; an assistant superintendent of secondary education; an assistant superintendent of human resources, who also negotiates the union contracts; a chief business officer; and assistant superintendents for facilities, student support services (suspensions/expulsions and special programs), and special education. It is trendy to have a cabinet-level position that is more outwardly focused on community engagement, although it's hard to find examples of that working very well. The larger districts may also have a deputy superintendent, who is more like a chief operating officer and whose function is coordination and making the trains run on time, or a chief academic officer, who might be more focused on curriculum and instruction. In smaller districts, several of these positions are combined.

Critics, including the employee unions, often point to this configuration and say it is top-heavy. However, if you look to the supposedly lean and mean private sector, any equivalent-sized company essentially has a vice president for each of these functions, or something similar. This critique often underestimates the complexity of running one of these places.

A large urban district like Santa Ana receives about 55 percent of its revenue in its general fund. This comes to the district on a reimbursement basis for average daily attendance, or ADA. The remaining 45 percent comes through a complex maze of categorical funding. There are thirty-five different categorical funds organized into five tiers. During the severe budget cuts of the 2009–2013 period, the five tiers were simplified into three tiers. The bottom tiers have more flexibility in how to spend the funds. There is heavy compliance from the state and federal government around categorical funds, which creates some bureaucracy on both ends. In the private sector, you would have marketing and sales that would drive revenue. In a typical school district, you have a one person or a team charged with reporting on how the funds are spent.

This discussion about how school districts get their revenue may seem overly detailed, but it is an important point. School districts are very risk-averse, whereas state and federal education agencies are very compliance-driven. These dynamics combined with other factors contribute to a culture of fear in school districts that is hard for outsiders to imagine. So when people talk about things like innovation and driving change through large organizations, it is very difficult to do through this maze of categorical programs, these compliance-driven cultures of fear, and the education gauntlet.

Effective July 1, 2013, California Gov. Jerry Brown made some significant adjustments to the maze through his Local Control Funding Formula. LCFF does two things: It allocates more funding to school districts with a higher percentage of low-income students and English language learners, who are more expensive to educate. And it simplifies the labyrinth of categorical funds.

You would think that this latter adjustment would be very popular with school superintendents. But in Randy's discussions, it became apparent that their satisfaction depended on the local school board. The superintendent's biggest fear was that the employee unions, facilitated by their friends on the school board, would swoop in and take advantage of this newfound flexibility and use it to increase pay at the expense of student support. Gov. Brown addressed this concern, to some degree, with modifications included in the May revise of his 2013–2014 budget. Beyond that, many superintendents worry about meddling boards. One superintendent from Central California explained, "We are from a farming community. Most of our parents, and school board members for that matter, are not highly educated. All this talk about API scores and 21st skills is meaningless to them. What they really care about is winning the football championship. Flexibility in their hands is a scary thought."

THINK Together convened a group of African American superintendents to talk about the crisis in educating African American students, particularly males. The superintendents spoke about the protection that the categorical funding system afforded them from their boards, which might not understand or see the benefit of some of the specialized support programs that are funded through the system. So they, too, saw this categorical funding as protection from their boards.

Randy has observed another dynamic that relates to the inter-relationship between the board, the superintendent, and the cabinet. Boards that are very active and reach down into the organization and try to micromanage create a very dysfunctional dynamic. Where this occurs, the superintendent and cabinet spend virtually all of their time managing the board rather than running the district.

School boards typically meet twice per month. If members are constantly requesting reports on this, that, and the other thing for the next meeting, then that is what the senior leadership spends its time on. High-performing boards, by contrast, set policies including clear expectations around staff reports so that they have adequate information to govern, hire the right superintendent, and give that superintendent the support they need to lead the system through the gauntlet. Most boards don't do that.

And most people don't know it, but superintendents shop for boards. Notoriously difficult boards have a hard time finding a good superintendent who wants to put their career on the line by having to deal with them. On rare occurrences, you find a particularly mission-driven superintendent who wants to take on the challenge or, more often, an assistant who rises through the ranks and begins to turn things around. But in general, high-performing boards attract high-performing superintendents.

Another challenge that involves both the board and superintendent is continuity. The average tenure of a large urban school superintendent in a district is about three years. Often, the first thing the new superintendent wants to do is make changes. In large organizations like these that are culturally resistant to change, it takes a few years to see the impact of those changes. Just as soon as they are beginning to be felt, hopefully in a positive way, the next superintendent comes in and charts a new course. This constant redirection adds to the cynicism and the resistance to change in the organization. If the organization, or even a portion of it, doesn't like the changes the superintendent is proposing, people tend to hunker down with the attitude that this too shall pass. And far too often it does.

The most effective superintendents start with working on the culture. Part of that is building trust, but there's a large culture of fear inside school districts that makes it difficult. This is counterintuitive from what outsiders might think. Outsiders see school districts as a government-run monopoly where everyone has job protections far beyond the private sector. They see complacency and people that can only get fired for severe abuse or neglect. But the culture of fear inside school districts is very real, and effective leaders must deal with it. That is one reason that trust is so crucial.

Dr. Steven Ladd, the superintendent in Elk Grove since 2004, emphasized the value of building a strong ethos and culture within a school district. "A strong culture can create its own gravitational pull," Ladd said. "It can help to mitigate the fluctuations of board members with different agendas. Elected officials come and go, but the system can survive the turnovers if the mission is about students. The rest of the issues we can figure out in a civil way."

This seems logical, but a focus on students and on civility can be rare commodities in school districts. It is often said that school districts are run for the benefit of adults and not the students. When Randy began this work full-time, his impression was that was absolutely the case. Rarely did he have a conversation with an administrator that involved what was good for students. The conversations were always about board politics, union politics, and money. In the last five years, as accountability for student performance has risen and become more public and a generation of leaders has emerged, this has begun to shift. Boards, unions, and money are still common topics, but student performance and preparing students for a radically different world are now common topics, too.

Here is how Ladd views his job: "The mission of the organization, in our case with 62,000 students, is to provide them with the tools they need (knowledge, employability skills, hard skills) at age-appropriate levels. Students need to learn take care of their health in the process; need to cultivate an appreciation of the arts, beauty, and environment; and be happy, contributing members of society in a global economy.

"The way we do that," Ladd continued, "is with strong teaching and learning. This leads to the development of talent, human capital, and 'a learning' culture within the organization. Professional development is very important. Over the last fifteen years, teachers and administrators have had to make the transition from the pre-standards era, to standards, and now to the Common Core State Standards. Continuing to build capacity in the teaching rank and file is one of our biggest challenges.

"How does one go about navigating this in a large organization as the world around us changes?" Ladd asked. "We do it by defining the mission, working as a team, through collaboration and with the belief that there are no shortcuts. It's not complicated, but it is complex. The challenge is building an integrated system that is producing the outcome related to how kids do once they leave your system.

"In addition, we have business responsibilities. Are we making good decisions? Are we being good stewards of taxpayer dollars? The funding perspective is very different. The budgeting process with the state is just ridiculous. When we reach our target funding level in 2021, we will be funded at the per-student level of 2007–08. On top of that, 88 percent of our budget is personnel-related. We have to build our budget, build it in public, and then negotiate 88 percent of it. But, we operate a people business and the return on investment is measured in student performance."

Finding the right leader for the right district can also revolve around work ethic. Is the culture workaholic or 9-to-5? In his district, Ladd said, "Elk Grove reduced 27 percent of their administrative positions during the economic downturn. Work continues to increase, and people are tired. When it comes to leadership and building a bench, we develop leadership capacity along with nuts-and-bolts management. When we promote from within, we have people working their way up through a variety of positions. This way they gain important product knowledge. If a person is selected from outside the district, we help them learn our culture. In either case, their success in their new position will be predicated on elements unrelated to their last job. So, we need to give them the support to be successful.

"One of the questions we ponder," Ladd continued, "is does the potential leader have the self-discipline to live in a lonely world?"

Ladd told Randy that the book *Gardens of Democracy* by Eric Liu and Nick Hanauer really resonated with him. The authors suggest that systems (schools) are often described mechanistically—with people being interchangeable parts. In the book they offer a different systems view, one as a garden. "A school system is like a garden. You've got to weed it, fertilize it. It definitely needs some sun. You can't plant incompatible species next to each other. This is very different from the manufacturing model. If you accept the garden model, your leadership and supports reflect this belief."

Should districts be managed from the top-down or up from the bottom? It's popular to say that schools should be freed from the suffocating centralized bureaucracy so that they can use their imagination and creativity to flourish. The .300 hitters do this, and this gets extrapolated into the notion that every school can, too. However, there is little evidence that the talent pool exists to make this successful at scale.

A few years ago, the Charles Stewart Mott Foundation was launching an initiative called "A New Day for Learning." It pulled together a focus group of education stakeholders for a daylong discussion. There were teachers and principals, along with people from universities, the arts, STEM, Ed Tech, and Extended Learning Time. At the start of the day, the facilitator went around the room and asked everyone what they liked and didn't like about the school day as it now exists. The teachers and principals said they were tired of teaching to the test and they wished that they could be freed from their constraints. Later in the day, freed from constraints, what emerged from their imagination and creativity looked pretty much like school looks today. It was the same with the university people.

And the same thing happened across California with the first round of School Improvement Grants. The bottom 5 percent of schools in the state were identified and were given the opportunity to receive an additional two million per school for three years. They were asked to create turnaround plans under one of four options:

1. Close the school and send the students to higher performing schools.

2. Convert to a charter school.

3. Fire the principal and at least 50 percent of the staff and give the new principal greater autonomy.

4. Replace the principal (except in specified situations), implement a rigorous staff evaluation and development system, institute comprehensive instructional reform, increase learning time and apply community-oriented school strategies, and provide greater operational flexibility and support for the school.

While Randy saw a few successful turnarounds, most of the turnaround schools simply did more of what they were already doing.

Let's think for a minute about who the teachers are. If you think in terms of a bell curve, the top 10 percent of teachers (the .300 hitters) are remarkable, passionate, mission-driven. The bottom 10 percent are the opposite, and that is the group that administrators would love to get rid of, although most superintendents tell Randy say it's actually 5 percent. The 80 percent in the middle are people who, with the proper direction and support, can do a credible job. But they are not the people that you want to put in charge of driving change. They can certainly have valuable input, but nothing in their background or skill set indicates that they are leaders of a transformation in education.

The argument against top-down management is that you have ineffective administrators at the top. Maybe the .300 hitter concept applies here, too. It certainly would if Reed Hastings is right. But if Randy is right, and two out three superintendents are pretty good and only the .300 hitters are strong enough to drive change bottom-up, then the law of averages is with top-down. And, it's not a mutually exclusive set of answers. Collaborative leaders build cross-sectional teams that enable input from all levels of the organization. So the solutions are neither top-down-driven nor bottom-up, figure-it-out-on-your-own. What often gets lost in the bottom-up approach is the ability to share best practices. The administrators have more of an opportunity to look across the district and across the education landscape to see what's working and figure out how to apply those lessons locally. Teachers and principals are too busy with the day-to-day responsibility of making it happen with students. To charge them with this additional responsibility is asking too much of professionals not adequately equipped to succeed at the task. The articulation and coherence you see in a system like Little Lake has no chance of emerging in the bottom-up choice-driven systems that seem to be coming into vogue today.

Where should superintendents come from? Districts are large, complex organizations; starting as teachers and coming up through the ranks as an administrator paired with additional university training often doesn't fully prepare someone for the job. In the 1990s, a retired military leader engineered a successful turnaround—although it later proved to be an oscillation—in Seattle that opened people's eyes to looking outside of school districts for leadership talent.

One of the people in the forefront of this type of thinking is philanthropist and entrepreneur Eli Broad. The Broad Education Foundation launched an innovative leadership development program called the Broad Academy. Originally designed to prepare crossover leaders from other fields to lead large urban districts, the academy was later expanded to include promising leaders from within the ranks of urban and suburban school systems. Critics including Diane Ravitch say this is part of the privatization of schools. But others, including Richard F. Elmore, codirector of Harvard's Doctor of Education Leadership program, contend that it fills a major gap in leadership development for school systems. There is little or no independent research on the performance of Broad-trained superintendents, but according to research from the Eli and Edythe Broad Foundation itself, 65 percent of academy graduates who have served as superintendents for at least three years are outperforming non-Broad comparison groups, based on state test scores, improvement in closing education gaps, and graduation rates.

Other education leaders such as Orange County Superintendent of Schools Dr. Al Mijares, Randy's old ally in Santa Ana, feel that the best superintendents are instructional leaders. Mijares hasn't been a big fan of the Broad approach, but says that it can work. "Even leaders that come up through the school ranks from a business or human resources background have to be on top of the instructional program. When decisions get made, superintendents must ask 'how will this impact instruction?'"

Randy thinks a good analogy can be drawn from business. If you look at Steve Jobs' phenomenal success at Apple, it was because he was a "product guy," passionate about Apple's creations. Jobs would say that Microsoft's downfall in recent years was that it was led by Steve Ballmer, a marketing guy who didn't have as much passion or insight into the product side of the business. Randy's view is that, pragmatically, there is probably not enough leadership talent emerging from the instructional side of school districts to provide first-rate leadership everywhere. Absent that, crossover leaders can be trained and should have a strong partner in leadership on the team with instructional chops. And, as Mijares suggests, as decisions get made, superintendents must ask, "How will this impact instruction?"

Schools

The next chapter will delve more deeply into how to drive performance at the student and school level, as well as at the systems level. This is the heart of the matter of teaching learning. Everything else in both the School Support Ecosystem and the School Industry

Ecosystem exist to support the teaching and learning that goes on in the classroom.

Parents and the Community

In the spring of 2013, Randy attended the National Charity League "Senior Presents" event for the local chapter. Randy's wife, Mary, was chapter president, and their daughters are quite active in the organization. The event is sort of a debutante ball, and the purpose is to present the senior class of girls and acknowledge their accomplishments in scholastics, community service, and in other activities such as athletics, the arts, or whatever their passion might be.

Most of the girls were headed off to first-rate colleges with a wide variety of experiences, successes, and a significant support system from their families and their communities. Randy was standing to the side with one of the other dads, talking about how much they admired this outstanding group of girls. Randy's friend said his daughter was finishing up her sophomore year at a private high school with a 4.5 GPA, was dancing ballet at a high level with plans to attend a summer ballet conservatory in New York, and had just returned from a mission trip to Kenya. Randy asked, to what do you attribute your daughter's, and these other girls', success? His friend replied simply, "It's the moms."

"These girls are all bright and capable and motivated. But they would never push themselves to these levels. It's the moms that drive them."

Randy pondered his friend's comments. While this was a mostly white upper-middle class group, what the man was describing was the "Tiger Mom" phenomenon. There was no question in Randy's mind that parents made a big difference.

Through his work at THINK Together, Randy had come to believe that raising children was a bit like an equation: Parents + School + Community = Strong, healthy, well-prepared young adult. This equation doesn't always pan out; there are always kids who have health problems or challenges or simply don't bring enough strength to the table. But this equation certainly establishes conditions for success.

In 2013, Richard V. Reeves and Kimberly Howard published a report for the Brookings Institute titled *The Parenting Gap*. "The United States suffers from gaps in income, education, and opportunity. The most important gap of all might be in parenting." Continuing, "We can argue about the size of the parenting effect, compared to genetics, economics, culture, schooling, and so on. There is no question, however, that the quality of parenting is one of the most – perhaps *the* most important contributor to a good, fair, responsible society."

The Parenting Gap uses something called the Social Genome Model data set which is based on the Bureau of Labor Statistics Children of the National Longitudinal Survey of Youth 1979 as their basis. The CNSLY measures parenting using the well-validated HOME-SF scale. This data set and tool are, in turn, used to identify characteristics of the strongest and weakest parents.

> Parenting quality is not randomly distributed across the population. There are strong links between parenting quality and income, race, education, and family type. Parents who have low income, are poorly educated, or are unmarried are more likely to fall into the weakest category. Almost half of the parents in the bottom income quintile fall into the category of weakest parents—and just three percent are among the strongest parents. Similarly, 45 percent of mothers with less than a high school degree are among the weakest parents and four percent of them are among the strongest parents. Forty-four percent of single mothers fall into the "weakest" category parent category, with just three percent in the strongest group. At the other end of the scale, higher levels of income, education, and family stability all strongly contribute to better parenting.

This *parenting gap* is a contributor to the *opportunity gap*. Reeves and Howard, "The relationship between parenting quality and a child's chances of doing well comes through in our analysis loud and clear. The following graph shows that children of the strongest parents succeed in each life stage at much higher rates than children of the weakest parents. By the end of adolescence, three out of four children with the strongest parents graduate high school with at least a 2.5 GPA, while avoiding being convicted of crime or becoming a teen parent. By contrast, only 30 percent of children with the weakest parents manage to meet these benchmarks.

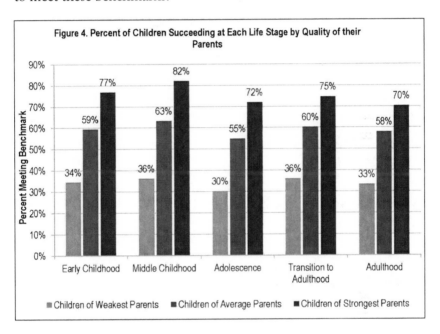

Figure 4. Percent of Children Succeeding at Each Life Stage by Quality of their Parents

Benchmarks for Success

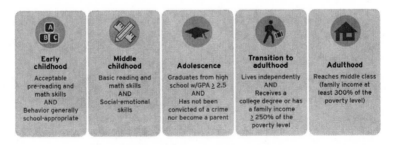

Brookings Institute study titled Parenting Gap by Richard V. Reeves and Kimberly Howard dated September 08, 2013.

Irvine vs. Santa Ana

One of the highest-performing school districts in the country is in Irvine, California. Near the other end of the spectrum is next door in Santa Ana. There are dramatic differences in income levels and parent education levels between the two. So when people say, as they often do, that Irvine has great schools and Santa Ana doesn't, is it really the schools that are different, or is it the parents? Let's take a look at the parents' education levels in the two districts:

	Irvine	Santa Ana
Graduate school	50%	2%
College graduate	68%	4%
Some college	23%	14%
High school graduate	99%	24%
Not a high school graduate	0%	57%

Source: California Department of Education

Impact on Teacher Expectations

Not long after Randy started the Shalimar Learning Center, volunteers reported that many of the elementary students were not being assigned homework. This was quite different than the homework expectations that schools had for the kids and grandkids of the Shalimar volunteers. Several of the volunteers went over to nearby Whittier Elementary to visit with the teachers, who told them they had stopped assigning homework because it never got done. The volunteers encouraged the teachers to start assigning homework again: "We're here now, and we can support it, at least for the students that come to the learning center." As a result, the teachers perked up, and so did the students.

What should a teacher do who gets caught in this situation? Remember, Southern California in the mid-1990s was awash in new immigrants. Children were coming in large waves from Mexico and Central America. The school systems weren't set up or equipped to deal with the influx. In the process, expectations were lowered in many places. The same thing occurred over time in communities across the country that had thirty, forty, fifty, even sixty years of families with deep dysfunction and generations of poverty. Communities got progressively worse as the kids who could make it out did, and the ones who didn't sunk to new lows, generation after generation. With that, teachers lowered expectations and fed into the downward spiral.

In *Waiting for "Superman,"* Green Dot charter schools founder Steve Barr posed the question, "Are the schools bad because the neighborhood is bad? Or is the neighborhood decayed because of rotten schools?" Is it an "inputs" question or an "outputs" question? Barr takes the position that the failure of the schools drives the neighborhood to lower and lower levels. However, Randy thinks it's both. If you go back to Al Mijares' description of schools as a manufacturing process, when the inputs were mostly white middle-class kids and a strong labor pool artificially supported by few work options for professional women, it yielded a certain result. When the inputs became immigrant children from cultures without a strong history of education and third or fourth generations of welfare families, and the labor pool is watered down, that yields a contrasting result.

With African American students, the dynamic has been a little different. African American kids who rose up and succeeded have now become middle class in sizable numbers. Those left behind have sunk lower and lower, with the attendant social ills of multi-generation poverty and the breakdown of the family unit. In new-immigrant neighborhoods, there is a hope and a drive that if they work hard, stay out of trouble, and get an education, their lives will be better. For the families where it doesn't work out that way for multiple generations, there is a palpable loss of hope and a disbelief that their lives can improve. These communities—whether it's the Bronx or Harlem in New York, or Detroit or Flint in Michigan, or Oakland, South Central LA, or San Bernardino in California—are some of the toughest places to work. Kids who study and want to succeed get called names like

"Oreo" (black on the outside, white on the inside) and are stigmatized for trying to succeed in the way the establishment wants them to. The American economy rewards skilled labor and knowledge with premium wages, but has few options for those without. Demonizing your brothers and sisters that are trying to succeed feeds into an extremely destructive cycle.

Randy and Dr. CynDee Zandes were working with San Bernardino's mayor and school leaders on a Promise Neighborhood project when eleven schools were tagged as failing. Randy and CynDee stayed engaged in the school turnaround process led by Deputy Superintendent Dr. Judy White. As touched on before, San Bernardino is California's Detroit. The city has suffered a decades-long erosion of job losses and economic setbacks, leading to a flight of talent and an in-migration of struggling people drawn by the cheap rent. In 2013, nearly half of its residents were on welfare, food stamps, Medicare, or all three. The city itself declared bankruptcy in August 2012. With weaker inputs into the system, the schools produced weaker and weaker outputs in the form of dropouts or poorly prepared graduates.

In a dramatic call to action, Judy White stood before her colleagues who were gathered to launch the turnaround process and declared: "For many years our schools have struggled. As they have struggled and the district has faced sanctions, we've hired consulting group after consulting group to try to help and improve our performance. Different consultants have different strategies, but they all had a common thread. The two things that every consultant has told us is that we have incredibly low expectations and no sense of urgency. Our parents have low expectations, our teachers have low expectations, our principals have low expectations, our central office leadership has low expectations, and our board has low expectations. And there is no urgency. That needs to change now!"

Fortunately, it's beginning to happen. With the leadership of the mayor, a new board majority has been elected and a terrific new superintendent, Dr. Dale Marsden, was hired. Meanwhile, Judy White became superintendent in nearby Moreno Valley. The district has launched a citywide strategic planning effort designed to build the will for change through a collective impact strategy. There are still lots of impediments and a long road ahead, but expectations are starting to change, and a plan has been put into place to drive that change forward.

8

Moneyball and the Wallpaper Effect

Author and journalist Michael Lewis wrote a best-selling book called *Moneyball: The Art of Winning an Unfair Game*. The book is about how the Oakland A's became one of the most successful franchises in Major League Baseball despite spending a small fraction each year on player salaries compared to their richest competitors like the New York Yankees. The book later became a successful movie starring Brad Pitt that garnered six Academy Award nominations and helped to accelerate the use of business analytics in industries far and wide.

Lewis' interest began with a simple question: How did one of the poorest teams in baseball, the Oakland Athletics, win so many games?

As Randy learned more about the Principal's Exchange and its work with the Little Lake school district, he saw a parallel to *Moneyball*. Like baseball, he surmised, education in America is an unfair game. And, as we've learned, there are plenty of reasons for this. The top 10 percent of the socioeconomic spectrum in America have world-class educations. The bottom third do not. And, as our PISA scores indicate, the middle of the spectrum is also not competitive globally. Unlike baseball, though, public education is much more than a game.

What they both have in common is the powerful influence of money. Lewis indicated that many people argued that baseball was ceasing to be an athletic competition and becoming a financial one. "The gap between rich and poor in baseball was far greater than in any other professional sport, and widening rapidly. The raw disparities meant that only rich teams could afford the best players. A poor team could afford only the maimed and the inept, and was almost certain to fail. Or so argued the people who ran baseball." However, there were lots of teams with big payrolls that failed miserably too.

Lewis wondered: "What was the A's secret? How did the second-poorest team in baseball, opposing ever greater mountains of cash, stand even the faintest chance of success, much less the ability to win more games than all but one of the other 29 teams? For that matter, what was it about baseball success that resisted so many rich men's attempt to buy it?" These were the questions that *Moneyball* sought to answer.

These were similar to the questions that Randy sought to answer as he continued his educational odyssey. How can we replicate the success of the kids at Shalimar at society-changing scale? How can we replicate and scale the success of low-income school districts like Little Lake? Why do some of the school districts with the highest per-pupil spending fail so spectacularly? And, why have so many education reforms failed?

It still matters how much money you have to invest in either baseball players or educating students, but it also matters how well you spend that money. "Oakland seemed to be playing a different game than everyone else. At the bottom of the Oakland experiment was a willingness to rethink baseball: how it is managed, how it is played, who is best suited to play, and why. Understanding that he would never have a Yankee-sized checkbook, the Oakland A's general manager, Billy Beane, had set about looking for efficiencies in the game. Looking for, in essence, new baseball knowledge."

How Oakland acquired this information was revolutionary. Lewis wrote: "In what amounted to a systemic scientific investigation of their sport, the Oakland front office had reexamined everything from the market price of foot speed to the inherent difference between the average major league player and the superior Triple-A one. That's how they found their bargains. Many of the players drafted or acquired by the Oakland A's had been victims of an unthinking prejudice rooted in baseball's traditions. The research and development department in the Oakland front office liberated these players from this prejudice, and allowed them to demonstrate their true worth."

In 2010, Ruth S. Johnson EdD and the Principal's Exchange's Robin Avelar LaSalle PhD published a college textbook called *Data Strategies to Uncover and Eliminate Hidden Inequities: The Wallpaper Effect,* a concept described briefly earlier. Randy read the book while on vacation in the summer of 2013 and recognized it instantly as *Moneyball* for education.

The Wallpaper Effect laid out a game plan for using "other data," things most school leaders today do not systematically analyze to drive the performance of low-income students, schools, and school districts, therein reducing or eliminating inequities. School districts like Little Lake that stuck to the game plan were the Oakland A's of public education.

As Randy floated around the pool at his brother Don's vacation home along the Colorado River, he shared what he was reading and thinking. Don, a lifer in the automobile business and now an executive in the major dealer division for the online advertiser the Auto Trader Group, injected the notion of "big data" into the conversation. He told Randy of how big data had transformed the car business in just the last four years.

Don described the car business this way: There are historically four segments to the industry: The consumer, the dealer, advertising and marketing, and the automakers that design and manufacture the cars. The auto industry was another industry that ran on myths and legends, particularly at the dealer level, somewhat like baseball and public education. Traditionally, automakers developed the product and sold it to dealers. They also controlled the branding and marketing. Dealers bought the cars from automakers and in turn advertised locally and sold the cars to the consumers, the end users.

The automakers' success with their product lines was a hit-and-miss proposition. If you were, say, a Ford dealer, some of the products may be hot-sellers while others may be dogs. To get the hot-selling products, dealers sometimes had to take some of the dogs off the hands of the automakers. The dealers, in turn, had to warehouse the inventory (a mix of dogs and hot-sellers), while they advertised it locally, and then had to turn around and sell it.

Historically, dealers advertised through a variety of methods, most of them very expensive. First, they locate themselves near high-traffic locations, often near freeways, highways, busy streets, or in auto malls, usually very expensive real estate. Then they would advertise on local television, radio, or in the newspaper. If you ran a full page ad in a paper like the *Los Angeles Times*, with circulation of more than one million readers in the 1990s, it could cost $20,000 or $30,000 per day. On any given day, 2 to 4 percent of the readers might be in the market for a car, and some smaller slice of that might be interested in the kind of car a given dealer is selling. The same dynamic might occur for radio and television advertising.

Meanwhile, before the Internet, the consumer had relatively limited amounts of information about the true cost of the cars or the margins at the local dealer level. So consumers would go to the dealer, enticed in by whatever method. They went through the tortuous negotiating process and left with a good deal, or not-so-good deal, based on their negotiating prowess, and whether they were buying a hot-seller or a dog.

As consumers went online in the late 1990s, things began to change. Buyers could access more information, so they showed up at dealers well-informed. This helped them to negotiate better deals, thus squeezing dealers' profit margins. Meanwhile, global manufacturing capacity continued to increase, outstripping demand even before the recession. Because many automakers had a glut of inventory, they pushed more and more product down the dealer's throats. The dealers had to finance the extra inventory, then advertise and discount heavily in order to move it.

In the meantime, newspapers and broadcast media became less

effective as buyers got more information online. New avenues of reaching consumers like Google and Auto Trader emerged, eviscerating newspaper's profits. High-margin classified advertising plummeted along with newspaper print readership. Using the *LA Times* as an example, circulation dropped from more than 1.2 million in 1990 to about 600,000 in 2013. And dealer profitability diminished as well. By the mid-2000s, many dealers made almost no profit selling cars, and instead made their profits running the back end of the dealership—service, parts, and finance.

In 2008, the economy collapsed as the real estate bubble burst. Two of the Big Three domestic automakers needed bailouts, and automakers across the globe were severely challenged. The game began to swiftly change. Global manufacturing was downsized or, more accurately, right-sized to demand. The dealers stopped buying the dog inventory from the automakers because they simply couldn't afford to. Meanwhile, the industry was awash in data. Data was being generated everywhere, from online inquiries to diagnostic data from the latest generation of connected vehicles.

The automotive industry began to capture and interpret that data, which provided insight and value. In so doing, the industry began to transform its understanding of the customer. It started to tailor customer interactions, marketing campaigns, and relationships to an extent that were previously unimaginable. Delving into these data streams drove much-needed change into the heart of the industry.

Manufacturers are now making fewer dog cars, dealers are able to keep leaner inventories, and customer satisfaction is up. So is profitability for both dealers and automakers. And it only promises to get better as the auto industry becomes more sophisticated in capturing and analyzing data and using it to drive performance throughout its ecosystem.

So, can data drive this kind of transformation in education? Let's take a look at the *Wallpaper Effect* and see how it might:

> The Wallpaper Effect's central focus is on the critical roles
> that data can play to expose information that can and should

compel schools and districts to rectify fundamental equity issues for students. Data refers to information that can be used to describe conditions in schools and districts that affect student's school experiences in either positive or negative ways. For many, data implies test scores. However, even when disaggregated, the common uses of such data offer limited change power.

In contrast, the other data, illustrated in the Wallpaper Effect, when used adeptly by educators working together in collegial groups, can help build "equity muscle," a term used throughout the book that equates to increased capacity to drive higher performance for all students. Other data can provide a lot of useful information about the academic culture of a school and how students are faring in the system while at the same time offering up clues about what needs to change.

The Wallpaper Effect offers five ways to use data to improve performance in the K–12 education system:

Role 1. Getting Real: Telling the Whole Story – A driving question for every decision in every educational institution should be: Is this in the best interests of our students…all of them? "This" can be anything, including instructional practices, materials, schedules, district systems, school policies, common routines, decisions about personnel, budgets, or facilities. Schools, districts, and communities need to better understand with crystal clarity what happens to diverse groups of students and determine whether inequities exist in their schooling. Rather than engaging in rhetoric about slow or fast students, caring or uncaring parents, capable or incapable teachers and administrators, well-grounded information can help pinpoint specific areas of concern in order to arrive at appropriate solutions and resource allocation. Careful analysis of data helps us dig deeper into our understanding of conditions affecting student success. Data can play an important role when indicators of school improvements are connected to short-and long-term higher learning outcomes for all students.

Role 2. Examining Institutional Heart – Data can help expose how certain educational practices reflect our situational belief systems. Because historical legacies and practices create institutional norms, many educators do not regularly engage in self-reflection about personal beliefs or their assumptions about student potential and ability. Skillful use of data can stimulate personal and systematic examination in ways that completely alter the type and quality of opportunities provided to students. Devoting time to highlight and do something about institutional biases must take place on an unremitting basis with all of those involved in the educational enterprise.

Role 3. Mobilizing for Action – When strategically used, data have the power to mobilize parents, students, educators, and the community at large. Schools should create opportunities for these groups to help collect, analyze, and represent data. This process builds ownership and understanding of the power and credibility of data. It also helps create a sense of urgency to engage in appropriate reforms for young people. We must not assume that parents and young people cannot collect, analyze, and represent data. Their voices are critical and compelling. Data presentations by a collective group of stakeholders lead to a richer dialogue about factors that contribute to outcomes, as well as the roles of different stakeholders to improve the future for children and communities.

Role 4. Stop, Look, and Listen: Caring Enough to Check Up – The excitement about a new endeavor can cause schools and districts to rush to implement well-intentioned reforms with no forethought as to how they will measure the impact of those reforms. We must resist this quick implementation temptation and devote time to determining how to measure the results of planned reforms prior to their implementation. A data-informed monitoring process allows for midcourse corrections, the reinforcement of positive directions and the celebration of success. Monitoring students longitudinally as they progress through the system tells us about their progress and what teachers, curriculum, and programs they have experienced. From this information, schools can describe conditions and patterns for individual or groups of students. Practices and policies can then be critically examined to determine whether they enhance or inhibit student progress. Data can uncover how some policies have differential impacts on different populations.

Role 5. Expect It and Inspect It – Nationally, the public is demanding greater accountability from schools. At the local level, parents and educators require information regarding the plans and progress made by educational institutions. Internal and external accountability systems require data. A school or district needs a plan for collecting, analyzing, and representing data that will answer key questions. No Child Left Behind launched a major accountability effort linked to funding and sanctions. While the politics around NCLB are complex, the notion that schools and districts should be accountable for student performance is straightforward and generally accepted. Individuals and organizations perform best when expectations are clear and progress is frequently monitored. Data are central to this effort.

Wallpaper Effect

Outcome data have the potential to produce a misleading picture of actual conditions in schools and districts, thereby creating a wallpaper effect. Outcome data, like wallpaper, can cover up cracks or other unwanted blemishes or surfaces. These data may show outcomes in an attractive light, but when the wallpaper is peeled off, problems surface once again, displaying more layers of wallpaper or major cracks.

Data used in schools and districts typically answer very narrow sets of questions about student outcomes. Yet, we argue that asking only the most superficial questions about performance outcomes can mislead and mask the organizational and systemic contributing factors (cracks) influencing those outcomes. There are other invisible data that are not mentioned publicly or are not a part of accountability measures, but are critical pieces of the puzzle nonetheless. These are the powerful data that influence outcomes, have long-term consequences for students, and are critical elements related to issues of equity, social justice, and performance. Brought under the microscope, these data have the potential to spotlight institutional behaviors and often paint a very different picture about true conditions that are incongruent with what we say we believe or want for students.

This examination of "other data" amounts to the same kind "systematic scientific investigation" of K–12 education that Lewis described for baseball and the Oakland A's. Baseball players had been victims of "unthinking prejudice rooted in baseball's traditions." The same is true for students in public education. "The research and development department in the Oakland front office liberated these players from prejudice, and allowed them to demonstrate their true worth," Lewis wrote. The same is true for the Principal's Exchange approach that has liberated students and allowed them to reach their full potential. This is being achieved as education leaders have implemented the approaches detailed in the Wallpaper Effect, which have come to be known as Response to Intervention for Systems (RtI-S).

Let's take a look at a couple more examples of how this is playing out. Lynwood, California, is another working-class town in LA County, next door to Compton. Over the last sixty years, this city of approximately 70,000 residents has changed from a predominantly white population, to a predominantly black population, to, in recent years, a predominantly Latino population. With each shift, it has gotten progressively poorer.

Lynwood, has produced a number of well-known people who reflect its changing demography: The late NFL Commissioner Pete Rozelle, Dodgers great "Duke" Snider, longtime NBA coach Rick Adelman, actor Kevin Costner, rap music impresario Suge Knight, tennis star Venus Williams, and Angels baseball infielder Efren Navarro were all born or raised there. Coincidentally, Randy Barth was also born in Lynwood, in 1958, toward the end of its majority white period.

For much of the last twenty years, the Lynwood Unified School District ranked near the bottom of student and school district performance. Several generations of leaders were suspected of and in some cases found guilty of financial malfeasance. In the spring of 2010, with the district finances in desperate shape, the state of California put Lynwood Unified on a watch list, giving it a year to put its finances in order or be subject to takeover by the state.

As bad as the district's finances were, the performance in the classroom was even worse. The high school graduation rate was 61 percent, the dropout rate was 43 percent, and the percentage of students completing their A-G requirements so they could enter college was below 20 percent. Its student demographics were 93 percent Latino, 7 percent African American, and 37 percent English learners, and 97 percent of students were impoverished.

In the summer of 2010, the school board hired a new administrative team led by Superintendent Eddie Velasquez, Deputy Superintendent and Chief Academic Officer Paul Gothold and Assistant Superintendent Gudiel Crosthwaite. Much of the central district staff had been laid off the previous spring, and nine of the seventeen schools had no principal in place a month before the new school year was to commence. Morale was about as low as it could go.

The new team hired the Principal's Exchange to conduct an audit to analyze strengths and weaknesses and make recommendations for a road map to move the district forward. At the same time, THINK Together was brought in to begin to build an Extended Learning Time system as part of the turnaround plan.

Sarah Gonzales, the new assistant principal at Firebaugh High School describes how PE helped her. I was "an idealistic young teacher that got plucked from the classroom and put into administration in the midst of a firestorm. Firebaugh had five principals in three years, one of whom landed in jail for inappropriate relationships with under-age kids. Morale was incredibly low and the school was a complete mess, really close to anarchy." Sarah, a graduate of Carlton College and Yale had come to Lynwood as a Teach for America teacher and stayed. "At the end of the first quarter we were doing a meta-reflection of our data and 98 percent of our students had a D or an F in algebra. I was at the end of my rope and I had no idea how to begin to address the situation.

"Robin gave me a strategy. She said identify your high need, medium need and low need teachers. With your high need teachers, visit their classrooms three to four times per week. With your medium need teachers, visit them two to three times per week. And your low-need teachers visit them once a week."

The high need teachers were teachers that had just quit teaching amidst the chaos that engulfed Firebaugh. Often they would be sitting at their desk on their cell phone and the students would be on their cell phones, with no teaching or learning taking place. This is what PE calls "not on my watch." Robin coached Sarah to visit those classrooms regularly and get the teaching and learning back on track. Sarah continued, "There are teachers that want to be able to teach, but just don't know how. So PE has a simple to use 'golden ticket lesson plan' that an administrator like Sarah could begin to coach her teachers on. It's an 'I do, we do, you do' approach of gradual release as the teacher works with the students. If the teacher has trouble with classroom management, coach them on that. If they had problems developing or delivering lessons, coach them on that. The approach is to find what they do well and build on their strengths."

Sarah said the approach saved her. "I was drowning. I just didn't know what to do. But Robin knew that I had been a good teacher myself and could draw on that skillset and experience to help others become better teachers. She broke what seemed like an overwhelming task down into something that was actionable that I could begin to do. With the game plan in place, we began to make some progress."

Across the district, the RtI-S system began to be put into place. At the high school level, the district stopped tracking students into remedial classes and began enrolling them in A–G classes surrounded by support systems that would enable students to be more successful.

At the elementary level, the district created common learning goals and a coherent curriculum approach. An assessment system was put into place to diagnose the specific strengths and weaknesses of each student. A plan for differentiated instruction was created to meet students at their level, then move them forward—whether they were behind, at, or even ahead of grade level in a given subject area. A team of intervention teachers helped support this during the school day, and THINK Together supported the strategy during the extended hours after school.

Results quickly began to improve. Out of a possible 136 grade-level targets that the state measures to determine Adequate Yearly Progress, Lynwood met just sixteen in 2011. By 2013, it had met seventy. Its API rose from 675 in 2009 to 723 in 2013. What's more, in 2012 and 2013, Lynwood was the most improved unified school district in the state. Students graduating from high school having met the college A–G requirements nearly doubled, from below 20 percent in 2010 to 38 percent in 2013.

And consistent with the approach that all students achieve, the percentage of African Americans graduating from high school rose from 55 to 75 percent at Sarah's Firebaugh High School and 59.7 to 70.7 percent at Lynwood High School from 2011 to 2012. These improvements far outpaced the gains in graduation rates elsewhere in the state and Los Angeles County.

What did it cost to engineer this turnaround? Not much. Lynwood paid the Principal's Exchange between $800,000 and $900,000 per year. Most of this amount was paid out of the district's Title II budget, which is a funding stream designated for professional development. In exchange for these fees, Principal's Exchange provided a detailed assessment of where things were, worked with the district to build the RtI-S system, trained and coached teachers and administrators to build their capacity to sustain the improvements, and built software tools to extract data from the district student information system so that administrators and teachers could gain actionable insights quickly enough to inform their practice. In a district with an operating budget of well over $100 million per year, this investment in RtI-S has tremendous leverage and increases the return on investment in the core operating budget of a school district.

At the end of the 2012–2013 school year, Eddie Velasquez stepped down as superintendent, and Paul Gothold was named to succeed him. Gudiel Crosthwaite stepped up and replaced Paul. The district hasn't missed a beat during this leadership transition because a clear path was set in place. Implementation of the Common Core curriculum is a logical next step to the groundwork that has been laid by the Principal's Exchange. PE conducted weeklong summer institutes for teachers and administrators to immerse them in Common Core and build their capacity to implement it successfully. This is far different from the Common Core implementation challenges we are seeing elsewhere across the country.

Randy observed another PE supported turnaround in a different kind of district that is worth taking a closer look at. East Whittier is a K–8 district serving a little over 9,000 students across thirteen schools and one early-education center. This district is not as poor or as low-performing as either Little Lake in 2002 or Lynwood in 2010. Still, it had significant pockets of students who were underperforming when you peeled back the wallpaper as Co-Superintendent Dr. Dorka Duron and Director of Categorical Programs Danelle Almaraz did.

East Whittier is a district that is 80 percent Hispanic, 14 percent white, and 6 percent other. It has 55 percent of students living in poverty and only 15 percent who are English learners. According to Danelle, PE had been working in the district for several years at their most challenging school, Ceres Elementary, with good results.

Several other schools fell into sanctions as their English Learning and Special Education sub-groups were underperforming in both English language arts and math. Again PE performed an audit. These audits are designed to identify both the weaknesses and the strengths— the hot spots, as PE calls them, as well as the sweet spots. The idea is to focus attention on the hot spots and build on the successes of the sweet spots. Robin Avelar LaSalle, whose sons play high school football, likens the approach to reading keys in football. You can't attack everything all at once; you have to understand where you are and attack the weaknesses. The same principles apply, but they are tailored for each district and targeted to the areas of greatest need. They are implemented by training existing staff so that they own the changes and are coached throughout the year so that those changes become ingrained as new habits.

Because of the varying demographics of the schools in the district, some schools had as few as two English learner students as others had as many as three hundred. With these kinds of disparities, there was no consistency in the curriculum and strategies to address this population. So, together with Dorka and Danelle, PE worked with the teachers and principals to align their curriculum and build their own common assessments, starting with English language arts. Building their own assessments caused a number of epiphanies for the teachers. For example, Danelle shared that one teacher taught synonyms a certain way, but the standardized tests asked about synonyms another way. This confused the students, causing them to score more poorly than they might otherwise. By unpacking the standards and building their own assessments, the teacher saw how she could adjust her approach in a way that enabled her students to learn synonyms better and reflect that proficiency on the test.

As teachers began teaching to the same standards and talking about it, the results improved. Mulberry Elementary improved seventy-one points in their API the first year. But their reaction was interesting. They asked, now that we've gotten out of sanction, we don't have to do this curriculum alignment stuff anymore right? Fortunately Dorka and Danelle, along with the principal, kept them on the right track.

Over time the teachers discovered the assessments from the textbooks lacked the rigor their students needed. They also learned that they could regroup students every four to six weeks based on the student's performance on the assessments, so that students were getting the level of support that they needed. Over time, the other schools saw this approach was working and wanted in. The methodology that was used in English language arts began to be applied to math as well.

Overall, the results in East Whittier were impressive. Looking at gains in AYP from English language arts over a five-year period from 2008–2013, there was a districtwide gain from 51.5 to 66.6 percent; English learners improved from 30.4 to 49.5 percent; Special Ed students improved from 22.7 to 41.1 percent, and students receiving free or reduced price meals moved from 38.6 to 58.6 percent (see graph).

EAST WHITTIER CITY MATH AYP

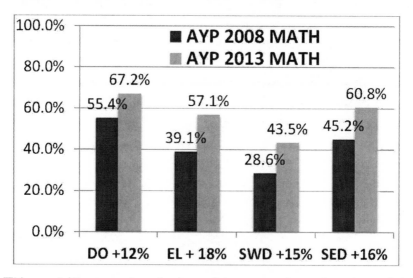

This graph illustrates the gains in proficiency rates for students in math in the East Whittier School District as a result of implementing the RtI-S methodology. The first bar is for student's districtwide (DO), the second for English learners, the third for students with disabilities and the fourth for socio-economically disadvantaged.

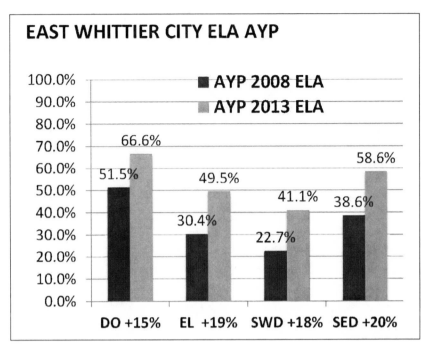

EAST WHITTIER CITY ELA AYP

■ AYP 2008 ELA
■ AYP 2013 ELA

DO +15%   EL +19%   SWD +18%   SED +20%

This graph illustrates the gains in proficiency rates for students in English language arts in the East Whittier School District as a result of implementing the RtI-S methodology. The first bar is for students district wide (DO), the second for English learners, the third for students with disabilities and the fourth for socio-economically disadvantaged.

For math there were similar-sized gains: districtwide, 55.4 to 67.3 percent; English learners, 39.1 to 57.1 percent; Special ed, 28.6 to 43.5 percent; and socio-economically disadvantaged, 45.2 to 60.8 percent. When you compare the East Whittier school performance against similar schools, they are outperforming their statewide peer group by 20 to 25 percent.

In 2014, a business group known as California Business for Education Excellence named East Whittier as one of just six school districts to its Honor Roll. CBEE's mission is to inform people about the achievement gap and its impacts on the workplace, influence the state's education improvement efforts through the use of actionable data that can improve teaching and learning, and improve public education systems and practices by harnessing actionable data and scaling the success of higher-performing schools.

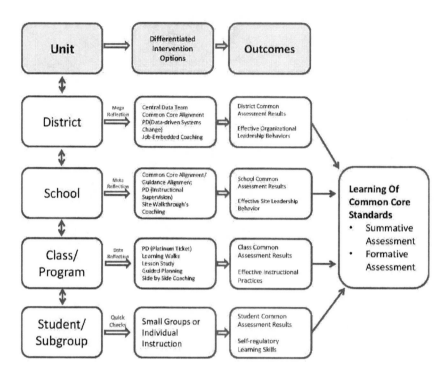

This chart depicts the Principal's Exchange Response to Interventions for Systems methodology applied at all levels of a school system in support of Common Core implementation.

As Randy studied the Principal's Exchange approach and compared it to the methodology used by other school consulting firms, he learned a few important things. First, most systems-change firms operate only at the leadership level, meaning they don't work directly with the teachers and get down into the classroom. Separately, there are a large number of firms that provide professional development for teachers but, too often it's not connected to the systems change work. PE's work involves professional development for teachers and connects to the systems-change work all throughout the district. This results in a highly aligned, cohesive, high performing system. As districts shift to Common Core implementation, adopting this kind of approach can help lead to a strong implementation across the system.

As the Wallpaper Effect indicates, the summative data captured in California's comprehensive Academic Performance Index can sometimes mask the performance of different subgroups of students. So, Randy did a comparison study of all forty-two THINK Together districts and examined proficiency rates by sub-group. He used Little Lake and East Whittier, as mature implementations of the RtI-S methodology, as benchmarks for comparison. Randy compared the proficiency rates of Latino students, low-socio economic students, English learner students and special ed students, in both English language arts and math. He did not compare African-American students because neither Little Lake nor East Whittier has a meaningful number of African-American students. Little Lake and East Whittier outperformed all of the other THINK Together districts, in most cases dramatically. (See charts on the following page and in Appendix 2.)

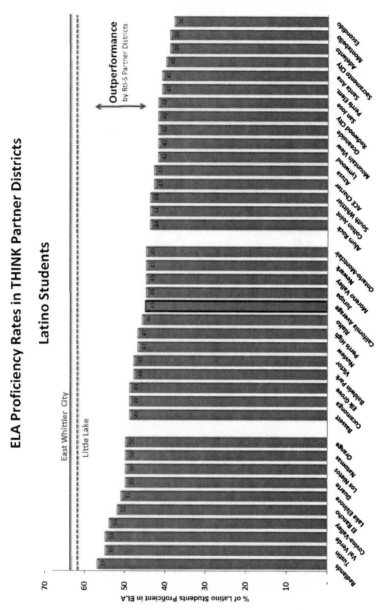

This graph benchmarks the proficiency rates for all Latino students in English language arts in East Whittier and Little Lake City School Districts (the benchmark Principal's Exchange RtI-S districts) versus all other THINK Together districts.

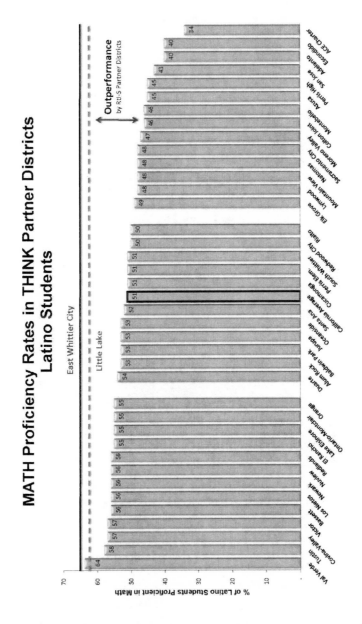

This graph benchmarks the proficiency rates for all Latino students in math in East Whittier and Little Lake City School Districts (the benchmark Principal's Exchange RtI-S districts) versus all other THINK Together districts.

9

The Man in the Mirror

Paolo Leon climbed into his car and started on the short commute to his office at MVE & Partners architectural firm. In just a few minutes, he would take the elevator up to the eighth floor of a gleaming granite and glass office tower at the corner of Main Street and MacArthur Boulevard in Irvine. The building is in the heart of one of the most thriving communities in America, and, coincidentally, just up the street from where Randy worked almost twenty years before, when he first met the three moms from Shalimar.

Paolo, now twenty-eight, reflected on his own short journey: Shalimar, Sage Hill, USC, MVE internship turned full-time gig, MBA from Chapman University, Taylor (another architecture firm), and back to MVE. He was extremely blessed, and he knew it. This last year, he married his high school sweetheart, Candice Romero. Candice was another scholarship recipient at Sage Hill who is doing well. She attended Chapman for her undergraduate studies and was now working as an ad manager for US Interactive Media.

Paolo, now a THINK Together board member, quietly chuckled as he thought about Randy. Over the years Randy often cited Paolo as an example of what was possible if our communities built a proper support system around all of its students. Randy liked to say that different students need different kinds of supports, and therefore we need an ecosystem of support to ensure that all kids reach their full potential. He'd say a student like Paolo would likely have made it without a THINK Together support system, but what THINK was able to do for a kid like Paolo was open doors to opportunity. The scholarship to Sage Hill, the internship at MVE that THINK helped facilitate, became gateways to Paolo's success.

At a recent board meeting, though, Paolo gently challenged Randy's thinking: "Randy likes to speculate that I would have been one of the kids to emerge from a tough situation, no matter what. I'm not so sure. THINK gave me a place to study, academic help, mentorships, scholarships … a lot of things. It is hard to separate out what made the difference and what didn't. For me, it took all of those things, plus support from my family and friends, and good schools. I don't know that you can parse it out and speculate on what you can leave in and what you can leave out."

What caused Paolo to be in such a reflective mood that morning? His first assignment back at MVE was on the design team for an apartment complex that the Irvine Company was building in San Diego. This is what it is all about, the investments that Donald Bren and the Irvine Company made through the years, coming full circle. The Irvine Company's tremendous success was owed to many factors, among them a commitment to planning and design and a long-term investment horizon. Its investments in THINK Together took the same approach, and now, young professionals like Paolo were providing a high return on that investment.

Education in our communities, in California, and across America, is the number one economic development issue. In a global economy with rapidly evolving technology, communities add value through an educated workforce. The communities where the workforce is highly educated—Silicon Valley, San Francisco, Orange County, Seattle, Austin, Boston—are the ones that are thriving. Even in those communities, the haves and have-nots divide sharply in line with education levels. The communities that lack an educated workforce—Detroit; Flint; San Bernardino; Brownsville, Texas—are at or near the bottom of the per-capita income ladder. In Chapter 7, we illustrated the stark contrast in the level of education among the parents in Irvine and Santa Ana. Not only do Irvine schools perform better as a result, but the economy in that community is thriving compared to Santa Ana.

What is heartening to see is that places like Pittsburgh, Pennsylvania, have turned things around. Once defined by heavy industry and blue-collar masses, Pittsburgh is now home to the fifth-most-educated young workforce (age 25–34) out of the forty top metropolitan areas in America. California is moving in the opposite direction. As we stated earlier, the over-fifty workforce is the most educated in the world, while its under-thirty-five workforce is the least educated in the developed world. As a result, economists estimate that California will have a shortage of one million college graduates by 2020.

Stubborn Skills Gap

In the fall of 2013, the Organization for Economic Cooperation and Development (OECD) produced what the *New York Times* called "an exhaustive report" on the global labor force. The report indicated that the American labor force was not merely slipping in comparison to that of its peers around the world, it had fallen dangerously behind.

"The OECD study," Eduardo Porter wrote in the *Times*, "lands in the midst of a contentious debate over whether the United States faces a skills shortage. Over the last couple of years, employers have been saying they can't find enough skilled workers." Jonathon Rockwell of the Brookings Institute says that the problem is getting bigger: "Just under a third of the existing jobs in the nation's one hundred largest metropolitan areas require a bachelor's degree or more, and about 43 percent of newly available jobs demand this degree. And, only 32 percent of adults over the age of twenty-five have one."

The *New York Times* article continued, "The OECD puts this deficit into an international context. It finds that advanced economies are generating very few jobs for workers with middling skills. Yet while other countries seem to have gotten the message, racing ahead to build skills, the American skill set is standing still."

"For instance, the youngest Koreans, age sixteen to twenty-four, scored forty-nine points more, on average, on literacy tests than the oldest cohort of fifty-five- to sixty-four-year-olds. Young Americans, by contrast, scored only nine points more than their elders. While younger cohorts in other countries are consistently better educated than older ones, in the United States (as we've seen in California) that is not always the case: thirty-year-olds in 2012 scored lower, on average, in literacy tests than thirty-year-olds in 1994."

The report noted, "Unless there is a significant change of direction, the work force skills of other OECD countries will be facing (and indeed are already facing) major and fast-increasing competitive challenges from emerging economies."

And yet, the report raised a couple of vexing questions: "The highly skilled in America earn a much larger wage premium over unskilled workers than in most, if not all, other advanced nations, where regulations, unions, and taxes tend to temper inequality. So, if the rewards for skills are so high, why is the supply of skilled workers so sluggish?" Andreas Schleicher, OECD's deputy director for education and skills responded, "The human capital base in America is quite thin. The American economy rewards skill very well, but the supply hasn't responded."

The United States was the first country to provide for universal high school education. Today, with its dropout rate, America has a weaker outcome in high school graduation rates than most OECD countries. The math and reading scores of American teenagers in OECD tests have not improved over the last ten years. And our college graduation rates have slipped substantially below those of other rich nations.

Immigration by less-educated workers from Latin America plays some role. But, as the OECD noted, "two-thirds of low-skilled Americans were born in the United States. And, America has a poor track record in improving immigrants' skills, both through the public education system and through employer training."

"Socioeconomic status is a barrier. Not only is inequality particularly steep, little is done to redress the opportunity deficit of poorer students. Public investment in the early education of disadvantaged children is meager, the report said. "But," noted Schleicher, "the skills deficit is not only a problem of poverty and marginalization. American college graduates perform worse than their peers elsewhere on skill tests. Looking at college diplomas, the US looks much better than looking at skills."

The other question is equally perplexing: "If the supply of skilled workers is so poor, how can the US remain such an innovative, comparatively agile economy? In other words, even if the American skill set is poor compared with that of its peers, who cares?" Schleicher answered: "Today, the American labor market is good at attracting talented foreigners, offering them more money than they could make elsewhere. Still, it might be risky to stake the nation's future on maintaining a steady stream of skill from abroad. What would happen if the other countries started rewarding their talented workers? What would happen if America's influx of talent stalled?"

Look no further than America's broken immigration system to answer that question. The tech industry has a semi-permanent shortage of 5,000 engineers in Silicon Valley alone. The 65,000 H1-B visas that allow entry for many of the imported engineers are snapped up in the first few days of the window opening each year. That is why companies like Facebook, IBM, and Microsoft are lobbying to expand the number of H1-B's to 180,000 as part of an immigration reform bill.

But that is not the only mismatch between America's labor force and the job market. The US military has struggled to find new recruits that are physically fit, don't already have police records, and that can pass aptitude tests. Increasingly, police departments across the country are struggling to find applicants. In Santa Ana, where Randy chairs the board of the Chamber of Commerce, employers have been vocal about the lack of qualified applicants for jobs in welding, auto repair, customer service, and other semi-skilled positions. As the baby boom retires, California is forecast to have massive shortages in nurses and teachers.

Leona

Had Randy not ventured east into San Bernardino County in 2007, he might never have met Leona Aronoff-Sadacca. She's now a THINK Together board member and one of its most generous benefactors. Leona was the owner of Gate City Beverage, a large beer distributor in Riverside and San Bernardino counties. Leona owned a number of other businesses in conjunction with Gate City, including a water company, a trucking company, and an insurance firm. With her companies headquartered in San Bernardino, Leona was deeply troubled by the decline in the city's fortunes following the closures of Norton Air Force Base and a number of large manufacturers. Its older housing stock and affordable rents made it a magnet for people living on the margins. As Leona began to liquidate her operating companies as she approached retirement, she was deeply committed to reinvesting back into the communities from which her own family's prosperity had sprung.

She was drawn to THINK Together after former tutor and board member Sam Anderson made a powerful case over lunch one day. She admitted she was dreading the lunch—not because she doesn't enjoy Sam's company, but rather because she knew "there's no such thing as a free lunch. I really wasn't interested in another organization." Sam managed to open her eyes to the possibilities at THINK Together.

"Because of him, I became involved, and I have not regretted it for one instant," Leona says now. "Education empowers. It gives you an opening. It gives you a foundation. It's like building a house—you have to have a strong foundation. Without a solid K–12 education, you do not have the foundation to be successful."

Two elements of THINK Together attracted her to the organization. First, she believes that private organizations need to support the public education system to make California stronger. Education will be the only way that the children of immigrants succeed. She thinks about her own life and remembers needing help when she first came to the United States as a Holocaust survivor. Her family fled Germany during the Nazi regime and hid in a farmhouse in the French countryside until the end of World War II. Leona was born in France while the family was in hiding. She immigrated to the Los Angeles when she was nine.

Given her history, her education investments leaned heavily toward Hebrew Union College in Los Angeles. But, Leona felt strongly about THINK Together as it began to partner with school districts in the Inland Empire. She was deeply troubled by the poor performance of many local schools and was impressed by THINK's ability to partner with schools to address this issue.

"In my position, you look at how you can make the biggest impact," Leona said. "Alone, I could not help this many children. I feel together, we can change our education system and ensure a bright future for the next generation. Without education, they are not going to make it." Leona leveraged her connections to help the organization in a variety of ways. She introduced THINK to some of the power brokers in the Inland Empire. She helped raise money in an area where philanthropy is scarce. And, she even seeded partnerships that brought opportunities to THINK Together students that helped create a model to close the opportunity gap for low-income students.

After she retired, Leona moved to Irvine's beautiful Shady Canyon. Shady Canyon is home to one of Southern California's great country clubs and many professional athletes and corporate executives. Leona had also gotten involved in the Pacific Symphony, one of Orange County's premiere arts organizations. John Forsythe, the symphony's longtime executive director, had long had a desire to expand the reach of the symphony beyond the county's elite audiences and into the broader community. It troubled John that low-income kids would have few chances to explore their interests in music in a serious way. Many schools cut their music programs as they doubled down on English and math during the accountability era. This shift was followed by devastating budget cuts during the great recession, creating a double whammy for arts programs in schools. Even where music programs survived, low-income parents could not afford the instruments kids needed nor the private lessons needed to compete to get into the better youth orchestras.

John, like many in the classical music world, was inspired by the El Sistema program in Venezuela. El Sistema, founded in 1975, became widely known when its most famous product, Los Angeles Philharmonic conductor Gustavo Dudamel, burst onto the world stage as a world class conductor in his mid-twenties. El Sistema's aim, much like THINK Together's, is to remove children from poverty's snares, like drugs, crime, gangs, and desperation. El Sistema's method, imagined by its founder, economist and trained musician José Antonio Abreu, was classical music. Orchestras and music training centers around the country were established to occupy young people with music study and to instill values that can come from playing in ensembles: a sense of community, commitment, and self-worth. Today, the program is estimated to reach 310,000 children and youth at approximately 280 locations across Venezuela.

The Pacific Symphony had tried for some time to launch a program in Santa Ana but had trouble navigating the district bureaucracy. Leona suggested it partner with THINK Together and offer the program to Santa Ana students through the after-school and summer programs. Assistant Superintendent Herman Mendez, a classically trained musician himself, and Tia Dwyer, THINK Together's Orange County general manager, had laid some important groundwork but couldn't get over the stumbling blocks to get it launched. With Leona's convening and Randy's partnership with Jane Russo and Dr. Cathie Olsky, the stumbling blocks were removed. Then, Leona put up the money to get it started. Out of those efforts, the Santa Ana Strings program was launched. For the last two years, professionals from the symphony and music teachers from SAUSD have collaborated to teach more than two hundred Santa Ana students the violin. This is Phase I of the Pacific Symphony's vision to build an El Sistema-like program in Santa Ana.

The following year, when the budget got tight, Leona stepped up with a $500,000 challenge grant to help raise money to keep THINK

Together moving forward. What motivated Leona to do something like that? "What you want to do at my age is find a way to leave a footprint," Leona said recently. "You want to see your funds working, and you want a way to know if you are hitting the mark." THINK's use of data to track performance gives Leona confidence that it is serious about hitting the mark.

The giving, she says, stems from the Jewish concept of *tikkun olam*, Hebrew for "healing the world." While the phrase comes from third century rabbinical teachings in the Mishnah book, today it's understood as being a force that improves the world. Tikkun olam suggests that everyone can have a hand in working toward the betterment of future generations and forces everyone to take ownership of the future. It's not a word that Randy and his early group of supporters might have used, but the concept seems to echo one from World Vision that had a great impact on Randy: "Let your heart be broken by the things that break the heart of God." Even if there are differences between these two concepts, there is enough in common to foster collaboration and to draw people from different political or faith traditions to act in concert for our children. "It is the collaboration, the positive vibe, and the sense of being with winners," that Leona says keeps her a very strong supporter of THINK Together programs.

Where There is No Vision, the People Perish

If America is going to remain a great nation, the rejuvenation and modernization of its public education system must be at the top of the list of priorities for the whole country. While public policy and the performance of the schools themselves play a central role, so does our culture. As we've seen through the stories in this book, Randy makes the case that it takes the parent, the school, and the community working together to provide a support system that enables children and youth to thrive. But let's not forget that students have to do the work. They must bring will to the table, or the rest is all for naught. In fact, US Education Secretary Arne Duncan recently pointed out that one of the reasons American students are falling behind is that too many parents and too many kids just don't take education seriously enough and don't put in the work necessary to really excel.

In *Waiting for "Superman,"* Davis Guggenheim showed clips of nearly every president going back a generation or more, declaring education a top priority or declaring themselves to be an "education president." But we've seen very little follow-through and action. Maybe that is because presidents, just like the rest of us, have to drive education change through the gauntlet. Lou Gerstner, the former chairman and CEO of IBM who famously turned the company around in the 1990s, has also been involved in school reform issues, and noted: "At IBM, I had sixteen divisions and it was too difficult to drive change through that structure, so we simplified it to six. In public education in America, we have over 15,000 school districts; each of them in its own way is involved with standards, curriculum, teacher selection, classroom rules, and so on. We have islands of excellence, but we fail to scale up systemic change." Education in America, right or wrong, is a bottom-up proposition. But that doesn't mean that the inspiration and the vision for change can't come from the person in the White House. In fact, it probably has to.

Reforming our schools needs to be a bottom-up as well as a top-down proposition. We need vision—one like John F. Kennedy's "we're going to the moon"—but paired with a consistent follow through that persists over time. Driving performance in education is a long-term proposition, and we have yet to have a president that has stayed on topic over time. George W. Bush worked in a bipartisan fashion with leaders like Democratic Sen. Ted Kennedy and Republican Reps. John Boehner and George Miller to pass No Child Left Behind. NCLB became very unpopular because it introduced accountability into a system that fundamentally lacked it. Then it set up system of sanctions without sufficient corresponding investments or effective systems of support. As former Secretary of Education for Massachusetts Paul Reville said, accountability and choice were "necessary, but insufficient."

Though we still need top-down vision, innovation is happening on the ground, bottom-up. We need contributions from all parts of the education system, driven through the gauntlet, to change the outcomes for our students at society-changing scale. There are a set of recommendations in Appendix 1 that are a start on moving this systems-change agenda forward.

Purpose and Culture

We can talk about schools and school reform and point our fingers at teachers unions and ineffective bureaucrats, etc., but change starts in our families, in our neighborhoods, and in our communities. It starts with *you*. Many families today, either in your community or your region, need help. America is a nation of immigrants. Our newer immigrants usually don't have the luxury of waiting three or four generations to send their kids to college like Randy's family and many others like his did. There were solid middle-class jobs available without a college education. But times have changed. Families in our lower-income communities probably didn't have successful experiences with the education system, so it is hard for them to create that for their kids. Add to that the disintegration of the family unit in certain communities, and it is an uphill battle to provide a support system that can help kids reach their full potential.

On the other side of the coin is service. Most, if not all, faith traditions teach that it is better to give than receive. Randy believes that we are happier when we are serving others and when we are connected to a purpose larger than ourselves. Many studies show that, and it is certainly embedded in various scriptures. Two very influential books, Viktor Frankl's *Man's Search for Meaning* and, more recently, Rick Warren's *Purpose Driven Life*, make the case for this in very compelling ways.

In *Man's Search for Meaning*, Frankl details his time in a Nazi concentration camp and makes keen observations about who survived and who didn't during that incredible ordeal. When all was taken away from people, Frankl observed, the people who survived were those with a higher purpose: loved ones to get back to, or a cause they cared very deeply about. Later, Frankl wrote: "Ever more people have the means to live, but nothing to live for."

In *Purpose Driven*, Warren makes the same case. Writing from a Christian perspective, he creates a road map for people to find purpose and meaning in their lives. His opening line says it all: "It's not about you." Both Frankl's and Warren's writings are aligned with Stephen Covey's work and the question he posed in *7 Habits* that changed Randy's life: "Picture yourself at your funeral. What do you want your life to have been about?"

Living a life of service changed and enriched Randy's life in ways he could never have imagined. The same is true for the dozens of volunteers at Shalimar who have volunteered faithfully for twenty years. That is also true for the Sam Andersons, the Sat Tamaribuchis, and the Leona Aronoff-Sadaccas that have served the organization in other ways. Their lives have been enriched and given more purpose and meaning because they help others. It's a win-win situation. They win, and the kids they help win, and our communities and our country are strengthened in the process.

Getting involved helps people in two other important ways: First, it helps connect you to other people who may not look or think like you. Usually when that occurs, you learn something, stereotypes are broken down, and communities are strengthened. Second, you will probably learn something about education that is quite different from what you might read or see in the media. Often, perception lags reality. The perception of what is happening in public education is heavily skewed by what is happening in the big urban districts in the major media markets. That looks very different than much of the rest of the country. But these perceptions color the education policy debates. If you get involved in education in your local community, there is a pretty good chance that you will develop a different perspective.

Graduation

On a beautiful early June evening in Newport Beach, the parking lot at St. Mark's Presbyterian Church was filling up fast. The cars were an odd assortment of old clunkers, beat-up pickup trucks, and well-worn economy cars, alongside late model Audi's, BMW's, Mercedes Benz and Tesla's. The people streaming into the elegant dining hall were equally diverse.

The occasion was the high school graduation celebration for THINK Together's legacy community-based programs, including the Shalimar Teen Center. The students and their humble, yet proud, families were there along with their teachers and some of the community volunteers that helped to tutor and mentor them. Joining them were some of the Shalimar alumni, young professionals who have returned to help the kids behind them graduate college and pursue their dreams, fully equipped to compete in a global economy. Also in attendance were donors and THINK Together board members who made these programs possible.

This is Randy's favorite night of the year. It represents the culmination of the collective work of the students, their parents, the school, and the community, and it is about the only time of year that all of these diverse players gather together in the same room. Better yet is the reason for the gathering, the high school graduation and the launch into college for these THINK Together students. This is the seventh year in a row that 100 percent of THINK Together seniors will head to college armed with scholarships and new laptop computers courtesy of THINK Together. Many of these students are the first in their family to graduate high school. Students attending THINK Together high school programs for four years are six times more likely than their demographic peers to go to college. THINK's high school programs are drop-in programs, so students self-select in. This means that the most motivated students often are the ones who attend. So, that positively skews the performance numbers when compared to the general population of similar high school students. It is impressive, nevertheless, and demonstrates that students with the greatest socioeconomic challenges can compete with anybody, given the proper support system and if they are willing to do the work.

As the program is about to begin, Randy slips into his seat next to Nadia Flores, the former Shalimar teen who now serves as THINK Together's director of community outreach. Nadia, dressed in a chic black blazer, has come a long way from the frumpy outfit she wore at the yogurt shop while serving her high school classmates. Recently recognized by *OC Metro* magazine as one of Orange County's rising stars on its "40 under 40" list, Nadia often takes the microphone at such events. When she does, she tells the audience how the course of her life was changed by THINK Together. When speaking to parents, she tells them that their children's path is being shaped, and she exhorts them to stay involved in their children's education, and make sure that they have the right classes in school and the right support system out of school.

Nadia's own journey has taken her around the globe. She traveled to Sweden as an exchange student, and to Japan, Brazil, Mexico, and Cuba as part of different educational programs at UC Santa Barbara's Global Studies Department. Her mother, back in Orange County, worked for Sam Anderson as a home-healthcare aide as his first wife fought a losing battle with cancer. Sam would later help Nadia as she sought her first job. Through his contacts, she was able to land a position at Univision, the Spanish-language television station. But the power that THINK Together had wielded in her life remained very important to her, so she returned from Los Angeles to Orange County to work with Randy.

"I want people who come from where I come from to be more than a statistic. I want them to dream big, to have more than a survival mentality. If they are only thinking survival, they cannot dream. I really believe that THINK can make a difference for our families. My story can help. It puts a face on the idea. It says, 'Yes, you can succeed.'"

Seated next to Nadia were two young women with a history similar to her own: Yessenia Delgado, seventeen, and her sister, Lizbet Pizaña, twenty. Their parents also were on hand to celebrate Yessenia's completion of the Shalimar program and her admission to UC Berkeley, where she plans to study psychology.

"What I got from Shalimar was attention," said Yessenia, who was accepted into ten of thirteen colleges where she sought admission. "I was in a program to help me get to college at school, but there were so many kids that I couldn't really ask questions. And, I had a lot of questions as I filled out college applications and scholarship request forms."

Sister Lizbet, was just finishing a two-year stint at Irvine Valley College and was on her way to Cal State Long Beach. She added that without THINK, "I probably wouldn't have graduated from high school. I really needed the support."

THINK Together alumnus Ever Arias is the evening's emcee. Ever opens the program welcoming Yessenia and all of the students who have participated in THINK Together programs over the years. We know, he remarked, "that growing up in the Shalimar neighborhood was difficult for me, my siblings, and many of my friends. But thanks to the Shalimar Teen Center, we had a safe place to go after school to do homework, study, or just socialize with friends." The previous year, Ever had earned his bachelor's degree in Chemistry from UC Riverside. Months later, he would be on his way to medical school, the first THINK Together alumni to do so. His dream is to return and practice medicine in a community like he grew up in, to help improve the wellness of those kinds of communities. This last year he spent time volunteering at the Shalimar Teen Center while he was preparing for the MCATs.

"I just want to say to our students tonight that I've been in your shoes. I know the obstacles you face and what your fears are," he said. "But I'm also here to tell you that those fears and obstacles can be overcome. Believe in yourself, and pursue your dreams."

There was no time in that night's program for him to share the story of his sister, America Arias. Just days before, America had won an Emmy Award as producer of the morning show for NBC's affiliate station KCRA 3 in Sacramento. The Arias family emigrated from Mexico when America was in middle school. Fortunately for them, they landed in the Shalimar neighborhood, where the kids participated in the THINK Together programs. America became the first in her family to graduate high school. She went on to Cal State Fullerton, where she was recognized as one of the "Top 100 Journalism Students in America," landing an internship at CNN along the way. She quickly catapulted herself into the competitive television news business. "One of the greatest benefits I received from my years at THINK Together was the inspiration I drew from volunteers— many of whom were college students," she said. "They instilled in me the vision that I, too, could attend college, graduate, and have a high paying job. I attribute my professional success today, in large part, to the support, tools, and encouragement I received at THINK Together."

Ever tells the high school graduates that he and his family are proof that the new graduates are on the right road. The graduates have closed the achievement gap that plagues so many communities like theirs: "My sister America went through the program and was the first in our family to graduate college. My sister Dulce was also part of the program, and she is pursuing her college degree. My youngest brother, Rafael, is in the elementary school program," Ever said. "None of us were destined to even graduate from high school. THINK Together changed the destiny of our family, and it can change your destiny as well."

Through headphones, Yessenia's parents hear the message translated from English to Spanish and smile. The mother, a housekeeper who finished nine years of school, and her father, a gardener with a fifth-grade education, then hold their breath as Yessenia takes the stage as the senior class representative and tells the audience: "THINK has helped shape me in so many ways. They have been my motivators in everything I do. They inspired me to dream and then provided me a real support system so that I could realize those dreams."

Yessenia was followed to the microphone by a parent from THINK Together's Highland Street Teen Center in Orange, Venancio Chavez. Unscripted, he speaks in Spanish about THINK Together and describes the organization as his children's "third leg of support. There are the parents, the school, and THINK Together. Without all three, my daughter would not be going to college. I thank God for THINK Together and for all you here in this room that have made the possibility of going to college a reality for my daughter."

Randy rises to take the microphone. He is tickled that Mr. Chavez's words echoed what were in his own remarks about the three elements of support for children. He looks out on a room packed with the people who have made this work possible for the last nineteen years. There was Bobbi Dauderman, who has tutored all these years, and her husband, Jerry, who now serves on the board. There were Bill and Jean Wenke, who have also tutored for twenty years and served on the board. There was Tony French, whose wife, Karen, tutored for many years before she succumbed to cancer, and Tony serves on the board. There was Sam Anderson and his wife, Susan; Betsy Tarbell and her husband, Don; Sat Tamaribuchi, the Irvine Company executive who made the original connection into the company, and so many more. And, there were second-generation supporters like Leona and Joe Sadacca and THINK's current board chair, Eric Boden and his wife, Connie.

As Randy looked into the faces in the audience, he reflected on their diversity. It was the changing face of California and the changing face of America. He remembered conversations he used to have with Pablo Diaz, who succeeded Mary as THINK's executive director in the late 1990s. Pablo and Randy used to talk about how THINK Together had become a place where diverse segments of a community—old and young, rich and poor, different ethnic groups and faith traditions, different political perspectives—could come together for the benefit of a community's children. And the people who invested their time, talent, and/or treasure were enriched as well. All of this strengthened the fabric of the community in the process.

Like Ever, Randy spoke of changing the destiny of families and of entire communities. Shalimar is still a tough neighborhood, but now, a college-going culture has been built there. More than three hundred THINK Together graduates from that one street have gone to college, and the first seventy-five or so have now graduated. These young men and women are architects and engineers, teachers and social workers, business people, and nonprofit executives. "Any street in America would be proud to have its children turn out this way," Randy said.

At the end of the evening, Randy climbed into his car for the twenty minute drive back to his home in Santa Ana and pondered the same question he had been thinking about for years. How do we replicate and scale the good things that are happening in public schools and in the programs that support them so that all of these kids can reach their full potential? He was proud of how far THINK Together had come and for the impact it had on students and families like the ones he had just spent the evening with. But even the more than 100,000 students THINK Together was now touching were just a drop in the bucket for California's 6.2 million students, let alone the more than 50 million students across America.

More than that, how do we replicate the work that Phil Pérez and his team are doing in Little Lake, or the other amazing islands of success in American public schools? And how do we build the capacity of parents to be good partners in their children's education? Some of it, Randy mused, comes down to policy, some comes down to practice, and some comes down to the allocation of resources so that America can invest in its children and its future. But much of it, Randy felt, comes down to each of us as individuals doing his or her own part. In doing so, we all connect to something larger than ourselves.

As he pulled onto his street, he remembered the turning point in his own life. He was in Martinique sorting his life out as he was navigating his divorce. Late one evening, he was cleaning up and getting ready for bed. The windows of his bungalow were wide open, letting in the balmy breeze that carried with it the fresh salt air and faint sounds of music from the Club Med discotheque. Randy stared into his own eyes in the bathroom mirror. "Who am I?" he wondered. "What do I want my life to be about? What do I want my legacy to be?" He lingered for a long time, deep in thought as he contemplated these questions. Then he splashed some cold water on his face as he returned to readying himself for bed. As he dried off, he could hear the lyrics of a Michael Jackson song wafting into his room:

I'm gonna make a change,
For once in my life
It's gonna feel real good,
Gonna make a difference
Gonna make it right

As I turn up the collar on my
Favorite winter coat
This wind is blowin' my mind
I see the kids in the street
With not enough to eat
Who am I to be blind, pretending not see
Their needs
A summer disregard,
A broken bottle top
And a one man's soul
They follow each other on the wind ya' know
'Cause they got nowhere to go
That's why I want you to know

I'm starting with the Man in the Mirror
I'm asking him to change his ways
And no message could have been any clearer
If you wanna make the world a better place
Then take a look at yourself and then make a change.

Epilogue

In recent months, as we were finishing up the book's final edits and winding our way through the publishing process, several things occurred that we thought were germane to the story of THINK Together.

Progress

In Orange County, a collaboration of county agencies each year produces a report called the *Conditions of Children in Orange County*. The report is a comprehensive examination of twenty-five primary areas that provide a look into the health, welfare, and educational well-being of the more than 700,000 children (ages 0-17) in this diverse county of more than 3 million people. Orange County matters. It is the sixth-most-populous county in the U.S., and it is very diverse. The K-12 students in the county are 48.7 percent Latino; 28.8 percent white; 17.3 percent Asian American, Pacific Islander, or Filipino; 1.5 percent black or African American; 0.4 percent Native American or Alaskan Native; and 3.3 percent multiracial or other. The county is economically diverse as well, with a high median income, $84,100, yet 50.4 percent of the county's students K-12 students qualify for free or reduced-price meals at school. Despite its wealth, or maybe because of it, Orange County remains one of "the most inaccessible places to live for low and moderate earners."

The twentieth edition of this report was released in late October 2014. The release coincided with the twentieth anniversary of the opening of the Shalimar Learning Center. The report's data caused Randy to reflect on the broad progress this county had made in the twenty years since he worked with those three mothers to open an after-school center in the Shalimar neighborhood. The county has made great progress in many important areas: College readiness has improved. The number of children involved in crime and in gangs has dropped. And health indicators such as immunization rates and children with healthcare coverage have improved, while infant mortality rates have dropped. The one indicator that went the wrong way by a significant amount was childhood obesity.

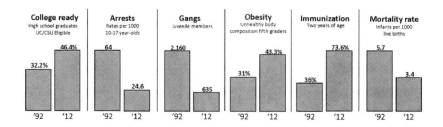

Randy's efforts at Shalimar, which later led to THINK Together, were but one of many efforts to address the alarming issues that Orange County faced twenty years ago. Since then, the efforts of a broad range of county agencies, nonprofit organizations, and faith-based groups, along with evolving efforts from schools, have resulted in real progress for children across many measures. But the county is increasingly a high-cost place to live and to do business. Therefore, Orange County must continue to try to improve the conditions for all children and to ensure the educational success of those on the wrong side of the economic divide if it is to maintain the long-term well-being of the county. Orange County, like much of California, can be a bellwether for the rest of the nation as America becomes more diverse and, increasingly, a nation divided by wealth gaps. The good news, illuminated in the *Conditions of Children* report, is that real progress can be made when communities come together around a common purpose.

The Gauntlet and Oscillation

In Chapter 7 we talked about the "gauntlet" and the range of factors that can conspire to, intentionally or unintentionally, harm the best interests of children. The gauntlet was on full display in Santa Ana in the fall of 2014. First, some background: After Donald Bren made his catalytic investment in Santa Ana, and THINK Together worked with the district to build an Extended Learning Time platform across the district that could engage the broader community and support the goals of the district, the classified employees union, CSEA, sued Santa Ana Unified for outsourcing jobs to THINK Together.

As mentioned previously, prior to the arrangement with THINK Together, the after-school programs had been run by a mix of teacher-led sites (17), THINK Together (13), classified-led (6), Boys & Girls Club (5), and YMCA (1). There were more than 300 classified staff who worked in the program, although many didn't work five days a week (they shared positions), and an audit showed many didn't meet NCLB standards (48 college units or passing the district Instructional Aide exam). Further, many district staff worked at different schools during the daytime than they did after school. So, as they finished up their duties at their primary school and traveled to another school for their extra duty, it was difficult to start the extended day program effectively.

When THINK Together took over, it hired about 100 of Santa Ana's classified staff who met the qualifications, were able to work five days per week, and could get to their extra-duty assignment in a timely manner. It matched the wages that the district was paying, which were higher than what THINK Together was paying, but the employees did not get their pension contribution on this extra-duty pay.

As a result, one of the Santa Ana classified staff that went to work for THINK Together sued the district. The state CSEA joined in the suit and broadened it to an outsourcing complaint. The matter went to trial in Superior Court in Orange County. The district argued that these jobs were grant-funded extra-duty pay and therefore were at-will employment and not subject to the protections of permanent positions under California Education Code Section 45103.

On February 9, 2012, the trial court determined the after-school tutoring positions held by the classified employees prior to the district's agreement with THINK Together were extra duty assignments "at will," rather than permanent classified school employment positions, and the employees who held those positions never obtained permanent status for the extra-duty hours they worked. Consequently, the trial court held, the district's agreement with THINK Together did not violate the provisions of Section 45103.1, and denied the peremptory writ of mandate requested by CSEA.

CSEA appealed the decision. On May 29, 2013, the California Court of Appeals reversed the Superior Court judgment and remanded the matter with directions to stay the proceedings as to the Education Code claims asserted by CSEA until it exhausted administrative remedies. The Court of Appeals felt that the proper venue to adjudicate this matter was the California Public Employee Relations Board (PERB) and not Superior Court. Eventually, the statute of limitations on the matter ran out on PERB.

During the years that the dispute was winding its way through the legal process, Santa Ana Unified had three superintendents. Jane Russo retired, and her replacement came and went in less than two years. During that turbulent two-year period, most of the cabinet left as well. So, a mostly new lineup with a different philosophy (and different legal counsel) was in charge when this matter came up again 2014.

In the middle of September, the new superintendent, Rick Miller, called Randy in for a meeting. Rick and a deputy superintendent told Randy and his Orange County general manager that they felt the district was on the wrong side of this matter and that they had significant legal exposure. To address this, they intended to bring the K-8 programs back in-house and operate the programs themselves. When

Randy pointed out that there were not likely enough classified staff within the district to operate the program, Rick indicated that the district was looking to hire many of THINK Together's part-time staff and create hundreds of new union positions. He said, "This about positions, not people." The district gave THINK Together 90-day notice and said the change would occur over the winter holiday break, starting in December.

The news shook Randy and the vast array of THINK Together stakeholders involved in various partnerships within the district. Some wanted to go to the media; some wanted to mobilize the thousands of parents served by the programs; some wanted to make it an issue in the school board race that was occurring that fall; and still others wanted to begin a recall campaign against the current school board.

Randy hired an attorney who had years of experience with school districts in these matters and formed a kitchen cabinet of key stakeholders that included the longtime mayor of Santa Ana, the head of the Children and Families Commission of Orange County, the Irvine Company, the head of the Samueli Foundation (a large STEM-funder), the head of the Orange County Business Council, and the Orange County Community Foundation. This group put pressure on the board to try to get the district to explore other legal options as well as other program solutions. But these options never really saw the light of day, and the district, with 4–1 support on the board, moved ahead with its plan.

As details emerged, it became apparent that Santa Ana Unified was giving a 40 percent raise to the new CSEA positions. In addition, the district planned to go back to operating the programs with part-time teacher site coordinators at a cost of $55 per hour plus benefits (compared to roughly $18 per hour for the full-time THINK staff). What's difficult about this model is that teachers need significant prep time, especially during the early days of this shift to Common Core, to do a good job during the school day. And, the site coordinator needs prep time to prepare daily lesson plans in multiple subjects for multiple grades. If classroom teachers do this job, they use up all the prep time, reducing their effectiveness in both places. A few heroic teachers can do this, but over time and over a large number of schools, this has proven to be a failed model.

To pay for these higher wages, the district is gutting the support system that THINK Together painstakingly built over time. With Local Control Funding and more money for schools due to a temporary tax increase (Prop. 30) backed by Gov. Jerry Brown, Santa Ana didn't seem worried about the higher costs and the loss of philanthropy. To the THINK Together stakeholders, this seemed very short-sighted. If the district has extra money, why isn't it being used to expand services to students? This change also illustrated a shift in philosophy at the district from a focus on collaboration and community engagement to a preference for control and running things in-house.

This situation provides a good look at the gauntlet in action. The state education code and funding mechanisms were factors in this situation, as were the school board, the superintendent (and superintendent turnover), the employee unions, parents, and the community. This decision was clearly profitable for adults in the district, but it remains to be seen how it will turn out for the students. Will the progress made in Santa Ana in recent years be built on and sustained, or will it be, as Reed Hastings generally observed, an oscillation?

Collective Impact

A school district headed in the opposite direction, philosophically, is San Bernardino. San Bernardino was used as a negative example in several ways earlier in the book. However, with some new school board members and a new superintendent, Dale Marsden, the last two years have launched a new era in San Bernardino schools.

As we pointed out earlier, San Bernardino has as tough of a set of socioeconomic conditions as just about anywhere in the country. To make matters worse, factions in the community were constantly at war with each other. Community stakeholders were pulling in different directions as the city and its schools struggled.

Dale and the new board decided to deploy a collective-impact approach to this difficult set of challenges. They set out to engage the broader community in a dialogue about their collective issues. Out of this dialogue, a thirty-seven member strategic planning committee was formed to build a strategic plan to move the district and the community forward in the same direction. These thirty-seven members included representatives of students, parents, teachers, principals, district administrators, school board members, the faith-based community, the nonprofit sector, business leaders, and higher education. Randy was a member of that team.

The process was facilitated by Dr. Lindsey Gunn of Cambridge Strategic Services. Over the course of several months, the strategic planning team came up with a plan that was then vetted by the community in a series of meetings. This process helped to raise awareness around the issues that the district and the community faced, helped diverse stakeholders broaden their own perspectives, and created relationships and buy-in from the community for the new plan and the changes that were going to need to occur for the district to move forward.

The new plan was called "Making Hope Happen Here." Under the plan, a new mission statement was adopted for the district, as well as a set of beliefs, a framework for excellence, and a set of nine strategic objectives with associated metrics to measure the district's progress toward its goals. As California shifts to a Local Control Funding environment and school districts are tasked with developing Local Control Accountability Plans (LCAPs) based on community input, this approach has made San Bernardino a leader in this arena.

Mission Statement

The mission of SBCUSD, the leading expert in human learning, is to ensure all students, cradle to career, develop the knowledge, skills, and proficiency required for college, career, civic, and economic success by inspiring and engaging them in a system distinguished by:

- High expectations for student and staff performance.
- Vital partnerships with families, community, and employers.
- Culturally proficient schools.
- Learning experiences beyond traditional boundaries of where and when.
- Safe, respectful, and welcoming environments.
- Beliefs

We believe that:

- Every person has value and deserves to realize full potential.
- Learning liberates the mind, the heart, the spirit, and instills hope.
- Relevance inspires motivation and excellence.
- Emotional, psychological, and physical well-being is significant in the pursuit of life, learning, and happiness.
- Cultural proficiency leads to equity and removes barriers to opportunity.
- Strong interpersonal relationships based in trust empower individuals and communities.
- Individuals and communities thrive in environments of mutual respect, value, and worth.

Basics for Excellence

Focus on Results Together
- We work collaboratively to produce exemplary outcomes for our SBCUSD community.

Service
- We achieve success by consistently and effectively serving others.

Sense of Purpose
- Our actions are focused and contribute to the attainment of our mission.

Positive Passion
- We experience enthusiasm and encouragement as evidenced by our excitement and joy in what we do every day.

Emotional Commitment
- We exhibit inspired behaviors that reflect pride, motivation, and empowerment through involvement.

Parameters of Trust
- We establish consistent parameters of trust that are characterized by honesty, transparency, and collaboration.

Professionalism
- We exhibit professionalism by providing superior customer service while adhering to quality professional standards.

Key Strategic Objectives

- Each student will develop and pursue an academic and career plan based on his or her interests and talents.
- Each student will demonstrate independent initiative, civic responsibility, and community pride.
- Each student will develop creativity through mastery of fundamental knowledge and applied skills.
- Each student will enjoy learning throughout life by learning how to learn.

These key strategic objectives are then further broken down into nine strategic objectives, each with specific actionable implementation plans and goals, and metrics to measure progress against these goals. The nine strategic objectives are:

1. Applied Learning
2. Learning Beyond the Boundaries
3. Coaching and Mentoring
4. High Expectations for All
5. Network of Alliances
6. College and Careers
7. Resource Acquisition & Allocation
8. Success & Accountability
9. Health, Wellness & Safety

Change is hard. Changing a culture within an organization is even harder. Changing the culture in a community with some of the deepest challenges in America is an incredible challenge. But, by getting a broad set of stakeholders in the community to work together to develop a plan, you begin to build the trust, the relationships, the shared purpose and vision, and the actionable plans that can begin to get you there. You begin to change the culture.

By doing this painstaking level of community engagement and buy-in, you start to give the organization the chance to build in the stability, together with the high expectations, that can attract the talent (and build the capacity of the talent that is there) to deliver on the new vision. Without this groundwork, the change is too hard and the obstacles are too great. But with it, a new culture can be built over time that gives these changes a chance to succeed and be more than an oscillation after Dale leaves (hopefully after a very long run) and the board turns over. Keep an eye on San Bernardino; it is a district to watch.

Scaling What Works

When Randy and his group of volunteers started this work, it was to answer three mothers' plea to "provide a safe place for our kids to go after school in the neighborhood, to get help with their academics." Later, their work morphed into responding to Al Mijares' challenge to build a system of support that could provide students with consistent help on a significant enough scale as to be meaningful more broadly.

As Randy became more and more involved with school improvement and school reform conversations, he often heard the comments around the concept of "turning islands of success in public education into continents of success." People would say, "Success doesn't travel well in public education." Noted school-change leader Michael Fullan often talks about the need for collaboration and shared learning across school districts. But all too often there aren't platforms to do this on a sustained basis.

As THINK Together began its own next-generation strategic planning dialogue, it began to ask some new questions. Can it leverage the infrastructure that it has built around schools and school districts to do other things that can help more kids reach their full potential and have an even greater impact on the achievement gap? Can its infrastructure be utilized as a shared learning platform to help share what's working across different school districts? It's not that Randy or THINK Together have all of the answers to what ails schools, but they have a unique view into where some of those answers might be. And they have a platform that could be utilized to help some of the things that work get to scale. THINK looked at the 42 school districts it was partnering with at the time. Those districts comprised more than 900,000 students. Half the states in America don't have that many students in them. What if THINK Together could help scale some of these other ideas that could reach these 900,000 students and beyond?

Randy and his board and leadership team, together with some of their school district partners, began to talk about what this could look like. Randy ran the idea by his longtime colleague Lillian French, who thought it was a great idea and suggested he start with Principal's Exchange. At this point, though Randy had long admired the organization's work, he had never met its CEO, Robin Avelar La Salle. Lillian arranged a lunch that began a dialogue between the two organizations.

Principal's Exchange does brilliant work, but it is small. To have a greater impact on more schools and more students, it needed to grow but didn't have the infrastructure or the capital. Both Robin and Randy felt that the PE model was both replicable and scalable. To grow, PE needed to hire some of the principals and administrators who had implemented their methodology effectively in their schools and school systems. THINK Together had the management capacity and infrastructure to help to begin to scale it, if they could find the growth capital.

So, THINK Together and Principal's Exchange have created a unique partnership to do just that. They have attracted their first round of growth capital, and Robin has hired nine key people to come to work with PE. Together with Stanford University, they have collaborated on a federal innovation grant application to help scale this work. Stanford is validating the impact and will do the evaluation work if the grant gets funded.

Jonathan Raymond, formerly superintendent of the Sacramento City Unified School District and now president of the Stuart Foundation, had another idea for the THINK Together platform. As superintendent of Sacramento City Unified, the eleventh-largest district in California, Jonathan took part in something called the Urban Education Dialogue. Sol Price, the founder of the Price Club (now part of Costco), started this gathering through his foundation. Price realized that running these large complex districts, in the public eye every day, was a difficult and lonely job. He thought it might be good if these peers could get together and compare notes and start a dialogue that might help each other professionally.

Price Philanthropies invited the superintendents of the twenty largest school districts in California to get together for a day or two, three times a year. They set their own agenda. Sometimes they would have a speaker on a topic they were all interested in. Sometimes they would do a book study. Sometimes, they would just talk among themselves. For Jonathan, it was the best professional development he had as a superintendent.

Jonathan pointed out to Randy, "There are more than a thousand school districts in California. I was fortunate to have access to this Urban Ed Dialogue as schools chief for one of the largest districts. But many of the other superintendents don't have access to that. What if you started another superintendents' dialogue off of your platform? It would be of great benefit to superintendents that don't have access to one."

Input from school partners like Lillian French and Jonathan Raymond led THINK Together to broaden its vision and mission as it developed its new strategic architecture. While THINK Together will remain California's largest Extended Learning Time provider, it is moving beyond ELT in the hope of having an even greater impact on student achievement.

Vision

Educational excellence and equity for all kids.

Mission

Create opportunities for all kids to discover their passions and reach their full potential.

We Believe In...

Harnessing the power of integrated partnerships and scalable, data-driven solutions to create and deliver innovative programs for kids.

Shared Learning Platform

THINK Together is building a unique statewide shared learning platform, including collaborative data sharing partnerships—which provide a lens into what's working—to help innovation move well within the public school system framework. We have the expertise to derive actionable insights from data and partner with school districts to develop customized solutions around large-scale implementation of leading practices.

What We Do

Early Learning
- Working with 0-5 year-olds to ensure they are ready to learn when they hit kindergarten

Expanded Learning
- After school and summer learning opportunities

Core Learning
- Customized solutions for core instruction during the school day using the Principal's Exchange Response to *Intervention for Systems.*

Learning Communities
- Convening professionals across organizations and school districts to foster collaboration and help to spread promising practices so more kids benefit.

Improving and optimizing education is tough work. It takes people working together, with trust and collaboration, to get things done. There are a lot of obstacles as we've seen through the gauntlet, but as communities and as a nation can never give up. The stakes are too high, both collectively as a country, and for families and individuals. Ultimately, our destiny depends on the success of our collective efforts in this endeavor. What will America's destiny be? What will *you* do to affect the outcome?

Appendix 1

Recommendations

This is not a perfect or exhaustive list, but rather some high-level recommendations that could make a huge difference. For those looking for the silver bullet, it's not here. As Phil Pérez says, "It's not sexy, and it may not get us on the cover of Educational Leadership, but if we do these things, we think our education system will be much higher performing than it is today."

Federal

Education spending at the federal level in 2012 was about $138 billion, or about 4 percent of the federal budget. This includes all of the education-related programs across the federal government. The US Department of Education appropriation was about sixty-six billion. The big buckets for this spending are:

Title 1 grants	21.2%
IDEA (Special Ed) grants to states	16.8%
Pell Grants	33.4%
Other programs	28.4%

New America Foundation, Federal Education Budget Project

The other big buckets of education-related spending in the federal budget are:

School nutrition programs	14.9 billion
Head Start	8.0 billion
Veterans education benefits	11.0 billion

In order for any federal investments to be sustainable, they must reside in a federal budget environment that is sustainable. America's current budget approach is not. Our budget favors older people versus young people. Stan Druckenmiller, the iconic hedge fund manager, has been out touring college campuses and talking about "generational theft," how America's budget priorities favor oldsters versus youngsters. Here are some highlights from Druckenmiller's presentation:

- Since 1960, federal entitlement transfers as a percentage of the federal budget have grown from 28 percent to 68 percent.
- Since 1970, Medicaid, Medicare and Social Security benefit per oldster has risen from 41 percent of per capita GDP to 72 percent.
- Oldsters are consuming more—Oldster consumption is up 164 percent over the last thirty years, while youngsters is up just 38 percent.
- With the Baby Boomers about to retire, oldster spending is about to explode.
- Since the 1960s, the poverty rate for oldsters has dropped from 35 percent to 9 percent, while the poverty rate for children has dropped from 28 percent to 22 percent.
- Birth rates are declining. In the 1950s women had an average of 3.7 children. Now they have 2.06. Those 1950s babies are about to turn sixty-five and start collecting benefits, and there will be fewer workers around to pay for those benefits.

- Meanwhile, life expectancy has gone up, so oldsters are living longer and taking more entitlements.

- Without adjustments, Baby Boomers' entitlements will consume 20 percent of GDP, which is the historical ceiling for tax revenues. This means the equivalent of the entire federal budget will be given to people that don't provide a current service.

- From now until 2050, the working age population (18–64) is forecast to grow by 17 percent. Oldsters will grow by 102 percent over the same time. Today, there are 4.8 workers supporting each retiree. By 2050, it will be 2.4. Without adjustments, taxes for workers will have to go through the roof.

Budget Reform

In 2010, the National Commission for Fiscal Responsibility and Reform came up with a proposal, known as the Simpson-Bowles deficit reduction plan that would reduce tax rates, close loopholes, broaden the tax base, and trim entitlements. This would modernize the tax code and reduce federal debt over the intermediate and long-term. Some version of this must be done, and sooner rather than later. Or, we will continue to under-invest in our future, and America will decline.

Immigration Reform

Closely tied to this dynamic is immigration. America needs comprehensive immigration reform. We need more people to immigrate to America and become productive members of our society to support the retiring Baby Boomers. And, we need a large-scale system of support around schools so that these immigrants can accelerate their productivity into the knowledge-based workforce.

Other Federal Recommendations

- Fund early-learning programs. There is strong evidence that this is the most important investment we as a nation can make in education. There is bipartisan support. Forget universal preschool; it's too expensive. Concentrate investments in low-income students and target kids up to age five. Give states the flexibility to design their programs to target the gaps in each state. That may vary depending on what is already in place. Move Head Start and Early Head Start to the Department of Education and integrate with this initiative.

- Continue to support school choice as an incubator for innovation and as a prod to the system. Don't overdo it, though, and don't expect it to be a silver bullet—it is not.

- Lighten up on compliance and become more outcomes-focused.

- Maintain strong accountability focus.

- Update the School Improvement Grant framework based on the evidence of what has worked in the early rounds of these investments and elsewhere in the school-turnaround environment.

State Recommendations

- Same as above: Work with feds to expand early learning, continue to promote some level of choice, make compliance systems more outcomes-focused.

- Promote local control accompanied by outcomes-based accountability systems. Accountability must be tied to a standards framework that links to global competitiveness. Avoid incentives to dumb standards down.

- Increase investments in support systems around schools in a structure that creates community schools (integrated support systems around low-income schools) including investments in expanded learning and mental health. Structure these with local matching funds requirements and other incentives to develop public-private partnerships and engage local communities.

- Stay the course on the implementation of Common Core and Next Generation Science standards. Invest in the support systems and professional development required to do this well over the long run. Just because this is hard does not mean it is not right.

- Create balanced teacher evaluation systems that include student performance, principal review, and peer review. As there is the potential for a big performance dip in the first few years of Common Core testing, take a hiatus on the student data portion of the teacher evaluation for two years as a new baseline is established, but then incorporate as part of a balanced evaluation system.

- Strengthen evaluation systems for principals and administrators, too. Create incentives to foster alignment and collaboration rather than scapegoating.

Local Recommendations

- Citizens: Improve your knowledge of what is going on your town's education system.

- Get stronger candidates to run for local school boards.

- School boards: Focus your attention on hiring a great superintendent. It is the most important decision you will make. Then, make sure the superintendent works with the community to develop a strategic plan with clear annual objectives. Measure progress toward those goals monthly. Trust, but verify. Provide your superintendent and his or her team with the support needed to be successful. Don't micromanage or meddle in their work. Put the performance of the organization ahead of your political career. Kids come first. If your organization is successful, your political career will be enhanced. Work on engaging the community, especially parents, constructively.

- Superintendents: As Michael Fullan says, "Love your people!" Build a culture of transparency and trust. We're not talking about blind trust, but a trust-but-verify culture. Over-communicate. Foster collaboration across the organization. Consider appointing the leader of each union to your superintendent's cabinet. Remember, culture eats strategy for breakfast.

- Superintendents: Conduct an audit of all your practices, your systems decisions-making frameworks, practices, and the resulting performance. Your system is built perfectly to get the results you are currently getting. If you want better results, you need to drive change. Take a look at the kind of frameworks used in places that have superior performance in similar settings as yours. We shared some examples from places like Little Lake, East Whittier, Elk Grove. Long Beach and Garden Grove have also had meaningful successes. Work with your community to develop meaningful strategic plans. Out of that, develop a set of annual strategic objectives that focus the community and the organization in a common direction. Measure your results including the near-term activities that will contribute to achieving the goals set out in your plan. Create dashboards that measure key indicators of your monthly progress toward your goals. Share these dashboards widely. Focus your board on the plan and the dashboards so that they don't try to micromanage the district. Stop jumping around so much, and stay in your jobs longer. Turnover is detrimental to high performance

- Superintendents: Invest in building the capacity of your principals. There are approximately 132,000 K–12 schools in America. If each one had a great principal, most of the rest of this would take care of itself. Jim Collins talks about building great organizations that support and drive high performance at the unit level. In school districts, this is the school principal. Build their capacity to be the instructional leader at their school. Build their mindset to be servant leaders to support their teachers and the other campus support staff who make things work. Build their capacity to create a strong culture at the school and foster collaboration. Build their capacity to use data to drive the performance of their teams, bottom-up, like we have seen in the Principal's Exchange schools.

- Teachers: Be lifelong learners, and build lifelong learners. The best teachers live this, but many don't. Many get stuck in a rut and burn out. One professor said to Randy, "I always want my students drinking from a running stream rather than a stagnant pond." Embrace Common Core and become a "guide by the side" for your students, rather than a "sage on the stage." Embrace technology and new ways of accessing knowledge for your students. Collaborate with your colleagues. Embrace the use of data to highlight successes and illuminate challenges. Adjust your lessons and approach based on what the data are telling you. Most of all, inspire your students! Many of us had one or two teachers whom we connected with that captured our imaginations and ignited the spirit within us. Be that teacher for your students.

- Parents: You are your child's first teacher. You can blame others all you want, but educating your child is your responsibility.

- Parents: Make education your top priority (after faith if you are a family of faith). Whatever your skill set or income level, make learning, school, and studying a top priority. Be engaged at school, and advocate for your children to make sure they have the classes and the support they need. Make sure your student is healthy, safe, and ready to learn. Set high expectations; kids will rise to your expectations. Make sure that they are engaged, and bring great attitudes and work ethic to school. Help them find their interest and passion so that it sparks a love of learning. Be a partner with your children's school and with the classroom teacher. Make sure that your children read. If they are young, read to them every day. Engage them in dialogue, and ask open-ended questions that make them think.

- Community: Citizens, get involved! We were all designed to serve. You can add meaning and purpose to your own life and make a difference in somebody else's life. It will be good for you and good for the community. It is what made America great. If you run a program or an organization, think about how you can collaborate strategically with others to magnify your impact. Don't collaborate just to collaborate; that is a waste of time. But think about the integrated support systems children and families need, and think about how your organization can collaborate with others to build that in your community.

- Philanthropists: The spirit of giving is part of what has made America great. But your desire to find the silver bullet can also be part of the problem. Think strategically, and think about how your investments can be leveraged and sustained. Social change takes years. One- and two-year grants spread around to lots of organizations may be good PR, but it is not going to change much. Make big, smart bets, and stay with them for the long run. It works in private investing—see Donald Bren in real estate and Warren Buffet in securities—and it is the best way to have impact in philanthropy, too.

Appendix 2

As mentioned in Chapter 8, Randy examined the proficiency rates of various subgroups of students in all of the forty-two school districts that THINK Together serves. He used Little Lake and East Whittier, the two districts with the most mature implementation of the Principal's Exchange RtI-S methodology, as benchmark districts. He then compared the performance of these subgroups against each other across districts. So, Latino students were compared to Latino students, English Learners were compared to English learners, low socio-economic were compared to low socio-economic and special education students were compared to special education students.

Little Lake and East Whittier have small African-American subgroups so he did not find the benchmarking of that subgroup especially insightful. Also, some of these school districts are K–12 districts and others are K–8 or K–6 so keep that in mind when comparing districts. Nevertheless, the trends that the graphs on the following pages illuminate are pretty consistent and reveal that a mature implementation of the RtI-S methodology yields between three and thirty point higher proficiency rates in both English language arts and math across subgroups in the THINK Together districts. This methodology revealed proficiency rates that were five to eighteen points higher than the California state averages for these subgroups.

Because this is a cost effective and highly replicable methodology, especially well-suited to support the implementation of Common

Core, we wanted to highlight this performance. Implementation of RtI-S leads to the kind of professional development and coherent systems-building approach that can lead to sustained excellence and not just an oscillation.

This graph benchmarks the proficiency rates for all English learner students in English language arts in East Whittier and Little Lake City School Districts (the benchmark Principal's Exchange RtI-S districts) versus all other THINK Together districts.

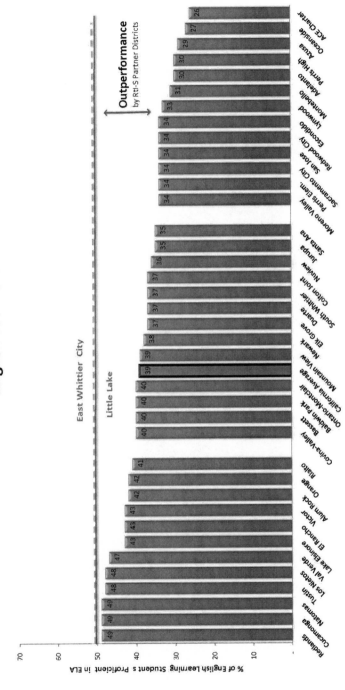

ELA Proficiency Rates in THINK Partner Districts English Learners

This graph benchmarks the proficiency rates for all English learner students in math in East Whittier and Little Lake City School Districts (the benchmark Principal's Exchange RtI-S districts) versus all other THINK Together districts.

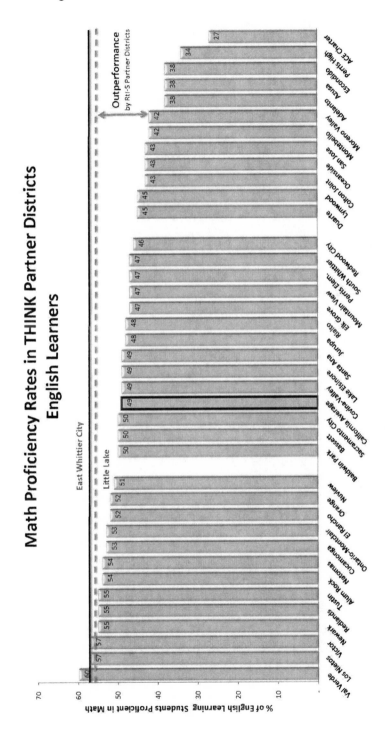

Math Proficiency Rates in THINK Partner Districts
English Learners

This graph benchmarks the proficiency rates for all socio-economically disadvantaged students in English language arts in East Whittier and Little Lake City School Districts (the benchmark Principal's Exchange RtI-S districts) versus all other THINK Together districts.

ELA Proficiency Rates in THINK Partner Districts Socioeconomically Disadvantaged

% of Socioeconomically Disadvantaged Students Proficient in ELA

Little Lake

East Whittier City

Outperformance by RtI-S Partner Districts

Redlands 56, Val Verde 54, Tustin 53, Covina-Valley 52, Lake Elsinore 51, Los Nietos 51, El Rancho 50, Baldwin Park 49, Bassett 49, Cucamonga 49, Duarte 49, Elk Grove 49, Alum Rock 48, Natomas 48, Orange 48, Nuview 47, Perris High 46, California Average 45, Ontario-Montclair 45, Victor 45, Moreno Valley 44, Newark 44, Rialto 44, ACE Charter 43, Colton Joint 43, Oceanside 43, South Whittier 43, Azusa 42, Perris Elem 42, Lynwood 41, Sacramento City 41, San Jose 41, Santa Ana 41, Mountain View 40, Redwood City 40, Montebello 39, Escondido 38, Adelanto 37

*This graph benchmarks the proficiency rates for all socio-economically dis-
advantaged students in math in East Whittier and Little Lake City School
Districts (the benchmark Principal's Exchange RtI-S districts) versus all
other THINK Together districts.*

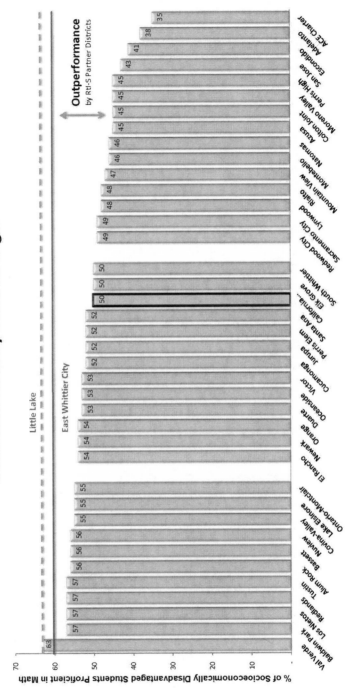

Math Proficiency Rates in THINK Partner Districts
Socioeconomically Disadvantaged

This graph benchmarks the proficiency rates for all Latino students in English language arts in East Whittier and Little Lake City School Districts (the benchmark Principal's Exchange RtI-S districts) versus all other THINK Together districts.

ELA Proficiency Rates in THINK Partner Districts

Latino Students

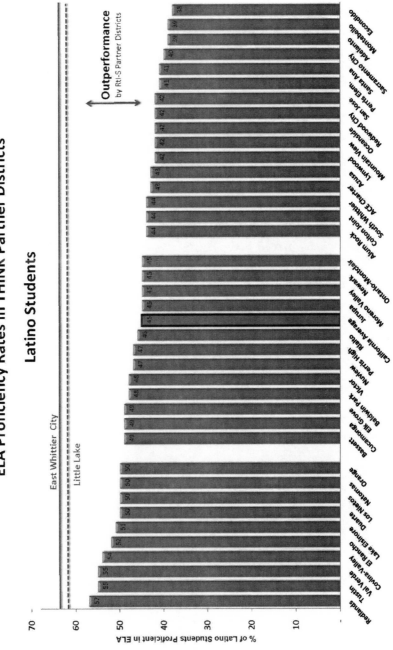

This graph benchmarks the proficiency rates for all Latino students in English language arts in East Whittier and Little Lake City School Districts (the benchmark Principal's Exchange RtI-S districts) versus all other THINK Together districts.

MATH Proficiency Rates in THINK Partner Districts Latino Students

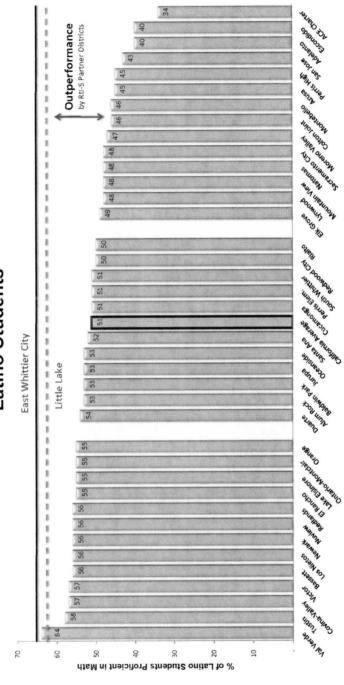

This graph benchmarks the proficiency rates for all special education students in English language arts in East Whittier and Little Lake City School Districts (the benchmark Principal's Exchange RtI-S districts) versus all other THINK Together districts.

ELA Proficiency Rates in THINK Partner Districts Special Education

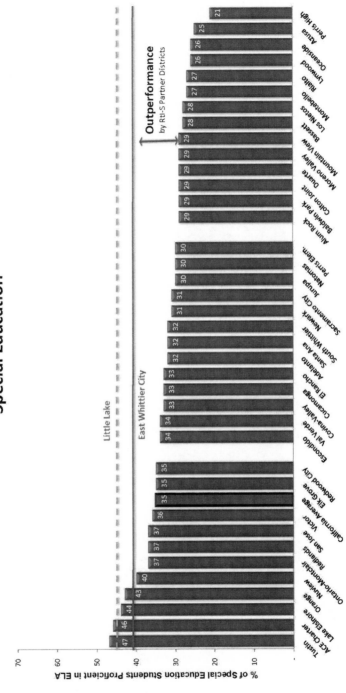

This graph benchmarks the proficiency rates for all special education students in math in East Whittier and Little Lake City School Districts (the benchmark Principal's Exchange RtI-S districts) versus all other THINK Together districts.

Math Proficiency Rates in THINK Partner Districts Special Education

Acknowledgments

I owe debts of gratitude to many people who helped in the creation of this book. First and foremost is my family: my wife Mary and our daughters Emily and Katie. I have a full-time gig as CEO of THINK Together that keeps me occupied sixty-plus hours per week. I write quite a bit anyway and so I thought I could knock off this book on nights and weekends over the course of about a year. It took three years instead. So, my family sacrificed quite a bit of their time with me (and vice-versa) over quite a long period of time during an important time (teenage years) in the life of our family. For their forbearance and understanding I am extremely grateful.

I also owe a debt of gratitude to the THINK Together Board of Directors. They afforded me a two-month sabbatical in the second year, ostensibly to finish the book. I didn't make as much progress during that time as I would have liked and wound up working on the manuscript for almost another full year.

I also owe a debt of gratitude to my coauthor, Jennifer Delson. As I said in the introduction, Jennifer came and rescued this project when it was lost in the weeds. She gave it form, brought other voices to broaden the perspective and brought insight into the families of the children that we serve. I especially want to thank the students, former students and their families, volunteers, and partners that opened themselves up and shared their stories with Jennifer and me.

I also owe a debt of gratitude to Steve Reich, our story editor who took what Jennifer had written and what I had written and fused it together into what is hopefully a coherent narrative with some insights that hopefully can inspire action on the part of various stakeholders that will improve the quality of our public K–12 school systems here in America. I also owe a debt of gratitude to our copy editor, Deirdre Edgar, who cleaned up our mistakes and made this a professional work for a first-time author.

I also owe a debt of gratitude to my two executive assistants, first Corina Martinez who was succeeded after the first year by Jennifer Matsuda. These two young capable people helped to coordinate all of these efforts and integrate them with my day job in ways that kept things moving along and productive for all of the various parties involved.

I also want to thank our publisher Wheatmark for taking these first-time authors through the publishing process in a rapidly changing book publishing world. I also want to thank our partners at eMaxx, Elefint Designs, and Dumont Marketing for their help in the design, marketing, and promotion of the book. I also want to thank Jennifer Mendez who runs the production department at THINK Together, for her assistance on the design and production of some of the marketing materials.

I owe a debt of gratitude to the school district superintendents that spent time with us sharing their experiences and insights, most of whom have been our great partners for years. These include Dr. Phil Perez from Little Lake, Jane Russo (now retired) from Santa Ana, Lillian French from Mountain View (El Monte), Dr. Steven Ladd from Elk Grove (just retired), Paul Gothold from Lynwood, Dr. Dorka Duron (now retired) from East Whittier, Dr. Al Mijares from the Orange County Department of Education, and many others who shared background and insights that have shaped our thinking and the work that we do each and every day.

I want to thank the team at the Principal's Exchange and especially Robin Avelar La Salle for giving us access and insight into their amazing work that we hope can get replicated and scaled as a result of the increased exposure from this book. Many more students, teachers and administrators deserve to know about the benefits of their great work.

I also want to thank our school partners. THINK Together is privileged to partner with forty-two school districts and 450 schools so that we can work together to create opportunities for all kids to discover their passion and reach their full potential. It's not always easy to partner with outsiders, and we appreciate the collaboration and sometimes the courage to stand up to stakeholders who would prefer to block these kinds of partnerships.

I also owe a huge debt to our THINK Together team. This is the most amazing group of professional colleagues and volunteers that I have had the honor to work with. Your creativity and passion has truly changed the destiny of thousands of children's lives. I so admire your talent, professionalism, and perseverance as we seek to do this noble work together.

I also owe a huge debt of gratitude to our generous donors, who without their generosity, our work would never have happened, nor would it be sustained.

I also owe a huge debt of gratitude to St. Andrew's Presbyterian Church. St. Andrew's helped me to develop in my faith; they raised me up as leader, and then supported this work as they sent me out into the world to serve others. My life has never been the same.

Finally, I want to thank all of the parents that have entrusted us with your beautiful and talented children. We believe it takes a village to raise a child and we are grateful to be part of your village. And to the children and youth that we serve, at the end of the day, any success that any of us have in this work is your success. All we can do is support you, but you have to bring the will and do the hard work. And if we all play our part, America *will* be great and good again.

Soli deo gloria.

Index

About the Authors

Randy Barth is the founder and CEO of THINK Together, a non-profit education company that provides academic support programs and other services at public schools statewide in California. A successful businessman for more than twenty years, he started his career as an investment adviser with various major Wall Street firms and later became a corporate CEO. He began his work in education as a volunteer after a gang shooting in Westside Costa Mesa in 1994. Barth holds a BA in Economics from UCLA and did graduate work at the Drucker School of Management, Claremont Graduate University.

Jennifer Delson, a freelance writer, was previously a reporter for the *Los Angeles Times* and *San Jose Mercury News*. As a reporter for twenty years, she gained recognition for capturing the texture of the lives of low-income families and stories of immigration. In her current capacity, she has written books, articles, and speeches for community leaders. She holds a bachelor's degree and master's degree in Latin American Studies from Wesleyan University and New York University respectively.

CPSIA information can be obtained at www.ICGtesting.com
Printed in the USA
BVOW07s1134060215

386597BV00002B/22/P